SCOTLAND
Counties & Towns

To Shetland Is →

Is.

OUTER HEBRIDES

ATLANTIC OCEAN

NORTH SEA

IRELAND

ENGLAND

Thurso
Wick
CAITHNESS

Stornoway
LEWIS

HARRIS

SUTHERLAND

Dornoch

ROSS & CROMARTY
Dingwall

Lossiemouth
Fraserburgh
Elgin
Banff
Peterhead
Nairn
MORAY
NAIRN
Inverness
BANFF
ABERDEEN

Portree
SKYE

INVERNESS

Aberdeen

Mallaig

Balmoral
Stonehaven
Braemar
KINCARDINE

Fort William

Blair Atholl
Pitlochry
ANGUS
Montrose
Forfar
Arbroath

Tobermory
MULL
Oban

Dunkeld
Dundee
PERTH
Perth
Cupar
St. Andrews
Inveraray
KINROSS
FIFE

DUMBARTON
CLACKMANNAN
Kirkcaldy
ARGYLL
Stirling
Alloa
North Berwick
STIRLING
Dunfermline
Dunbar
Leith
JURA
Falkirk
Haddington
Dumbarton
Linlithgow
EAST
Greenock
WEST
Edinburgh
LOTHIAN
Berwick-on-Tweed
ISLAY
Paisley
Glasgow
LOTHIAN
MIDLOTHIAN
BUTE
Motherwell
BERWICK
RENFREW
LANARK
Peebles
KINTYRE
Ardrossan
Lanark
Galashiels
ARRAN
Kilmarnock
PEEBLES
Selkirk
Melrose
Prestwick
SELKIRK
Hawick
Ayr
ROXBURGH

AYR

DUMFRIES

KIRKCUDBRIGHT
Dumfries
WIGTOWN
Gretna
Stranraer
Kirkcudbright

SCOTLAND

ROYAL ARMS OF SCOTLAND
(*Public Register of All Arms and Bearings in Scotland Vol. I*)

SCOTLAND

A Description of Scotland and Scottish Life

Edited by

HENRY W. MEIKLE
C.B.E., D.Litt., LL.D.

His Majesty's Historiographer in Scotland

THOMAS NELSON AND SONS LTD
LONDON EDINBURGH PARIS MELBOURNE
TORONTO AND NEW YORK

THOMAS NELSON AND SONS LTD
Parkside Works Edinburgh 9
3 Henrietta Street London WC2
312 Flinders Street Melbourne C1
91–93 Wellington Street West   Toronto 1

THOMAS NELSON AND SONS
385 Madison Avenue New York 17

SOCIÉTÉ FRANÇAISE D'ÉDITIONS NELSON
25 Rue Denfert-Rochereau Paris Ve

———

First published June 1947

PREFACE

CURIOSITY about Scotland has existed from the earliest times. For the ancient world it was a dark and mysterious country, a part of *Ultima Thule*, at the end of the earth. In the Middle Ages the Scot abroad as soldier of fortune, teacher, student, and trader was better known than the Scot at home. Even when the tragic fate of Mary Queen of Scots stirred Western Christendom, the land of her birth was largely a *terra incognita*. In the eighteenth century the poems of *Ossian* revealed to an enthusiastic Europe what seemed to be the very soul of the Celtic genius of Scotland, but few travellers were tempted to try to discover " windy Morven and echoing Sora and Selma with its silent halls." The famous Dr. Johnson who, greatly daring, left his beloved London to tour the Western Isles in 1773, was welcomed on his return to Edinburgh, so he tells us, as if he had made " a voyage to Nova Zembla and suffered five persecutions in Japan." The dangers and fatigues of travel and the lack of communications afforded little opportunity for the appreciation of the wilder beauties of Nature. Johnson's friend, Oliver Goldsmith, declared that in Scotland " hills and woods intercept every prospect."

It was the poems and novels of Sir Walter Scott in the next century which revealed the romance of Scotland to every civilized country, and awakened the desire to see

> Caledonia stern and wild,
> Meet nurse for a poetic child !
> Land of brown heath and shaggy wood,
> Land of the mountain and the flood.

Thousands flocked to view the Trossachs and other scenes of *The Lady of the Lake* ; and it is on record that the receipts from the tax on post-horses, at this time an easy means of transport along the rapidly developing system of roads, increased in an extraordinary degree with each edition of the poem. The word " tourist " was added to the language.

The spell of the " Wizard of the North " and of such later writers as Robert Louis Stevenson is still unbroken. But industry and commerce have also their romance, to be found in the ship-building yards and engineering works on the Clyde, in the skill of the world-famous agricultural research stations, the craftsmanship of the woollen mills, the potential power of hydro-electric schemes, and in the many new enterprises of to-day.

This book, instigated by the Scottish Council (Development and Industry), is designed to introduce Scotland to every kind of visitor, whatever his interests and whatever his native land. It should prove of special interest to the friends of Scotland everywhere, to the Scot at home, and to the Scot from overseas coming for the first time to the land of his forefathers. The writing of the chapters has been entrusted to leading authorities. The country, its people, its history and institutions, its work, its culture, and its sport, in short, its way of life, are all dealt with so as to give a picture of Scotland as it was and as it is. These aspects are further portrayed in the numerous illustrations which may afterwards serve to awaken pleasant memories.

Thanks are due to the contributors for their co-operation and readiness to conform to the general plan. The help given by Government Departments and by Mr. Ian Finlay, who read the proofs and made many valuable suggestions, is also gratefully acknowledged.

HENRY W. MEIKLE

CONTENTS

vii

CONTENTS

viii

LIST OF PLATES

Plates to illustrate 'Architecture,' between pages 178 and 179

PLATES IN COLOUR

SCOTLAND

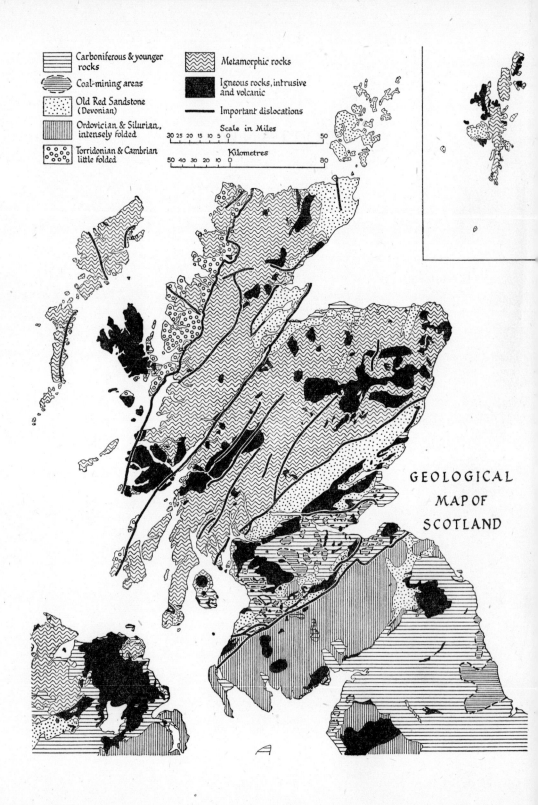

Carboniferous & younger rocks

Coal-mining areas

Old Red Sandstone (Devonian)

Ordovician & Silurian, intensely folded

Torridonian & Cambrian little folded

Metamorphic rocks

Igneous rocks, intrusive and volcanic

Important dislocations

Scale in Miles
30 25 20 15 10 5 0   50

Kilometres
50 40 30 20 10 0   80

GEOLOGICAL
MAP OF
SCOTLAND

PHYSICAL FEATURES AND SCENERY

In many of its physical qualities Scotland is akin to Norway, to Ireland, and Wales, and even to Cornwall and Brittany : all of these belong to the Atlantic fringe of Europe, and they have in common many features of their geological structure and of their climate and vegetation. But Scotland faces the North Sea as well as the open ocean, and this contrast in aspect is effective in a number of ways. There is again the fundamental division into highland and lowland, denoting difference not merely of height but also of soil and of human opportunity. The greater part of the Lowlands may be called mid-Scotland, the most habitable land of the Scots, which is shut off from the greater English Lowland by relatively barren hills, now known as the Southern Uplands, that formed the long-contested Border.

This Central Lowland, always the most fertile part of the country, has achieved special prosperity in the past two centuries through the exploitation of its wealth in coal, iron, and oil-shale. It has ever been the heartland of the nation, inviting as it did the fusion of Gael and Anglian, and offering the chief basis of economic strength : it now contains four-fifths of the population.

The reasons for this very uneven distribution of the Scottish people will be appreciated better when the character of the three natural divisions of the land—the Southern Uplands; mid-Scotland and the smaller lowland north of Aberdeen; the Highlands and Islands—has been described. The description will deal equally with the populous central part and with the larger highland regions and the islands, since it is in these outer tracts that many visitors will naturally spend their time.

But before particular description attention must be given to several more general aspects of the natural environment which are fundamental to life. Of these none is likely to affect the visitor's impressions so much as the climate, even if his own experience be short, and thus limited to weather rather than climate.

The passage of atmospheric depressions from the ocean dominates the weather, and so the climate, everywhere on the Atlantic fringe of Europe, and this throughout the whole year. But the number and intensity of these is greatest over the Northern Isles of Scotland, which might well have been the site of a Temple of the Winds.

As a result storm-waves have cut the finest sea-cliffs of Europe in Orkney and the adjacent mainland. Nevertheless passage by air to the Outer Isles is rarely interrupted. Elsewhere the depressions are thought of chiefly for the rain they cause and the alternation of warm and cool air-currents they induce. Their effect is least during the spring when east winds commonly prevail, and this consequently is the driest season: the continental air retards the rise in temperature, but there is much sunshine. Then weak depressions combine with long daylight to make June the finest month in Scotland, especially in the Western Highlands. July and August, the usual holiday months, are warmer but in most years they are wetter. Finer weather often occurs again during parts of September and October, while the fall in temperature is gradual ; but there is less regularity here. These facts are worthy of the visitor's attention ; they are vital in the economy of the country. The farmer has little to fear for the growth of his crops, but there is risk of some loss from excessive rain about the harvest time.

Pronounced difference in climate is to be noted between the east and west, accentuated, of course, by the height of the interior. In winter, air from the surface of the Atlantic Drift keeps temperature high ; the average for January in the Outer Hebrides, c. 42° F. (5·6° C.) exceeds that of Bordeaux, 900 miles (1,450 km.) farther south. Near the east coast it is colder by 2° F., severe frost is much more frequent, and snowfalls are particularly heavy in the north-eastern part of Scotland. The contrast in rainfall is even more marked on account of the abrupt rise of moist winds on the Western Highlands. Most of these mountains receive over 60 in. (152 cm.) in the year and on the highest parts double this amount. Moreover, the number of rainy days is greater in the west. Along much of the east coast the rainfall is under 30 in. (76 cm.). Thus on the Atlantic side the equable but damp climate promotes the growth, at lower altitudes, of plants such as grasses and, save where wind is excessive, also of trees ; but the wet autumn does not favour corn. The high rainfall on these mountains makes them an important source of water-power, some of which is already utilized.

It may be said that the scenic character of a land comes mainly from its forms and colours with attendant light, shadow, and tone, all provided by nature ; but the structures set up by man play a part, and these may be harmonious or the reverse. It follows that the typical weather is important, and particularly among the mountains : the rapid change from gloom to sunshine has its special

2

Plate 1   Ben Nevis (4,406 ft.), the highest mountain in the British Isles

(Photo : Robert M. Adam)

Plate 2   The skyline of Mamore Forest in the Grampian Mountains seen
from Ben Nevis.   The summits are the remnants of an old plateau

*(Photo : Crown Copyright ;   reproduced from a photograph supplied by the Director of
the Geological Survey, by permission of H.M. Stationery Office)*

reward for the eye in the brilliance of sunlit slopes contrasted with those still partly veiled in cloud. Most of the surface is clad in humble but varied vegetation, and this is spattered with the "stone-glint" —sunlight reflected from wet rock. The scene is mirrored in the lochs, salt or fresh, and water rushes and tumbles in every ravine and glen. The ancient forests have been carelessly destroyed, and little remains of the natural woods of pine (*P. sylvestris*) and birch that once covered much of the mountains, but the oak-woods of the lowest slopes are still found in many glens. Woods planted during the last 150 years, chiefly of European conifers, have been greatly depleted during the two world wars; and those of the National Forestry Commission, also mainly of fir, pine, and larch, are as yet under twenty-five years old. Forests therefore are incidental and rarely dominate the scenery.

Apart then from colour due to vegetation and the atmosphere, the landscape is a matter of shape of hill and valley and the pattern of land and sea, lake, and river. So the form of Scotland may now be examined in order to understand the nature of its surface by reference to its origin. This concerns geology, but special attention need be given only to a few facts selected from the long geological history of this ancient fragment of the earth's crust. Scotland includes rocks of nearly all the ages, but few of those which remain were formed later than the Carboniferous Period, perhaps 200 million years ago. From these and others much older an immense load of younger strata has been almost certainly removed by denudation. In contrast to the great age of the rocks the present surface has been produced within the last few million years of the Tertiary and Quaternary Periods during which the vast amount of erosion was accomplished. This produced a rather smooth surface of no great height which cut across rocks exceedingly varied in age, hardness, and structure; and the general tilt was probably towards the east. To see the result of this in the existing landscape we have only to climb any of the higher summits, where the view will reveal ridge after ridge standing at heights that differ but little. These are remnants of the old surface (Plate 2).

It may be noted here that each of the three main tracts of Scotland is built of characteristic rocks. Thus the Highlands are composed mainly of gneiss, granite, quartzite, and other hard crystalline rocks. The Southern Uplands are of closely folded sediments like grits, shales, and greywacke with some granite and lava. In mid-Scotland the hills are built chiefly of volcanic rocks, but the lower land is underlain by Old Red Sandstone and the various Carboniferous strata, including coal.

The earth storm which caused the up-building of the Alps had distant repercussions in the fracturing of this tough rocky crust near the western edge of the old land, and along the resulting cracks volcanoes arose, to leave remnants in the islands such as Mull and Skye. After this slabs of the crust subsided along this line to form the sea-bed between the Outer and the Inner Hebrides, while the Irish Sea to the south had a similar origin. The Outer Hebrides remain as a fragment of the old land, much of them still little above the ocean. But greater slabs on the mainland were raised up, with great dislocation on the western seaboard, preparing the way for the present indented coast. Thus the mountains attained their present general altitudes. During this uplift the rivers began to deepen their valleys, tributaries developed where weaker rocks were exposed ; and so the old surface became carved up into a series of tabular blocks, the present mountain and hill groups. The shorter, steeper, and more powerful rivers of the west were the better carvers : hence the closer mesh of deep valleys here, and the greater prominence of single mountains in the western Highlands.

These events led to the last great episodes of geological history, those of the Glacial Period. The land now stood high and had a greater precipitation : climate degenerated and snow, and then ice, accumulated. Eventually Scotland became enveloped in a thick cap of ice which moved outward from centres in the Highlands and in the Southern Uplands. The entire Lowlands were swept by the moving ice, which also filled the basin of the Irish Sea ; while the Scottish ice met the greater mass pressing westward from Scandinavia on the plain now flooded by the North Sea. Two leading features of Scottish geography are due to this glacial episode. The Lowlands are covered almost everywhere by the rock-waste left by the ice on its recession, chiefly as boulder-clay or till but also as sand and gravel where deposited by river water from the glaciers ; and these deposits form the basis of the present cultivated soils. Secondly, the most distinctive scenic character of the mountains, the glens, the lochs, and the corries are due to erosion by glaciers, and subsidiary features have been wrought by torrential rivers which succeeded them.

The abundance of deep lakes suggests great resources in water-power, and they are in fact considerable : much electricity is already being generated and further sources are soon to be tapped.

4

But the glens have been carved so deeply that the greater lakes do not stand at high levels. Consequently the potential power is less than it might seem to be.

As the ice finally melted away the land rose up slightly, for it had yielded under the weight of the ice-cap. When this happened the sea receded, to leave strips of its former beaches as an irregular fringe of almost flat land along the coasts. Many of these raised beaches provide very good agricultural land.

The map of Scotland derives some of its boldest and simplest lines from geological fractures that are much older than the events so far described. Thus Glen More, which severs the Northern Highlands from the rest, is a straight line of ancient weakness. This dislocation extends from Tarbat Ness S.S.W. to Islay, a distance of 190 miles (300 km.), and it marks not merely vertical but also great lateral displacement of the rock-slabs separated by it. The Central Lowland is divided sharply from the Highlands and from the Southern Uplands by parallel escarpments extending across Scotland from S.W. to N.E. They correspond to old faults which bring the exposure of the weaker rocks of the Lowland abruptly against the harder materials to north and south. Within the Highlands again, many other ancient faults running parallel to Glen More have affected the relief. Moreover, the almost straight character of much of the north and east coasts suggest the existence, under the sea, of similar lines of weakness with this trend, coupled with others from west to east.

The many separate groups of hills in mid-Scotland are built largely of volcanic rocks corresponding in age to one or other of the two formations of sediments which, being softer, are found underlying the lower land. These are the reddish Devonian rocks or Old Red Sandstone, and the sandstones, shales, limestones, and coal of Carboniferous age.

While the entire belt may be regarded as a broad down-fold to which these sediments owe their preservation, with the older (Devonian) rocks exposed near the two margins, the strata have also been bent and broken in other directions. Consequently the youngest rocks, which are the coal-measures, have been stripped away from the various up-folds. Thus there remain three separate coal-basins, in the west, centre, and east. The character of these, and of the surrounding country, is further affected by fractures and volcanic intrusions extending from west to east. The large Central coalfield has hitherto been the most important, and in addition to

5

coal, it yielded iron ore and fireclay. But the iron ore is not rich enough for present use and the output of coal is declining. The greater reserves remain in the Ayrshire coalfield and especially in the Eastern coalfield, divided between Fife and the Lothians. The oldest Carboniferous rocks in places contain oil-shale, which in West Lothian has been mined since 1860 for the extraction of oil and by-products by distillation.

The southern hills are noted for their uniformity, in height, form, and vegetation. In altitude they are mostly between 1,000 and 2,000 feet (c. 300–600 m.). Their rounded or even flat summits, often capped with dark peat, give way in graceful grassy slopes to many deep and narrow valleys and to some, known as the Dales, which have been widened in part by glaciers. There is, however, a marked exception to all this in the west, where, instead of the monotonous crumpled sedimentary rock, intrusive granites are exposed. Hence in Galloway, the region lying west of Nithsdale, a core of rugged mountains gives a foretaste of the scenery of the Highlands. Although only of moderate height—2,764 feet (842 m.) in Merrick—this group formed the centre from which the southern ice radiated and scoured the valleys to form deep glens, leaving Loch Doon and other lakes to fill the deeper hollows. East of Nithsdale less rugged, but still impressive features due to similar causes, are the glens leading to the Enterkin and Mennock Passes in the Lowther Hills and comparable scenery about St. Mary's Loch below Hartfell.

The waters of the Galloway hills, fed by high rainfall, steep rivers, and the lakes, have been harnessed and furnish electricity to the region and to northern England. The River Nith, in contrast to the others, occupies a deep furrow of great age which severs the Southern Uplands and so offers an easy way for road and rail between the lowlands of the Solway Firth and Ayrshire. Nithsdale combines the beauty of low woods backed by high hills, and rich farmland is seen in the wider hollows where red Permian sandstones are preserved in the dale. Annandale to the east, while similar, starts among the hills north of Moffat, and the main route from Carlisle to the north must climb to over 1,000 feet (c. 300 m.) to reach the upper Clyde valley. The scenery of the lowlands bordering the Irish Sea is unique and constitutes the principal charm of Galloway. The rivers Ken, Cree, and others end in estuaries with woods to the edge of tidewater. In the peninsulas rugged hills

6

Plate 3 Incoming tide on the Galloway coast

*(Photo: Alfred Furness; reproduced from 'The Scottish Scene'
by permission of George Allen & Unwin Ltd.)*

Plate 4　Kirkcudbright, one of the old seaports of the Solway Firth

(Photo: Alfred Furness; reproduced from 'The Scottish Scene' by permission of George Allen & Unwin Ltd.)

alternate with areas of rounded hummocks—some of ice-scoured rock, others of boulder-clay deposited by the ice and forming good farmland—and many hollows once under lake or swamp have been drained. In contrast are the coastal flats, the raised beaches which border the Solway and form the isthmus in Wigtownshire. Throughout all this lowland most of the whitewashed farms are concerned with well-tended herds of dairy cattle. The historic route to northern Ireland was fixed, like the modern road and railway, by bridges at the heads of the estuaries ; there too are the old seaports, such as Dumfries and Kirkcudbright, now little used, but the latter has a special charm. Near to tracts of good land are the notable ruined abbeys—Sweetheart, Dundrennan, and Glenluce—while at Whithorn in the far west is the earliest Christian site in Scotland.

The basin of the River Tweed comprises three concentric zones of different height, each with distinctive landscape. Highest is the main plateau of the Uplands already mentioned, deeply scored by the gashes of the upper Tweed and its tributaries. This is the domain of the hill-sheep. Next is a broad lower step or platform, from about 1,200 to 400 feet in height, in which the rivers still flow in rather narrow valleys. But the land is arable and more populous while cattle mingle with the sheep. Throughout both these zones woodland is confined mainly to plantations, a chief purpose of which is to give shelter to the stock. The Cheviot stands forward from the high platform to hem in the second step on the south, and the same volcanic rocks that build it also form the eastern rim of the latter. The Tweed cuts through these in a last winding stretch. This is the site of Dryburgh Abbey, while that of Melrose stands a little to westward. Overlooking these is the three-peaked hill of Eildon, relic of a separate intrusion, and this gave the name to an important Roman station, Trimontium, where roads met, as they do still at St. Boswells, nearby. The third or lowest step is the plain known as The Merse or " Border " that lay open to English armies in the past. It is the continuation of the lowland of Northumbria. Here a hummocky land of boulder-clay has been drained to form excellent farmland dotted with some ornamental woodland about the greater houses. Through it the Tweed passes in large curves bordered by terraces on one of which stands the picturesque town and ruined abbey of Kelso.

The beauty of the Tweed valley throughout is largely due to the woods which clothe so many of the steeper hill-slopes and the river banks; the same is true of the tributaries such as the Ettrick, the Teviot, and the Jed, the latter with its red cliffs providing a wonderful setting for the ruined abbey of Jedburgh.

Medieval woollen crafts have given place to the modern textile industry in the small towns of Tweeddale and the neighbouring valleys, with fine cloth the product of Galashiels and nearby towns, knitted goods in Hawick, and rayon in Jedburgh.

Under the name of the Lammermuir Hills the eastern end of the Uplands extends to the coast, lower than elsewhere but still a considerable barrier to the route northward from Berwick-on-Tweed. This follows at first the cliff top, but turns inland to follow a valley to the hill-crest. Thus the finest sea-cliffs are hidden from the route, but they may be visited from the old fishing village of St. Abbs.

Mid-Scotland falls naturally into a number of lowland districts separated by the ranges of hills and by the three firths. South of the Firth of Forth is the ancient province of Lothian, now three counties, but nature divided it into two parts by the Pentland Hills. This narrow range, an old geological feature limited by fractures, ends abruptly six miles from the coast; and the gap is occupied by Edinburgh, which from early times has controlled movement through it as well as the trade of the port of Leith. Unfortunately the manner of the city's growth has tended to hamper free movement of modern transport. But this in turn is largely due to the nature of the site. Rome with its hills is matched by Edinburgh which now covers several ridges parallel with the coast, while the massive hill, Arthur's Seat, acts as an eastern barrier. The craggy slopes, unusual in cities, are of volcanic rocks, and are steepest toward the west where they were trimmed by moving ice. Below such a rock the old Edinburgh arose, protected by its castle and a wall within which a growing population had to build its houses high, facing narrow streets. In contrast the " new town," of the eighteenth century, was built on a spacious plan, but it is left to the future to rectify the faults of later extensions much less worthy.

The scenery of eastern Lothian is well seen from the railway or the main road, but better by a wide view from the Garleton Hills beside Haddington, a typical Scottish market town of dignity. The rolling reddish land with prosperous farms contrasts with the woods of many estates and is backed by the slopes of the Lammermuirs. The coast is fringed by a series of famous golf-courses, sand-dunes, and fine beaches ; the volcanic crags of North Berwick and the Bass, and the ruined castles of Tantallon and Dunbar, are points of interest. Nearer Edinburgh are wooded gorges where the few crossings are marked by the fine castles that held them—Roslin and Crichton in ruin and Borthwick, still intact. Musselburgh, at the mouth of the Esk, retains the charm of an older period, but conceals its Roman origin. Collieries interrupt an otherwise rural landscape but paper-mills are hidden in the gorge.

West of the Pentlands views are more restricted by rocky hills and by the red mounds formed of the waste of heated oil-shale : west of these, collieries of the Central coalfield are in evidence. But the steep and wooded coast and the islands, among them Inchcolm with its ruined priory, form a fitting background for the graceful lines of the Forth Bridge. In a hollow hidden from the Firth is Linlithgow with its ancient castle and church commanding the land-route, and in a lovely setting by a lake.

Stirling is the very heart of Scotland : the central node of routes commands the visitor to halt. The castle and town resemble Edinburgh without its modern extension. The view from the former shows the critical gap between the Gargunnock Hills and the steep Ochils with the rich flats bordering the winding estuary of the Forth. Through the gap the southern rim of the Highlands appears in panorama.

The peninsula of Fife, with the lake-basin of Kinross, has the Ochil Hills as a northern barrier, and may be said to turn its face to the Forth. Thus while the hollows of the interior are fertile and, with old burghs backed by volcanic hills, have their own beauty, it is the south coast which is the most interesting part. Here are the old seaports, important when ships were small, and some still vigorous fishing ports, from Culross in the west—a charming "museum piece" easily visited from Dunfermline—to Crail in the east : behind them is the raised beach, well cultivated. But there is also coal-mining and a great coal-port at Methil. The old textile industry of Fife, especially linen, is modernized at Dunfermline. Kirkcaldy has expanded as a maker of linoleum ; ships are broken up at Inverkeithing and alumina refined at Burntisland, while at Rosyth is the naval dockyard.

On the east coast there is the single gem of St. Andrews, standing apart in peninsular isolation and great dignity, a town unique in Scotland. The renown of its ancient university scarcely exceeds that of its golf-links.

From Falkirk with its iron-works and the busy port of Grange-mouth, on the Forth, a low defile leads westward overlooked by green slopes on both sides. This was followed by the Roman defences in the past : to-day it is a main artery of traffic and leads to the industrial heart of Scotland, about the lower Clyde. But the traveller, with time, should see the whole basin from the Campsie Fells to the north, or should climb Tinto Hill, 2,335 feet (712 m.), near Symington in the south. The River Clyde is then seen to pass suddenly from an open valley in a broad rolling upland with pastoral farms to a narrow trench. The change occurs near Lanark at the Falls of Clyde, which are still beautiful though captured for electricity. The narrow valley which the river follows to Hamilton is a rural landscape specially pretty in spring, for there are many fruit-orchards. From Hamilton the wooded banks of the winding Clyde lead to the old strategic bridge of Bothwell defended by a castle. This now faces a park containing the birthplace of David Livingstone, the missionary-explorer. The flanking uplands are dominated by collieries and iron and steel factories, as at Wishaw, Motherwell, Airdrie, and Coatbridge.

Glasgow, with over a million inhabitants, has grown outwards from a bridge-head, the lowest bridge of the Clyde and centre of a web of routes. North of the river the site is hilly—many whale-back ridges or drumlins like those crowned by the ancient cathedral and the university—but there is no dominating crag. Glasgow owes its commercial supremacy largely to the initiative of its citizens in deepening the estuary progressively. This has allowed the port to develop as trans-Atlantic trade increased. It also led the iron and steel industry of the coalfield to be applied to shipbuilding and encouraged the host of varied manufactures with which the city is concerned. Thus the visitor should make the passage to the outer Firth by water past the great shipyards, past the ancient port of Dumbarton with its castle perched on a rock—one of the gates to the Highlands—and on to Greenock and Gourock. Clydeside is a scene of great activity afloat and ashore, backed by strips of farmland and rugged heights.

From Glasgow bridge a main route leads to Ayrshire across the raised-beach to Paisley with its ancient abbey and now large cotton-mills, and thence through the defile of Lochwinnoch through the green Renfrew Hills past factories devoted to cotton and other industries. But after Kilmarnock the lowland of Ayrshire is seen to be chiefly an agricultural country ; for the Ayrshire coalfield has not

Plate 5 The Southern Uplands, showing the triple peaks of the Eildon Hills overlooking the River Tweed. A view taken from Bemersyde

(*Photo : Robert M. Adam*)

Plate 6   The mountain peaks of Arran, showing Cir Mhor and
Caisteal Abhail

(*Photo : Robert M. Adam*)

Plate 7 A winter view in Glen Garry, a beautiful glen in
west Inverness-shire

(Photo : Robert M. Adam)

Plate 8   The Pass of Killiecrankie and the River Garry, Perthshire, on
the route from Pitlochry to Blair Atholl

(*Photo : Robert M. Adam*)

caused manufactures to dominate the landscape. It is a natural region of great rural charm typified by many winding and wooded valleys with ancient strongholds near the bridges, trim villages and scattered white farms. Dairy cattle are everywhere. The high eastern horizon is formed by encircling moors, and westward the bold profiles of Arran and the Highland peninsulas rise from the sea. The natural centre is the old town of Ayr which adjoins the new airport of Prestwick. The coast shows bold cliffs in the south and long beaches fringed by famous golf-links in the north. But two headlands jut out to shelter the modernized ports of Troon and Ardrossan on sites resembling those of ancient Tyre and Sidon.

North of the Firth of Tay the Sidlaw Hills, like the Ochils built of lavas, form the background of Dundee, a seaport and large city known chiefly in the past century for its manufacture of jute and other fibres. Near the head of the Firth the River Tay penetrates the hard rock of the defile of Perth to emerge upon a rich plain, the Carse of Gowrie, a rural landscape. But the old city of Perth fills the gap and its factories, which deal with textiles, including dyeing, and with glass and other materials, cannot mar the beauty of the setting. The view from Kinnoull Hill discloses the Tay emerging from the Highlands and passing in majestic sweeps across Strathmore amid fine woodland. This plain of Strathmore is a singularly uniform belt lying in front of the Highland rim and extending through the counties of Angus and Kincardine almost to the coast near Stonehaven. It is one of the famous agricultural regions but contains a number of ancient small towns like Brechin with its cathedral. The red soil and the many rivers with wooded banks give character to the plain and the Highland glens and plateau form the background. The coast to the east is marked by bold cliffs of red sandstone, by the two old towns Arbroath and Montrose, and by fishing villages.

The North-Eastern Lowland forms a very distinctive region. It is approached along the top of rugged sea-cliffs by a route once guarded by Dunnottar Castle, perched on the brink, but Aberdeen is at the real entrance and is the regional capital. The city still betrays its dual origin, small towns at the mouths of the rivers Don and Dee, each in past times having a university and the former also a cathedral. Nearly all the buildings in Aberdeen are of the pale granite of the district, and the bright effect is little spoiled by the varied factories or by the great fishing industry. This lowland

has no sharp inland edge, since there are many basins along the
Dee, Don, and Deveron separated by the Highland foothills. The
greater area is the rolling plain of Buchan rimmed by great cliffs
in north and east, but south of the River Ythan by continuous beach
to Aberdeen. The small towns like Turiff and Huntly are ancient
agricultural centres. The large fishing towns Peterhead and Fraserburgh give way along the north coast to smaller picturesque villages
peopled by a vigorous and distinctive fisher-folk.

West of the Spey the crystalline rocks are replaced by sandstones, and the lowland or " Laigh " of Moray and Nairn is a
plain of raised beach with gentle hills. The climate here, as on the
coast across the Moray Firth, is notably mild, dry, and sunny, and
this favours the farmer as well as the tourist who may enjoy golf
and bathing on fine links and beaches. Elgin with its ruined cathedral is the regional centre, but Inverness, though called " capital of
the Highlands," also links this lowland with the narrow and indented
fringe of the three inner Firths of Beauly, Cromarty, and Dornoch.
Here Ben Wyvis and lesser mountains rise abruptly from lowland
woods and rich farmland, while sea appears in all the long views.
Farther away is the separate and different landscape of Caithness :
a lowland too but wind-swept and bare, with much heathery peat
interspersed by green farmland. The sea-cliffs cut in sandstone
with outlying pinnacles are unsurpassed for scenery of this kind
save perhaps in Orkney.

The Highlands have many entrances, each a deep glen with a
town or village at its mouth. East of the Tay, however, in the
Grampian Highlands, the valleys do not provide easy through-
routes since most main roads do not penetrate the summit plateau
which is 70 miles (112 km.) long from east to west. The exception
is the road from Blairgowrie to Braemar on the Dee by the Cairnwell
Pass. This ascends Glen Shee, which resembles the several glens of
Angus farther east. All are glacial troughs with rugged heads and
shoulders ; but they contain few lochs. The Dee valley offers an
approach to these mountains by rail or road from Aberdeen, with
scenery of most varied beauty throughout. The district has the
merit of smaller rainfall than the other mountains. Because of this,
heather (*Calluna vulgaris*) is the dominant vegetation, much more
so than in the wetter west ; in August its bloom transforms the
warm brown of winter into rich purple. The redder bell-heather
(*Erica cinerea*), on the driest slopes, flowers in June. Heather is

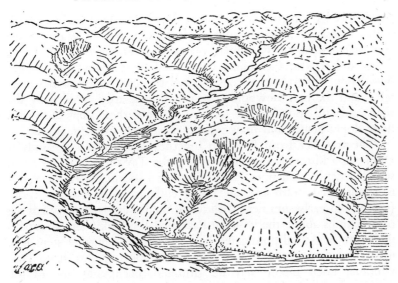

Diagrammatic air-view showing: part of a sea-loch with terrace of raised beach; a main glen with three steps and a loch; tributary glens with ravines at their mouths; also four corries.

burned every few years to promote young growth for the hill-sheep and the grouse.

The Central and Western Highlands are entered at Dunkeld, Crieff, Callander, and Dumbarton, but the approaches from the sea are much more numerous because most of the glens which prolong the greater sea-lochs have motor-roads and several have railways as well.

The terms *glen* and *strath* applied to valleys in the Highlands may be taken generally to indicate somewhat different types of scenery. The glen is narrow and has steep sides—usually typical troughs like those of the Alps or Norway but with lower mountains. The rock is often visible on the bottom as well as on the sides, but many of the deeper hollows are filled by lakes. The strath is broader and is floored by the debris of the ice, of rivers, or of former lakes; thus it offers much more cultivable ground and has a larger population. But valleys of both types derive beauty and interest from the rapid change of scene they offer. If, for example, the traveller enters the Highlands from Callander to visit the Trossachs and Loch Katrine, westwards, or to follow the railway northwards to Loch Lubnaig, he must in each case ascend an abrupt rocky step

13

cut deeply by a torrential river in a thickly wooded ravine. Such is the Trossachs, a beauty-spot made famous by Sir Walter Scott and matched at many similar places throughout the Highlands. Glens and straths, then, may be likened to stairways, the longer ones having several steep steps marked by rock, wood, and water-fall; and the best viewpoints are often necessarily avoided by the road and still more by the railway. Above these steps the valley floor slopes gently and may contain meadows, swamps, or lake.

The traveller from Perth to Inverness enters the Highlands at Dunkeld, a historical key-point where the Tay threads a rocky and wooded defile. Then, to Pitlochry, now a tourist resort, the valley is a cultivated strath and the sandy cliffs are golden with broom (*Genista*) in early summer. Following the River Garry onwards the route climbs above the wooded Pass of Killiecrankie and so attains the strath of Atholl dominated by Blair Castle. Further steps lead up to the notch in the high plateau, and beyond this, from Dal-whinnie, Loch Ericht may be glimpsed, occupying one of the deepest glens. And so to Strathspey, the widest of the straths. It is littered with moraines and mounds of gravel. The remnants of old pine forest, the open heath and birchwoods, the river and lakes attract many visitors to the villages—enlarged for this reason.

The valleys of the Dee and Don have most of the features so far described, especially the Dee above Ballater, the railway terminus, but the lower parts of both include partly cultivated basins, separated by abrupt ridges of granite hills through which the rivers flow in beautiful wooded gorges.

In the Northern Highlands each of the valleys open to the east offer types of beauty comparable with those south of Glen More; but the glens of the Atlantic slope, being steeper, have the valley steps closer together and the gorges cut through them are more rugged. The mountains also are much rougher: so these western glens, of which Glen Coe and Glen Spean are excellent accessible examples, are renowned for their grandeur, which is perhaps appreciated best when they are approached by way of the sea-lochs with the towering heights enclosing the inner parts.

Villages in the Highlands are usually situated where glens meet or at the ends of lochs. A few have been rebuilt on a plan in the last century, but in most, cottages of different ages stand in irregular groups; or they may be widely scattered, as crofts, along road or shore, and few houses are without flowers in their little gardens. Stately buildings are rare, but the castles of the greater Highland

Plate 9   The peak of Suilven, to the south of Loch Assynt in west
Sutherlandshire

(*Photo : Robert M. Adam*)

Plate 10   Sunset over Mull.   A view taken from the Isle of Kerrera across the Firth of Lorne

(*Photo : Robert M. Adam*)

chiefs are still harmonious features of the scene. They were the nuclei of former clan territories, *e.g.* Blair, already mentioned ; Dunstaffnage on Loch Etive—Campbell ; Achnacarry near Loch Lochy—Camerons ; Duart, Isle of Mull—MacLeans ; Dunvegan in Skye—MacLeods ; and Beaufort near Beauly—Frasers. Much more conspicuous but less harmoniously built are the numerous modern mansions and " shooting lodges " to be found in most of the glens.

While it is possible to see the Highlands from road or rail and ship, to appreciate their grandeur completely one must climb here and there. Thus alone can one explore the higher tributary glens from which the torrents have worn deep gashes down to the main valleys. And above these lie the corries, the rocky amphitheatres which held their glaciers long after the great ice sheets had melted. Where several corries are adjacent the rounded mountain top is replaced by a peak with jagged ridges thrusting out between the hollows. The corries are the haunts of red deer in summer and of the raven and the eagle. Thus the summits of such mountains as the Cairngorm group in the east, or Ben Nevis, Ben Cruachan, and very many others in the west, have forms usually classed as " alpine." And this is true of the higher islands as well. The Cuillin Hills in Skye, for example—favoured by mountaineers— suggest that the top part of some group of the Alps has been cut off and set down beside the sea !

The view from any mountain among the Inner Hebrides presents a marvellous panorama of land and sea which may be compared with many in Greece. But the range of colour is peculiar to this Atlantic atmosphere. Most of the Outer Hebrides again are low, and their beauty derives largely from the innumerable lakes and sea-lochs, from the immense stretches of pale sand fringed by natural meadow, and from the ocean itself. The homes of the islanders, too, who are both crofters and fishers, lie within sight of the sea.

The two groups of the Northern Isles differ in some respects. In Shetland rocks, vegetation, and life resemble those of the Western Isles rather than of Orkney, whereas the latter group possesses a much greater amount of good soil and a more prosperous agri- culture. Orkney is an outlier of the sandstone plateau of Caithness to which its character is allied. But the charm of both groups lies in the fine cliffs and shores, in the intricate pattern of land and water, and in all the characteristics of a people whose livelihood comes from both these elements.

FLORA AND AFFORESTATION

STANDING on the " Continental Shelf" of North-Western Europe, the British Isles, physiographically, are only a small detached portion of Europe. The separation from Europe took place in recent geological time and the flora of Britain, as might be expected, is a replica in miniature of that of the neighbouring continent, the greater part of it having reached our islands, since glacial times, over a connecting land bridge. Just as that of the British Isles is a reduced Continental one, so is the Scottish Flora a somewhat reduced English one. Moreover it is a flora comparatively poor in actual number of species, for there are approximately only 1,050 species represented there. The paucity of species is especially true in regard to trees. The only important native conifer, for instance, is the Scots pine ; other conifers which flourish with us, the European larch, the Douglas fir, and the Norway spruce, have all been introduced. And likewise the hardwoods, for the beech, sycamore, lime, and horse-chestnut, common in various parts of the country, are not indigenous, though the birch, oak, ash, elm, rowan (mountain ash), hazel, and alder are truly native.

Originally there was in Scotland a great forest-covered zone which rose almost from sea-level to an altitude of 1,000 feet or in Perthshire to 1,250 feet. But here man has wrought great changes in the flora. Many of the wild flowers are weeds of cultivation, and the existing woodlands show an inter-mixture of introduced European and North American trees. However, along streams in the valleys such native species as oak, alder, and birch are frequent. From Central Europe and Southern Britain the beech has been introduced and mixed oak and beech woods are common, with the beech generally dominant.

At a higher elevation than the oak and beech, and up to an extreme limit of 2,000 feet, the three dominant trees are the Scots pine, the larch, generally believed to have been introduced into Scotland in 1738 but recorded by Sutherland as growing in the Edinburgh Physic Garden (now, on another site, the Royal Botanic Garden) in 1683, and the birch. Wind exposure rather than low temperature is the main factor in determining the altitudinal tree limit in Scotland. On the low exposed hills of the Pentlands swept

16

with winds from the sea, conifers only occasionally attain an altitude of 1,500 feet, and then are often stunted. On the other hand, in the Grampians the Scots pine is able to find sheltered places at higher altitudes and ascends to 1,750 feet. There can be no doubt but that this tree is the native one in this sub-alpine zone, and descendants of the ancient Caledonian Forest are believed still to be found here and there, as in the Black Wood of Rannoch, on the southern shores of Loch Rannoch, and in Rothiemurchus Forest in Strathspey. The ground flora of the pine woods contains some of our most interesting and beautiful plants : *Linnaea*, a slender creeping evergreen shrub with pink sweet-scented twin flowers, a rare plant which not many years ago was collected in bunches by the school-children of Fochabers in Morayshire to take to their teachers ; the wintergreens or *Pyrolas* with their flowers like lily of the valley ; the white starry-flowered chickweed wintergreen, and *Goodyera*, the creeping lady's tresses orchid.

Scotland spells heather moors, so prominent a physical feature is the moorland of our country ; but not all our moorland is of the heather type. Travelling through Scotland one is forcibly impressed by the different colour of the slopes of our high hills ; they are either green like the Breadalbane range or brown or pinkish-purple like the Rannoch mountains. The former is the green-pasture type of moorland, the latter the heather type. They develop according to the habitat. If the soil is rich in calcium, magnesium, and potassium, pasture-moorland prevails, and on such moorland, especially on southern slopes, there occurs one of the world's most widely distributed plants, the bracken fern ; though one of the most obnoxious and injurious weeds of pastoral Scotland it is at the same time one of our most beautiful plants, from the time it unfolds its light green fronds early in the year, until it stains the moorland with rich gold in the autumn. On the other hand, if the soil be poor in mineral salts, or is of a peaty nature, then the grass gives place to heather (*Calluna*) and thus is formed the pinkish-purple moorland —the grouse moor of the Highlands. Heather reaches its maximum development in Britain and North-Western Europe ; eastwards and southwards in Europe it is never found in the great unbroken stretches we know in Scotland, where from times immemorial it has probably formed a conspicuous feature of our landscape. No doubt climatic conditions are partly responsible for this, for in Russia the limits of the plant are marked by a change from the moist conditions obtaining in North-West Europe to those of the continental steppes. But man also has played his part. He has done so firstly by deforestation, for it has been concluded that most heather moorland was formerly covered by trees ; and secondly, by regular burning, man actually *cultivates* the heather, causing young growth to spring up and so producing food for grouse and other game birds.

As few plants apart from the heather are able to survive this periodic burning, the heather does not have many plant associates. But if the moor be fairly dry and sunny, there may commonly occur the mountain whortleberry and the blaeberry with their pink bell-flowers and dark blue berries, the pink minute-flowered and black-fruited crowberry, the cloudberry with fan-shaped leaves, large white handsome flowers and orange-yellow raspberry-like fruit, and the bell heather, this last sometimes forming great spectacular purple stretches, as in July on Dinnet Moor in Aberdeenshire. On wetter moorland there may abound several species of sedge, the slender cranberry carrying on fragile stems large pink flowers and dark red fruits, the heavily perfumed bog-myrtle, the golden-flowered bog-asphodel, and its rarer cousin the Scotch asphodel with greenish-white flowers, and those fascinating plants the butterworts and sundews which, because of the sticky glands covering their leaves, are able to capture insects and, more important, feed on the digestible portions of their prey. Given excessively wet conditions, cotton grass, relatively insignificant when in flower but conspicuous enough when the long white silky hairs of the fruit are brightening the moor, forms with *Sphagnum* (the bog-moss) those patches of bog so characteristic a feature of Scottish moors. These cover the soil below the heather bushes and gradually invade neighbouring conifer woods.

In prehistoric times, bog-moss covered great tracts of country. It does so to-day in Northern Europe, but in Britain it usually forms small sheets and is of comparatively little importance. In the past, however, it was the plant mainly responsible for the formation of the peat on which the moor is founded. With an extraordinary power of absorbing water, the bog-moss covers the soil with a layer of sodden vegetation which finally dies and is added to the surface of the soil. Layer upon layer of this wet vegetation accumulates and the soil becomes water-logged and cut off from free air. There is little disintegration of plant tissues, and peat is formed which, as on Rannoch Moor and the Western Islands, may be many feet in thickness. Thus, growing and spreading very rapidly, this

Plate 11   Scots Pines near Loch Rannoch, probable descendants of the
ancient Caledonian Forest

(*Photo : Robert M. Adam*)

Plate 12   Birch trees on the shore of Loch Pityoulish, Strathspey

(*Photo : Robert M. Adam*)

Plate 13   At the pond in the Royal Botanic Garden, Edinburgh

(*Photo : Robert M. Adam*)

Plate 14 A herd of red deer with a Royal Stag in velvet in the foreground
(*Photo : Seton Gordon*)

insignificant plant has in the past advanced on to the forests, conquered them, buried them—and preserved them—in the peat. Therefore by careful examination of peat, especially of the pollen preserved therein, it is possible to trace with a high degree of accuracy the evolution of the vegetation from the Ice Age onwards. With the retreat of the ice, birch and willow seem to have been the first trees to appear. Pine came shortly afterwards and pine and birch forests were formed. After the hazel had gained some dominance in many parts, the oak, alder, and elm arrived, forming mixed oak woods, and the forests of Scotland had then reached their maximum development. But then followed a great and rapid formation of peat which overwhelmed much of the forest, and often tree stumps have been revealed embedded in the peat. Later, no doubt as the climate grew less wet and much warmer, the forests again triumphed, only to yield once again to the moor. To-day, afforestation tries to regain the moor for the forest.

In this process of afforestation the moor has to be drained, that is, excess water, the prime factor in peat formation, has to be removed. Next, available and necessary food elements must be supplied to the moor in the form of manure. For a very long time the Highlander has used those large brown seaweeds, popularly known as " kelp," as a manure for the reclaiming of the moor for agricultural purposes. To-day, basic slag is the manure commonly in use owing to the lack of lime and phosphate in the peat. After draining and manuring, the moor is then planted. In Eastern and North-Eastern Scotland, Scots pine grows well, but in the wetter Western Scotland where drainage is more difficult, Sitka and Norway spruce, especially the former, are most profitable. While no complete systematic survey of afforestable land has been made for Scotland, it is estimated that there are some two million acres which may lend themselves to planting. This is, of course, one of the main problems of the Forestry Commission (Scotland), established under the Forestry Act of 1919. Though much remains to be done, considerable progress has been made. Approximately 5,000 acres were planted in 1945 and again in 1946, chiefly in the districts of Argyll and Dumfries. The total area planted by 1946 amounted to 181,248 acres.

Not all afforestation has been at the expense of the moorland, as anyone who has visited the Culbin Sands in Morayshire will realize. This six-mile stretch of sand west of the River Findhorn has been described as the most extraordinary physical phenomenon in

Scotland. In 1694 the estate of Culbin was overwhelmed by drifting sand, and now huge accumulations of this sand extend inland in places almost to two miles, sometimes forming sandhills 100 feet or more high. Little or no vegetation covers these hills ; they are constantly moving, driven farther east by the prevailing western winds. But thanks to the Forestry Commission, the eastward drift is slowly but surely being checked, for several hundreds of acres have been planted with marram grass as well as with Corsican pine and other conifers in a successful effort to fix the sand.

Though Scotland, strictly speaking, is a dissected tableland of no very great elevation, yet it may be regarded as a mountainous country. There are, for instance, some 276 distinct mountains with 543 mountain-tops which attain a height of 3,000 feet or over. All are situated in the Highlands, and with the exception of Blaven and the Cuillins in Skye and Ben More in Mull, all are on the mainland. It is little wonder therefore that our mountain flora has always commanded the greatest interest from both amateur and professional botanists. The plants on the upper regions of our high hills are alpine or arctic in character with their typical low growth, wiry stems, and reduced hairy or fleshy leaves. While but few of them are genuinely alpine, in that they are to be found in the Alps of Central Europe, many are common members of the flora of North European, Asiatic, and North American mountains, and of arctic and sub-arctic regions throughout the Northern Hemisphere. For this reason this element in our flora is best designated Arctic-Alpine. Some of these plants are fairly abundant and widely distributed, either growing on exposed rock surfaces with or without much soil, or on the loose porous soil of the actual mountain summit. The purple, the starry, and the yellow mountain saxifrages ; the fern-leaved alpine meadow rue, and the alpine lady's mantle ; the mountain avens, oak-leaved and white-flowered ; the creeping azalea forming carpets of shiny leaves starred all over with red flowers ; the moss-campion, dwarf mountain cousin of the pink— all are plants of this nature. Others, on the other hand, are remarkable for their rarity, being confined in their few known localities to a very small area. For instance, on the wet rocky ledges of the Cuillin, and nowhere else, grows the alpine rock cress. The drooping saxifrage, rarely producing flowers but propagating itself by means of small bulbils produced in the axils of the leaves, is confined to the schistose rocks on the summit of Ben Lawers. The blue heath, heather-like and with large lilac bells, is known only from the Sow of Atholl, and the handsome sow-thistle with blue dandelion flowers only on the great granite precipices of the Eastern Coire of Lochnagar and on the adjacent hills of Angus.

Though a large number of Arctic-Alpines are common to all the mountains of the Scottish Highlands, many are concentrated in Perthshire, especially in Breadalbane, and in Angus, particularly in Clova. Thus on the ranges of mountains stretching from Ben Lui north-eastwards, and including Ben Heasgarnich, Meall nan Tarmachan, Creag an Lochan, Ben Lawers, Ben Vrackie, Caenlochan, Canness, and the hills of Clova, we have in addition to the more widely distributed plants many of our rarer boreal species, and both climatic and edaphic (or soil) factors are responsible. For on this mountain mass there are outcrops of a series of highly metamorphosed rocks known as the Lawers-Caenlochan Schist. This schist is rich in mineral salts and weathers into a fine friable porous soil, whilst the more resistent rocks form ledges where many species find lodgement. But passing from west to east along the Lawers-Caenlochan Schist, where we have the same general edaphic conditions, the number of species increases and the vegetation tends to become more boreal in character. This is almost certainly an expression of climatic conditions for the east is much drier and colder than the west, approaching in fact the more extreme conditions of the arctic.

Scotland is not all moor and mountain. She has her hedgerows fragrant with honeysuckle and white and pink wild-roses, blue and purple and yellow with vetches and vetchlings, white-starred with stitchworts, golden with ragwort. She has her meadows, rich with orchids and brilliant with the tall rosy-red spikes of the loosestrife and willow-herb, creamy masses of meadow sweet, white and pale pink drifts of cow-parsnip and angelica, pink heads of field-thistles, yellow heads of sow-thistles. And she has her lochans and tarns bordered with reeds and rushes and bright with yellow and white water-lilies, the bog-bean—close ally of the gentian—and the slender water-lobelia with nodding pale-lilac flowers.

Some of the most remarkable plants in our flora are to be found in lochans such as these. In the islands of Skye and Coll grows a plant widely distributed in North America, *Eriocaulon septangulare*—the pipewort. Its tuft of short grassy leaves is fixed to the peaty floor of the lochan, and its pin-cushion head of small mottled black-and-white flowers is carried above the surface of the water. In the island of Coll there is also the white-flowered lady's tresses orchid and the blue-eyed grass, like some miniature blue iris, and the slender *Naias* is on the mainland—in Perthshire—as well as in Skye and in North and South Uist. The particular interest of these plants lies in their geographical distribution. Apart from their Scottish stations and the few North-West European records of *Naias*, they are native only of temperate North America where they are widespread, and of Ireland. Such a distribution would seem to indicate a former closer relationship than at present exists between the north temperate floras on the two sides of the Atlantic. When the North Atlantic was much narrower than at present, or perhaps when our islands were joined to America by a land connection, these plants probably migrated eastwards from America by way of what is now Greenland and Iceland, either before or during the Ice Age. They are thus in all probability living relics and a testimony of a long lost continent.

Plate 15   Sea birds on the cliffs of the island of Berneray in the Outer Hebrides
(*Photo : Robert M. Adam*)

Plate 16 A golden eagle sheltering an eaglet with her wing from the
rays of the sun

(*Photo : Seton Gordon*)

FAUNA

FOR its size Scotland has a fauna which is rich and varied. The elk has gone; the last wolf was killed two centuries ago, but yet the wild red deer remains and adds charm and character to many a desolate moorland and hillside. The male red deer is a stag; the female a hind; the young a calf or a fawn. A stag with twelve points or tines to his horns is called a Royal, and is the prize of every sportsman. Each spring in March or April a stag "casts" his antlers—that is, they fall from his head. The new horns grow quickly, and by July may be fully formed. They are covered with soft skin known to stalkers as "velvet," and a stag is not considered ready to be shot until the velvet has left the horns, an event which takes place in late August or early September. Under ordinary conditions stags do not take to the water, but if necessary they can swim far. The roe deer may sometimes be found on the same ground as the red deer, but does not go so high on the hills, preferring the shelter of forests of birch and pine. It is a graceful little deer, full of energy, leaping easily with great bounds through long heather.

During the war years the fox greatly increased throughout Scotland, taking heavy toll of lambs and grouse. Forty lambs were killed by foxes on one common grazing during the spring of 1943, in a district of the Island of Skye, where before 1939 the fox was almost unknown. Like the fox, the fierce wild cat has spread widely during the years of war, and is now found in districts where it has been unknown during living memory. The wild cat is the most savage of British animals, and has indeed been pronounced untameable. It is curious that so savage a creature should ever associate with the domestic cat. Yet in districts where the wild cat has always been found, the domestic cat does on occasion mate with the wild tom. The kittens make excellent ratters and mousers. Wild cats are sometimes seen in strange places. One was watched in a raven's nest on a rock; another was disturbed at a peregrine falcon's eyrie on a rock sixty feet high, lost its footing and fell, bounding and bumping like a football the whole sixty feet, at the end striking a wire fence with great violence, and then running off as if nothing had happened. Sometimes a wild cat makes her home in a hollow tree. Like the red deer the wild cat can swim strongly should occasion demand it.

The stoat, a bloodthirsty small animal, is also a good swimmer. In winter it turns white in Scotland, and this white dress during a snowless winter is a disservice to it, for it can be seen at a considerable distance. The weasel, which is smaller than the stoat, is less common in most districts.

The badger is seldom seen, for it is nocturnal in its habits. It is an animal of strong individuality, intelligent and attractive, and scrupulously clean in its habits. In one forest area at least it is on the increase, and here it is popular, for it wages war on the rabbits which are destructive to young plantations. The red squirrel—a more attractive animal than the alien grey squirrel which has unfortunately been introduced into the islands, and has spread to the detriment of the native species—is also popular where forestry is an industry. The red squirrel can be tamed with ease and the beauty of its movements admired from close quarters.

Otters frequent most of the rivers and streams of Scotland, and also the rocky coastline. They are as much at home in the sea as in fresh water. They are fond of salmon, but are fastidious in their food, for they take bites only from the shoulder of the fish and leave the remainder. The otter is a great wanderer, and its tracks may sometimes be seen in the snow as it crosses some high hill pass in winter to change its fishing ground from one Highland river to another. In spring, too, otters travel great distances in order to feed upon frogs' spawn (and also no doubt on the frogs themselves) of which they are very fond.

One of the rarest Scottish animals is the pine marten. This long furred animal, which has on occasion been mistaken for a large squirrel, is found chiefly in the north-west Highlands. It was once, as its name implies, found in the old Caledonian forest of Scots pine, but its chief haunts at the present day are in straggling birch woods or on the open moor. Like the badger and the wild cat, the marten is mainly nocturnal, and is rarely seen. In autumn it is partial to rowan and other hill berries, and although on occasion it may take a farmer's chicken, it is nothing like so destructive as the fox or the wild cat, and deserves protection.

No article on the fauna of Scotland would be complete without a description of what is indeed the heaviest mammal in this country —the grey or Atlantic seal. Since the common seal is sometimes grey, and the Atlantic seal sometimes almost coal black, the name Atlantic seal is preferable to grey seal. The bull Atlantic seal is a huge beast, weighing at times over fifty stone. This seal is unique among

Scottish animals in that the season for bearing its young is not early summer, but autumn, from late September until early November. The common seal has its young in May or June. In Scotland, Atlantic seals have two widely different breeding haunts. They frequent either uninhabited islands, or inaccessible caves on the mainland coasts. The cow seals make their appearance off their islands in September and later go ashore to have their pups. These little creatures are land animals for the first month of their lives. They may on occasion be born out of sight of the Atlantic and 300 feet above it. They lie on the short grass or heather where they were born, and are suckled by the mother, who is then for a time a land animal also, and keeps guard over her pup, for which she is ready to give her life. There is no more wonderful experience for the nature lover than to visit an island where there is an Atlantic seal nursery. It is not easy to land on these islands, for the Atlantic swell in autumn almost always breaks heavily on their shores, and a wait of several weeks may be necessary before a suitable day occurs. The baby seals lie to the number of fifty to a hundred, perhaps even more, in the autumn sunshine, and the air is filled with a bleating as of lambs, but pitched in a higher key. Some of the seals sleep so soundly that they can be approached closely and even touched before they awaken. A few of the braver mother seals remain with their young, and roar and moan savagely if approached. A young Atlantic seal which had been washed by heavy seas from its island and had lost its mother was kept as a pet for some weeks by a nature lover, and each time the lady of the house went upstairs the little seal followed her.

Scotland shelters in its fields or on its hills two species of hares— the brown hare and the blue or mountain hare. The brown hare is the larger of the two. The blue or mountain hare turns white in winter, and retains its white fur long after the hills are free of snow so that it is a most conspicuous object.

Of the birds of Scotland pride of place must be given to the golden eagle. This magnificent bird is always a joy to watch, especially as he sails regally through the blue sky, and he may indeed be said to be the very spirit of the hills. Scotland was formerly the nesting-place of both the golden eagle and the sea or white-tailed eagle, but poisoning, trapping, and shooting have caused the sea eagle to become extinct in this country. The golden eagle also has no enemy but man. Amongst men he has two classes of enemy. In the first place there is the owner of a grouse moor whose keepers tell him that he cannot expect grouse and eagles. Pole traps are still used, illegally, for trapping eagles : the fact that the bird may be protected by law is no deterrent to those who seek its life. In the second class of enemy is the egg collector. Collectors will offer gamekeepers and shepherds as much as ten pounds for a well-marked clutch of eagle's eggs.

Both male and female share in the duties of incubating the eggs, which take six weeks to hatch. A pair of eagles under observation were found to be most regular in the hour of their change over, which took place at six o'clock in the evening by Greenwich time. On one occasion the female made a magnificent stoop from a great height. She alighted at the edge of the nest and stood there, quietly and expectantly, for some minutes. The male seemed reluctant to leave the eggs and his wife was evidently communicating with him without sound. At last he rose and launched out over the cliff while his mate settled herself on the eggs. There was a strong wind blowing, and the eagle flying away from the eyrie travelled at impressive speed—he might have been the spirit of the storm. On another occasion the male eagle was sunning himself on the top of the cliff when he was set upon and mobbed by a pair of ravens. These angry birds so annoyed him that he was forced to take wing and with the ravens in close pursuit sailed swiftly down to the eyrie. Before he had reached it the ravens left him, and his mate rising to her feet in greeting as he arrived, almost at once flew off, the relieving bird, of a darker plumage than his mate, taking over the charge of the eggs. He showed extreme care in settling down upon and brooding the precious eggs, lowering himself very slowly on to them and then gently tucking them away beneath his plumage.

The peregrine falcon is another king of the air, more dashing, and more ruthless than the eagle. The peregrine sometimes kills for the love of killing and leaves the prey to fall to the ground while he speeds on to some fresh attack. Merlin and kestrel are found in Scotland, but that small and dashing hawk the " hobby," which has been known to capture swifts on the wing, is found only in England. The buzzard, a lethargic bird, has considerably increased in Scotland, but the graceful hen harrier has decreased in some of its last nesting haunts. Recently this fine bird has attempted to establish itself on the mainland of Scotland, but has been shot and trapped ruthlessly.

Grouse and ptarmigan have decreased during the war years,

and the stock of both is lower than for a generation. Many factors contribute to this decrease. The eagle has been blamed, but the eagle is no more numerous than in 1939; indeed it has greatly decreased on the south-eastern fringe of its territory, although in the west it is holding its own. The red grouse is the only bird that the British Islands can claim for their very own. It has been introduced into other parts of Europe, and in some countries has thriven, but Britain, and more especially Scotland, is its home. The red grouse is considered to have come from ptarmigan stock. As the Ice Age receded and the winters became less severe, it was no longer necessary for the ptarmigan on the lower ground to assume a white plumage, and thus in time was evolved the race of red grouse. In winter the ptarmigan in the purity of their white dress rival the surrounding snows. " They will," as an old shepherd once said, " be the last birds left alive when the world grows cold." Ptarmigan on the nest are sometimes close sitters. I have taken an egg from beneath a sitting ptarmigan and replaced it without causing the bird to rise from her nest.

An even tamer bird than the ptarmigan is the dotterel, a bird not unlike the golden plover but smaller, which has its summer home on the high Scottish hills. The hen dotterel is agreeable to laying the three eggs but, this done, she takes no further interest in them, and the husband has to hatch them unaided. He is sometimes extraordinarily tame. Like the eagle, the dotterel is much sought after by egg collectors, and it is so tame and friendly that the nest is easy to find.

In a short article it is impossible to include all Scottish birds. High over the cities of Edinburgh and Glasgow the swift sails of a summer evening, and in the country districts swallows, house martins, and sand martins hawk for insects. Sand martins nest in gravel pits. The mavis or song thrush, the handsome blackbird, the large missel-thrush, greatest of Scottish-nesting thrushes, are all common in Scotland. So, too, are the chaffinch, the greenfinch, the minute golden-crested wren, and the oyster-catcher and sand-piper which haunt Highland rivers in summer. The blackheaded gull nests on hill lochs, and the herring gull frequents fishing-ports and even the cities such as Edinburgh and Aberdeen. In spring the moors echo with the love song of the curlew or whaup and the rollicking cry of the lapwing. Indeed, the beauty and variety of its wild life are distinctive features of Scotland and add greatly to its charm.

ARCHÆOLOGY

FOR a small country Scotland is singularly rich in prehistoric monuments. If these cannot compare in size with those of more favoured lands, they may claim a peculiar interest through their variety. Behind this variety there lies a circumstance of great historical importance. Situated at the extreme north-west corner of the Old World, Scotland has at various times received into her bosom, and has offered an ultimate sanctuary to, racial immigrations and cultural streams emanating from three diverse quarters—from the Mediterranean, *via* Spain, Brittany, and Ireland ; from the Alpine regions, *via* the Rhine valley and the Low Countries ; and from the Baltic, *via* the Northern Isles.

The oldest of our Scottish monuments belong to the first of these cultural streams. They are the chambered burial cairns of the men of the New Stone Age, a Mediterranean stock who, more than four thousand years ago, reached our western shores by the route just indicated, and thence slowly overspread the country to north and east. Such cairns are usually elongated in shape, and contain an internal chamber or gallery, often subdivided by partitions, which served as a family ossuary, wherein the representatives of one kindred were buried over a long succession of generations. Both inhumation and cremation were employed, though there is evidence that the former was the older rite. In Sutherland, Caithness, and Orkney these chambered cairns sometimes have curious projecting horns. The most imposing of our chambered cairns is Maeshowe in Orkney, which measures 92 feet in diameter and 36 feet in height, and rises from a ditch 40 feet across. It is one of the most impressive prehistoric monuments in northern Europe. Unfortunately it was pillaged by *Jorsalafarar*, Scandinavian pilgrims to Jerusalem, probably in the twelfth century, and they have left their inscriptions on the walls of the beautifully built internal chamber.

At the beginning of the Bronze Age, about 1800 B.C., new races were entering Scotland by her eastern seaboard, coming overseas from Holland and Belgium. They were a round-headed folk, whereas the chambered cairn builders for the most part had long skulls. At first the new-comers inhumed their dead singly in short stone cists, but very soon cremation became the rule, and the ashes were gathered into or underneath a cinerary urn. Where there is a cairn it is round, and some of the great round cairns of this period, placed as they usually are on commanding situations, rank among the most impressive of our prehistoric monuments.

To the later Bronze Age belong the circles of standing stones, popularly known as Druidical Circles. In these, Scotland is especially rich. Several distinct types occur, notably one peculiar to the north-east, marked out by a large recumbent stone generally on the south-western side. Recent investigation of these recumbent stone circles shows that in some cases they remained in use as burial places until the Iron Age, and perhaps even down into Roman-British times.

On many of our standing stones, and also on live rock surfaces, cup marks are found. These are small circular sinkings, tending to occur in groups ; the cups are sometimes surrounded with rings, and may be connected by channels. What purpose they served is quite unknown, but they represent a Mediterranean cult, which reached Scotland by her western approaches.

It is in the northern isles that we first obtain clear evidence about the habitations of the living. At Skara Brae in Orkney a famous village has been unearthed, consisting of a group of eight huts built of stones not laid in cement, and blanketed about with the midden deposits of the householders, who in this way sought to provide shelter for themselves against the pitiless winds and the driving sand. At Rinyo, also in Orkney, a second such village was discovered. The relics found in both show they were inhabited in New Stone Age times. A more advanced civilization was displayed by a third village, at Jarlshof in Shetland, where the principal occupation can be dated to the latter part of the Bronze Age.

In the more central parts of the country, and on land that has escaped cultivation, groups of hut circles are often found, associated with stock pounds and other indications of a primitive agricultural community. Sometimes these hut circles have underground chambers, known as earth-houses, which are especially frequent in Aberdeenshire. Remains found in the earth-houses show that they were lived in, doubtless as winter quarters. They were in occupation at the time of the Roman invasion, because Roman objects are sometimes found in them, and in two cases Roman stones have been used to build them. These earth-houses are very cleverly constructed. Their dry-built side walls are corbelled out in their upper portion until the space between them is narrow enough to be spanned by enormous lintels. Some of these earth-houses are as much as 80 feet in length. In the Outer Isles, wheel-shaped earth-houses of very elaborate design are found.

Another class of habitation which was used in Scotland during Romano-British times was the crannog or lake-dwelling erected on piles, or formed of stones and earth pegged down by a wooden girdle. In the Highlands, there are records of such lake-dwellings having been constructed as late as the sixteenth century.

Towards the close of the prehistoric period we find for the first time defensive works, not seldom of enormous size and strength. This must mean that the population was becoming denser, that its pressure on the means of subsistence was causing inter-tribal stress, and that larger political units were in course of formation. Some of these hill-forts have massive ramparts of earth-work; others have stone walls, built without cement, but in some cases strengthened by bonding timbers after a fashion which Caesar has described to us in his account of some of the Gaulish hill-top towns which he besieged. When the beams of such a wall were set on fire, by the conflagration of the hutments within, the result is a vitrified wall. Of these vitrified forts, Scotland has some very fine examples, such as Finhaven in Angus or Tap o' Noth in Aberdeenshire. Some of our larger hill forts are really hill-top towns, like those in Gaul already referred to. Of these, the most famous is Traprain Law in East Lothian. This town of the Votadini was inhabited during the first four centuries of our era, by a people in trading relations with the Romans. Within its ramparts, about the year 400, was buried the celebrated hoard of Roman silver known as the Treasure of Traprain, discovered in 1919. This is the loot of Roman villas and churches, probably from Gaul, and was doubtless buried on the hill by Saxon or Frisian pirates. It is now in the National Museum of Antiquities, Edinburgh.

The constructive capacity of our prehistoric inhabitants reached its climax in the brochs. These are peculiar to Scotland, and of them she may well be proud. They are mostly found in the extreme north and west, but there is one in Stirlingshire and another in the Merse. The only one that now survives in anything like a complete state is the Broch of Mousa, in Shetland, which is 45 feet in height. The typical broch is a hollow tower of dry-built masonry, enclosing a central court, in which there was usually a wooden penthouse. The walls of the tower are hollowed into a series of galleries, and a stair winding round the circumference of the tower leads up to

Plate 17 (*Above*) Standing Stones at Callanish, near Stornoway, a
'Druidical Circle' of the later Bronze Age   (*Photo : Valentine*)
(*Below*) Maeshowe, Orkney : a chambered burial cairn of the New
Stone Age   (*Photo : T. Kent*)

Plate 18   Skara Brae, Orkney, a village of the New Stone Age
(*Above*) A General View.   (*Below*) Interior of one of the stone huts

(*Photos : T. Kent*)

the parapet on top of its wall. The relics found in these structures show that they were chiefly occupied in the first and second centuries of the Christian era. In the Western Isles, numerous small forts, known as *duns*, are found, mostly on rocky sites. Many of these have galleries resembling those of the brochs ; but whether the broch was evolved from the galleried *dun*, or whether the latter is the degenerated representative of the broch, is a matter of dispute. It is at all events certain that not a few *duns*, like some of the crannogs, continued to be occupied until late in the Middle Ages.

Although the Romans never subjugated Scotland, they occupied it as far north as the Tay valley, and their marching camps stretch on beyond that up into Aberdeenshire. In Agricola's time (A.D. 80) there was a legionary fort at Inchtuthil on the Tay ; and in the next century under the Emperor Antoninus Pius, the governor Lollius Urbicus built, in the year 142, his famous Wall across the 37 miles of isthmus between the Forth and Clyde. The Wall was 14 feet in width, carefully built of coursed sods resting on a stone bed, and was probably 10 or 12 feet high. East of Falkirk, it consists not of sods but of simple earth. Outside was a dry ditch. The garrison were housed in forts, probably nineteen in number, placed on an average about 2 miles apart. A network of built roads, secured by forts at strategic points, enabled the Romans to police the country behind the Wall. Quite a number of Roman forts in Scotland, apart from those on the Wall, have now been explored. The most famous are Ardoch in Perthshire, Birrens in Dumfries-shire, and Newstead near Melrose. The garrisons of all these forts, including those along the Wall itself, were light armed auxiliaries, the heavy legions being quartered in the fortresses of Chester, York, and Caerleon, far to the south. The legions were a field force employed for a serious campaign, but too valuable for the rough and tumble of frontier warfare.

At the close of the Roman period Christianity entered Scotland through the mission of St. Ninian, who planted his monastery at *Candida Casa*, now Whithorn in Galloway, in the year 397. Our oldest Christian monuments are accordingly found in Galloway, and exhibit inscriptions in the base Latin of the later Empire, together with the Chi-Rho monogram so common upon Christian tombs on the Continent from the fourth century onwards.

By this time the inhabitants of Scotland were mainly of a Celtic race, and had developed a very considerable degree of civilization. In the dark ages that followed the collapse of the Roman Empire, this native civilization, in the eastern lowlands north of the Forth, reached its climax in the wonderful art of our Celtic sculptured stones. The oldest class of these fascinating monuments are untooled or nearly so, and the ornamentation, which is incised, exhibits human and animal figures, executed with the utmost verve and realism, as well as those mysterious geometrical and other forms known as Pictish symbolism. The meaning of these is entirely unknown. Later on, in the ninth and tenth centuries, these figure subjects are carved in relief, and highly enriched with interlaced work and other forms of Celtic ornamentation, and are associated with a Celtic cross ; while the monument itself now is much more carefully shaped and dressed. Lastly, the symbolism and figure sculpture pass out of use, and the cross alone remains. In the eastern low-lands, the cross is almost always graven on a slab, but in the western Highlands and Islands, where Irish influence was strong, the cross is usually free-standing. In the eastern lowlands, this very brilliant Celtic monumental art was killed by the Anglo-Norman penetration of the twelfth and thirteenth centuries, which brought the medieval art of Continental Europe in its train. But in the west it continued to flourish, and to burgeon forth in ever fresh forms of attractive-ness, quaintly blending Celtic and Gothic motives, until it was finally extinguished by the Calvinism which followed upon the Reformation.

To the general student, the chief interest of our Celtic sculptured stones is the vivid light which they cast upon the life and customs, the armour, weapons, and costume, civil and ecclesiastical, of those far-off times. We have scenes of hunting and scenes of war, with horse and foot engaged in disciplined formation ; chariots or covered wagons ; musical instruments both wind and stringed ; seafaring scenes, with rowing and sailing craft ; clerics on their missionary journeys, with cloak and staff and scrip ; and ceremonial occasions of various kinds. As the scanty chronicles of those times are almost wholly silent upon such matters, the information which these sculptured monuments yield us is precious indeed.

Scotland contains some fifteen monuments with inscrip-tions in the ogham alphabet, a form of writing generally believed to have been introduced from Ireland. In Ireland and Wales these inscriptions can usually be read without much difficulty, but un-fortunately in Scotland the number of versions of our oghams is in each case about equal to the number of scholars who have endeavoured to decipher them.

By far the most important of our early sculptured stones in Scotland is the Ruthwell Cross, nine miles from Dumfries. This is one of the noblest Dark Age monuments in Western Europe. In addition to figure sculpture of the highest artistic merit, exhibiting strong Hellenistic influence, this splendid cross, which dates probably from the seventh century, has inscriptions in Latin and in Anglian runes. The latter inscription contains part of an old English poem of great beauty and pathos, in which the cross itself narrates the part which it played in the tragedy of Calvary :

> Then the young Hero, Who was mightiest God,
>   Strong and with steadfast mind,
> Up to the cross with steps unfaltering trod,
>   There to redeem mankind.
> I trembled, but I durst not fail,
>   I on my shoulder bare the glorious King.
> They pierce my sides with many a darksome nail,
>   And on us both their cruel curses fling.

Long after the inscription had been successfully read upon the cross, a copy of the poem turned up in a tenth-century manuscript in the conventual library at Vercelli in Italy. Thus this famous cross must be regarded " not only as a finger post in the history of Christian art, but as a landmark in the history of English literature."

Apart from the sculptured stones, the monuments of the Celtic Church are hardly impressive. They include certain early monastic sites in the Hebrides, notably Eileach an Naoimh with its beehive huts ; the remarkable hermit's cell on the island of Inchcolm, in the Firth of Forth ; and two round towers of Irish type at Brechin and Abernethy. The latter stands free as it was built, but the Brechin tower is now incorporated into the medieval cathedral. Such towers were erected by the Celtic clergy as a refuge for themselves and their holy things during the period when the Norse sea-rovers ravaged our land. The Brechin tower is the earlier of the two, and the Abernethy tower shows Romanesque influence in its upper part.

Throughout the whole range of the prehistoric and early Christian periods in Scotland caves were inhabited. Among the most ancient traces of human life in our country must be classed the worked antlers and charcoal found along with the remains of an Arctic fauna in a cave at Inchnadamph, in Sutherland. The hunter folk must have dwelt there when northern Scotland had hardly yet emerged from the Ice Age. Other caves, in the old cliffs of the 25-foot beach at Oban, reveal a primitive fishing population who lived by collecting oysters and periwinkles, and harpooning fish and seals. At Covesea near Elgin a cave has been excavated which was occupied in the Bronze and Iron Ages, by a community who in the latest period used Roman pottery and brooches and barbarous imitations of Roman coins. The well-known caves on the Fife coast show carvings of Pictish symbols and Celtic crosses, and were doubtless inhabited by hermits, like St. Ninian's famous cave near Whithorn.

Plate 19 The Broch of Mousa, Shetland, the most perfect example in
existence of a Pictish broch or castle

(Photo : Valentine)

Plate 20   Round Tower, Abernethy, erected by the Celtic clergy as
a refuge against Norse invasions

(*Photo : Valentine*)

HISTORY

NOT the least surprising feature of the island of Britain is the existence of more than one nation within its narrow limits. Geographical conditions alone fail to account for these different nationalities. Not the stage and its scenery but the story of the drama explains their gradual evolution. The curtain rises in North Britain with the tramp of the Roman legions under the famous Agricola. They merely cross the stage leaving behind them little but the relics of a military occupation. When the curtain rises again at the beginning of the sixth century we find the country in the possession of four peoples—the Picts, the Scots, the Britons, and the Angles. The Picts, apparently a Celtic people, occupied the territory north of the Forth and Clyde. The Scots, also Celtic immigrants but from Northern Ireland, had established in the west of Scotland the small kingdom of Dalriada, corresponding mainly to the modern Argyllshire. To the south of the Firth of Clyde lay Strathclyde, the kingdom of the Britons, the original Celtic inhabitants of South Britain, who had been driven north and west by the Anglo-Saxon invaders after the departure of the Romans. Lastly, between Strathclyde and the coast south of the Firth of Forth was Northumbria, the Teutonic kingdom of the Anglian invaders from the north of the Elbe.

TERRITORIAL UNITY

How did these four kingdoms become one ? As in other European countries, the main impulse towards unity came from religion. The Scots were already nominally Christian when they left the island of St. Patrick. In 563 their fellow-countryman, St. Columba of royal descent, sailing from Ireland " the Isle of Saints " with twelve companions, landed on the island of Iona off the west coast of Dalriada, where he set up his first monastery. Two years later he went on a mission to Brude, King of the Picts. The hostile gates of his rude fortress at Inverness flew open, we are told, at the sign of the cross, and the King's " conversion " was followed by that of his people. St. Mungo or Kentigern, in after times the patron saint of Glasgow, brought Christianity to the Britons of Strathclyde, and St. Cuthbert laboured among the Angles of Lothian between the Firth of Forth and the River Tweed, which was to become the eastern part of the boundary between Scotland and England.

The second impulse came from the aggression of foreign foes, especially the Norsemen. These raiders, the scourge of western Christendom, conquered the Orkney and Shetland Islands, the North, and the Hebrides Islands off the west coast, where they settled permanently. A common faith and a common danger brought Scot and Pict together, and in 844 Kenneth MacAlpin, King of the Scots, became ruler over both peoples. For many years the rulers of Alba, as the united kingdoms were called, endeavoured to extend their boundaries southwards, but it was not until 1018 that Malcolm II (1005–1034) defeated the Northumbrians at Carham on the River Tweed, and acquired the fertile district of Lothian. During his reign he succeeded in placing his grandson Duncan, the Duncan of Shakespeare's *Macbeth*, on the throne of Strathclyde. Malcolm was the first to be called King of Scotland.

CONSOLIDATION

Territorial unity, excluding the conquests of the Norsemen, had thus been achieved but the welding of Scot, Briton, and Angle, differing in speech, custom, and law, had still to be accomplished. It began during the reign of Malcolm III (1058–1093), who was a contemporary of William the Norman, Conqueror of England. Refugees from across the Border increased the English element among the inhabitants south of the Firth of Forth, and Malcolm's marriage with the fugitive English princess Margaret began a gradual process whereby the interests of the Scottish monarchy became detached from the Celtic Gaelic-speaking north—the Highlands— and identified with the Teutonic English-speaking south—Lothian.

The southern customs introduced in Church and government through the influence of Margaret, Queen and Saint—her chapel is in Edinburgh Castle—were furthered by her sons, especially David I (1124–1153). He had spent some years at the court of the King of England, and he returned to Scotland with Anglo-Norman knights in his train whom he rewarded with extensive grants of land. They and their descendants, the Bruces, Balliols, Comyns and other baronial families, thus frequently owed a double allegiance, to the King of Scotland for the domains they held from him and to the King of England for those south of the Border. It was through them that Scotland became a feudal state and was brought within the orbit of western civilization. The Church provided a channel for the new ideas. The isolated Columban monasteries were supplanted by those of orders of monks organized throughout Christendom. Bishoprics were increased, parishes created, burghs grew up round the monasteries and castles, and trade developed.

David also succeeded in making good his claims to parts of Northern England. His son, Malcolm IV (1153–1165), failed to hold them, and his grandson, William the Lyon (1165–1214), captured in an attempt to recover them, was forced for fifteen years to acknowledge the King of England as Scotland's overlord : but from Richard I, eager to raise money for a crusade, he was able to redeem his country's freedom. For the next hundred years the relations between the two countries were on the whole friendly. The Scottish rulers were able to consolidate and develop their Kingdom, and to regain those districts which had been lost either by the conquests of the Norsemen or by Celtic revolts against the innovations introduced from the south. Thus Alexander II (1214–1249) reconquered Argyll, and Alexander III (1249–1286) defeated King Hakon of Norway at the battle of Largs and reunited the western islands of his kingdom. When Alexander was killed by the fall of his horse over a cliff, Scotland, according to a modern historian, was "relatively to her resources, the most prosperous country in Europe." The oldest fragment of her literature laments Alexander's untimely death as the end of a Golden Age :

> Quhen Alysandyr oure Kyng wes dede,
>
> ★   ★   ★   ★   ★   ★   ★   ★   ★
>
> Oure gold wes changyd in to lede.
>   Cryst, borne in to Vyrgynté
> Succoure Scotland and remede,
>   That stad [is in] pirplexyté.

THE WAR OF INDEPENDENCE

That "pirplexyté" was a disputed succession. Margaret, "the Maid of Norway," infant grand-daughter and heiress of Alexander III, died on her way to Scotland (1290). Edward I, one of the most powerful of the English kings, constituted himself arbiter among the claimants to the throne, and coerced them into acknowledging him as Scotland's overlord. Many of the rivals already owed him allegiance for their lands in England, as did Edward himself to the

King of France for his French domains. He decided in favour of John Balliol. His brief reign (1292–1296) was disastrous. Edward's rigorous insistence on his feudal rights provoked Balliol to resistance. When Edward called upon him as his vassal to aid him in a war with France, Balliol rebelled and in 1295 concluded a treaty with the French king. Thus began the Franco-Scottish Alliance, which, owing to the dread and hatred of England, the common foe, lasted for over 260 years. During that period Scotland was influenced by French culture and institutions, and even to-day the memories of the " Auld Alliance," as it is called, form a sentimental tie between the two countries.

Balliol's resistance was short-lived. He was defeated and forced to abdicate. The Scottish barons, many with landed interests in both countries, submitted and Scotland was governed by English officials. By their oppression the Scots were goaded into revolt and found a leader in Sir William Wallace. The skilful leadership of this commoner, feebly supported by the jealous barons, drove the English out of many of their strongholds. In the end he was betrayed, and after trial in Westminster Hall, London, suffered the ignominy and barbarities of a traitor's death from a king to whom he had never sworn allegiance. He is one of Scotland's national heroes, and the romantic story of his exploits told in verse by Henry the Minstrel—" Blind Harry "—in the fifteenth century long inspired the patriotism of the Scottish people.

A new champion arose in Robert Bruce, Earl of Carrick, grandson of one of the chief claimants of the throne when Balliol was chosen. Like many of the Scottish barons, he held large estates in England and was a trusted supporter of the king. In a fit of anger he slew his rival, John Comyn, in a church in Dumfries. Outlawed by King Edward and excommunicated by the Pope for sacrilege, Bruce committed himself to Scotland's cause. Of the magnates of the realm, only five earls, four bishops, and an abbot were present when he hurriedly had himself crowned king at Scone, near Perth, in 1306. A circlet of gold replaced the ancient crown. The " Stone of Destiny," held to be the very pillow of the patriarch Jacob when he dreamt at Bethel, and on which previous Scottish kings had been crowned, had been carried off by King Edward to London, where it still forms part of the coronation chair in Westminster Abbey.

By his skill and patience and his human qualities, Bruce won a place in the hearts of the Scots which blotted out the memories

Plate 21   Iona Cathedral and St. Oran's Chapel, the cradle of Christianity
in Scotland

(*Photo : Valentine*)

Plate 22   Edinburgh Castle, showing the Changing of the Guard

(*Photo : Valentine*)

of his early career. Undaunted by early defeats, he gradually fought his way to success until Stirling Castle was the only fortress held by the oppressors. To its relief, Edward II, son of Edward I, the "Hammer of the Scots," led a mighty host which suffered the greatest rout in English history at the Battle of Bannockburn, near Stirling, on 24th June 1314. The struggle was prolonged for another fourteen years, and the spirit that animated the Scots found its noblest expression in 1320 in an appeal to the Pope made by the barons assembled at Arbroath. In their own behalf, and " for the rest of the barons, freeholders and the whole community of the realm of Scotland " they declared : " It is not for glory, riches or honours that we fight : it is for liberty alone which no good man relinquishes but with life." In 1328, the year before Bruce's death, England recognized the independence of Scotland. Even Bruce's unworthy son, David II (1329–1371), prepared to barter his country's freedom, could not undo his father's achievement.

The War of Independence is the greatest event in Scotland's history. It confirmed its existence as a separate nation and state ; and though poverty-stricken and distracted by continual warfare with the " Auld Enemy " and torn by internal feuds, she was to emerge strong in the spirit of liberty and freedom. As her poet Barbour wrote, two generations after Bruce :

> A ! fredome is a noble thing !
> Fredome mays man to haiff liking ;   *makes*
> Fredome all solace to man giffis ;
> He levys at es that frely levys.   *lives/ease*

THE CROWN AND THE BARONS

As in feudal Europe, the struggle between the Crown and the barons was the main characteristic of Scotland during the later Middle Ages. The barons had grown " overmighty subjects " by the large estates, confiscated from the supporters of the English, with which Bruce had rewarded his adherents. The advent of the famous line of Stewart to the throne in the person of Robert II (1371–1390) through the marriage of Bruce's daughter to the King's Steward brought no prestige to the Crown. The barons regarded him and his successor, Robert III (1390–1406), as one of themselves. During a long series of royal minorities the country suffered the woes " when the King is a child." There were seven between 1329 and 1561 and it has been calculated that the Crown was strong for only a fifth of that period.

James I (1406–1437) had been captured as a boy on his way to France, and was for eighteen years a state prisoner in England. On his return to Scotland (1424), he set about restoring order with a ruthlessness which led to his assassination. His son, James II (1437–1460), succeeded in crushing the powerful house of Douglas, descended from Bruce's comrade-in-arms, the "good Sir James"; but James III (1460–1488) displayed personal qualities which rendered him obnoxious to a rude baronage. They hanged his favourites—a musician, an architect, and others—and eventually rose in revolt. The King fell by an assassin's knife after his defeat at Sauchieburn, near Stirling.

His son, James IV (1488–1513), young and vigorous, made his power felt in every part of the kingdom. The Lord of the Isles and his vassal chiefs in the Highlands were brought into subjection. In the Borders, the wild southern region adjoining England, law and order were imposed by frequent courts of justice. The royal arsenal was equipped with cannon—such as Mons Meg, still to be seen in Edinburgh Castle. A navy was built of which the *Great Michael* was the largest ship afloat. Learning was not neglected. To the two existing universities of St. Andrews (1412) and Glasgow (1451) a third at Aberdeen was added (1495). The fourth was not founded in Edinburgh until 1582. An Education Act required the barons and freeholders to send their eldest sons to the grammar schools. Printing was introduced from France, and William Dunbar, Gavin Douglas, and other poets and writers added lustre to the Court.

James's prestige was enhanced by the conditions of European diplomacy. England, France, Spain, and the Empire all strove to secure Scotland's support as a makeweight in the new-born conception of "the balance of power." In 1503 James had married Margaret, daughter of Henry VII, King of England—"the marriage of the Thistle and the Rose"—a marriage which was to lead to the union of the Crowns of both countries in 1603. But when Henry VIII went to war with France, James, true to the Franco-Scottish alliance, invaded England and fell with the flower of the realm at Flodden in 1513, a disaster still commemorated annually in the Border town of Selkirk.

The Reformation

The troubles of the minority of his son, James V (1513–1542), were complicated by dissensions regarding religion and foreign policy. When his personal rule began, an English party had arisen, favourable to the Lutheran doctrines infiltrating from the Continent, and supported by King Henry VIII of England, who broke with the Pope and enriched the Crown with the spoils of the Church. A sincere Catholic, dependent on the Churchmen to strengthen the Crown, James turned a deaf ear to his uncle Henry's advice to follow his example. When England and France were at feud, James sided with Scotland's old ally. His army was routed at Solway Moss, and the King, dying broken-hearted, was succeeded by his daughter, the famous Mary Stewart. Henry VIII raised the old claim of overlordship over Scotland, and the young queen was sent for safety to France and betrothed to the Dauphin. The French sent an expeditionary force to Scotland which helped to drive out the English and peace was restored.

It was during the regency of Mary of Lorraine, who ruled Scotland for her daughter still in France, that the religious revolution, the Reformation, came to a head. The Church was corrupt and too late endeavoured to amend its ways, while the reformers were full of zeal. Protestantism, however, owing to its English sympathies, was deemed unpatriotic, and for a time the Catholic French party maintained their ascendancy. But when the Regent began to treat Scotland as a province of France, especially after Mary's marriage to the Dauphin, dread of French domination replaced the ancient hatred of England and the number of Protestants increased. They were inspired by John Knox, home from exile in Geneva where he had played a part in Calvin's city, ruled " according to the Evangel and the Word of God." When they rose in rebellion Elizabeth, Queen of England, anxious for the security of her Protestant realm, lent her aid. Victory was assured by the Treaty of Edinburgh (1560). All connection with Rome was severed, a Calvinistic Confession of Faith was drawn up by Knox and his colleagues and ratified by the Scottish Parliament, and the Franco-Scottish Alliance came to an end.

" No historical personage outside Scripture," it has been said, " is better known to the world at large than Mary Stewart " (1542–1567). Historians, poets, and romancers of every country have been fascinated by her tragic story. The early years of her rule when she returned a widowed queen from France (1561) were indeed peaceful. She acquiesced at first in a Protestant Scotland in the hope of ultimately reigning over a united Catholic Britain. It was the refusal of her cousin, Elizabeth of England, the " Virgin Queen," to recognize Mary as her successor that was the beginning of the tragedy. There followed the well-known series of events—her marriage to Darnley, himself a claimant to the English throne—the assassination of her secretary Rizzio, dragged from her presence in the supper-room in Holyrood Palace—the murder of Darnley—her marriage to Bothwell, justly suspected of his death—their final parting at Carberry Hill—her imprisonment in Lochleven Castle— her dramatic escape—her defeat at Langside—her flight into England —her execution at Fotheringay Castle in 1587 after eighteen years' imprisonment.

THE CROWN AND THE KIRK

During the seventeenth century the history of Scotland as of Western Europe generally was characterized by those wars of religion which arose out of the Reformation. In Scotland they had their origin in the struggles of James VI, Mary's son (1567–1625), after the usual turbulent minority, to assert the power of the Crown. A judicious distribution of the lands of the old Church won over the nobles. But a new opposition had arisen. The Scottish Reformation had been a popular movement effected not by the Crown and ministers of State as in England but by ministers of religion such as John Knox. In the Presbyterian Church of Scotland—the Kirk—all the ministers had equal status ; there were no archbishops or bishops ; laymen as well as ministers composed its ecclesiastical courts. The highest, the General Assembly, in contrast to the feudal Scottish Parliament, dating from the end of the thirteenth century, was a democratic body. The pulpit in every church provided a means of expounding the theocratic views of its leaders, derived from Geneva. To control this new force, James succeeded in gradually imposing bishops, nominated by himself, upon the Kirk. These he hoped would also bring about a uniformity with the Episcopal Church of England : for he was as resolute as his mother to succeed to the throne of that country. In 1603, on the death of Queen Elizabeth, he realized his ambition, and as the descendant of James IV of Scotland and Margaret of England became James I, King of England and Ireland.

Plate 23   Stirling Castle, on the River Forth, commanding the entrance
to the Highlands

(*Photo : Valentine*)

Plate 24   Melrose Abbey, a Cistercian abbey founded by King David I
in 1136 ; one of the most famous abbeys in Scotland

(*Photo : Robert M. Adam*)

Plate 25 Dunfermline Abbey, founded as a priory for Benedictines by
Margaret, wife of Malcolm Canmore, and consecrated as an abbey in the
reign of David I. The view shows the nave, the only part remaining intact

(Photo : Robert M. Adam)

Plate 26 James III, from the painting by Van der Goes
in the National Gallery of Scotland. It is not certain
whether the figure behind the King is his son or his
brother

(By gracious permission of His Majesty the King)

The Union of the Crowns constituted a purely personal tie and Scotland and England remained separate states each with its own government and parliament. But it immensely increased the power and prestige of the Scottish monarch. It was no idle boast of James that from London he was able to rule Scotland with his pen as none of his ancestors had been able to do with the sword. The Episcopal organization of the Kirk was completed. His son, Charles I (1625–1649), a conscientious Episcopalian, again in the interest of uniformity, forced a liturgy on the Kirk which caused the Scots to suspect him of re-introducing Roman Catholicism. National indignation found vent in the National Covenant (1638), the subscribers to which denounced the ecclesiastical innovations. Headed by the nobles, whom Charles had alienated by an endeavour to reclaim the Church lands, the " Covenanters " took up arms and the King was forced to give way ; for his struggles with the Scots coincided with his quarrel with his opponents in England. When the Civil War broke out there, the Scots, doubting the King's sincerity, sided with the English Parliamentarians. As a further safeguard they insisted on a religious treaty, the Solemn League and Covenant (1643), by which, in return for military aid, the English bound themselves to establish Presbyterianism in Great Britain and Ireland.

The Scots played a notable part in the Civil War, but their hopes of a Presbyterian Britain were frustrated by the rise of Oliver Comwell and his followers, believers in the rights of separate congregations of worshippers, to whom Presbyterianism was as obnoxious as Episcopacy. Mutual distrust ensued, and after the execution of King Charles by Cromwell and his army (1649), the Scots came to terms with his son Charles II, whom force of circumstances compelled to sign both Covenants. At Dunbar (1650) and Worcester (1651) the Scottish armies were shattered, and for nine years Scotland lay under the alien yoke of Cromwell and his successor, while the King was an exile on the Continent.

On the fall of the Cromwellian régime the Scots enthusiastically welcomed the restoration of Charles II (1660) to the Kingdoms of Scotland, England, and Ireland. The nobles had learnt their lesson and were henceforth strenuous supporters of the Crown, and Charles became an absolute monarch. Repudiating the Covenants —" Presbyterianism," he said, " is no religion for a gentleman "— he restored Episcopacy, but, wiser than his father, did not re-introduce episcopal ritual. The Covenanters refused to accept the compromise, and many of the ministers were expelled from their parishes.

43

The attempts of Charles and of his brother and successor, James VII of Scotland and II of England (1685–1689), to dragoon these recusants into submission constitute the dismal records of their reigns. Many accepted the liberty of preaching offered by a series of "Indulgences," but a stubborn minority braved torture and the gibbet to the end. The stories of these sufferers for long remained the much-prized reading of a large proportion of the Scottish people, and the graves of the martyrs are still piously preserved especially in the South-east and South-west.

The real intention of the "Indulgences" offered to the Covenanters by King James was to benefit his co-religionists, the Roman Catholics, in his attempt to bring Scotland back to the old faith. But few even of the subservient nobility were prepared to win the royal favour by adopting the King's religion. Both Episcopalians and Presbyterians offered a passive resistance, and when events in England forced James to seek safety in flight to France, Scotland was also ripe for change. Following the English, the Scots offered the Crown to William of Orange and his wife Mary (1689), both of the House of Stewart, on terms which involved a revolution in Church and State. The Presbyterian Church was restored virtually as it is to-day, all oppressive measures were disavowed, and the Scottish Parliament secured its independence by the abolition of a Committee, the Lords of the Articles, which during most of the century had rendered it subservient to the royal will.

THE UNION

The controversy between the Kirk and the Crown was now ended by the establishment of Presbyterianism. "Trade," wrote a Scot, "is the golden ball for which all the nations of the world are contending." There was no free trade between England and Scotland, and the Scots were also excluded from trading with the English colonies. During the seventeenth century her adventurous sons had had to carve careers for themselves as soldiers of fortune in the armies of France or of Gustavus Adolphus, or as traders in Poland and the Baltic lands. Under the authority of their now independent parliament they determined to establish a colony of their own at Darien, on the isthmus of Panama, which would serve as a centre of trade between the east and the west. A deadly climate, the hostility of the Spaniards who claimed the territory, and lack of experience brought disaster on a scheme in which the Scots with characteristic perfervid enthusiasm—the " *praefervidum ingenium Scotorum*," according to the dictum of their great Renaissance scholar, George Buchanan—had invested almost all their available capital. In their indignation they laid the blame wholly on King William and the English merchants who had placed every obstacle in the way of the enterprise. The failure of the Darien scheme rendered a closer union between the two countries an economic necessity for Scotland. New capital and freedom of trade could alone save her from financial ruin. For England a union was a political necessity. Scottish commercial enterprise had revealed the danger of two independent parliaments with separate foreign policies under one sovereign. While the Scots had been fighting the Spaniards in Darien, William as King of England had been engaged in delicate negotiations with the Spanish Government. Ancient enmities and recent wrongs delayed the union until the reign of William's successor, Queen Anne (1702–1714). It was the subject of long and fierce debates in the Parliament Hall in Edinburgh, now the peaceful *salle des pas perdus* of the Scottish law courts. At length, in 1707, an Act of Union was adopted by both parliaments. The Scottish and the English legislatures were merged in the Parliament of Great Britain, sitting in Westminster, London, to which Scotland sent forty-five (now seventy-four) commoners and sixteen peers. She retained her own Church (and the educational system which it then controlled) and her own legal system. Free trade was established between Scotland and England and the colonial markets were thrown open to the Scots. The Darien subscribers were compensated, thus providing the capital for future industry and commerce. England gained security by the settlement of the Crown of Great Britain (on the death of Queen Anne without heirs) on Sophia of Hanover, a descendant of James VI, a settlement which the Scots had refused to adopt until their own grievances were removed.

Modern Scotland

The Union marks the beginning of modern Scotland and of modern Britain. In the free intercourse which ensued between the two countries and in the commercial prosperity common to both, old hatreds gradually disappeared. It was in the strength of union at home that Britain in the eighteenth century won her victories abroad and gained that colonial empire in which the Scots were to play a part out of all proportion to their numbers.

In the early stages of the new conditions, however, friction was inevitable ; and the Jacobites, as the adherents of the exiled House of Stewart were called, did not fail to take advantage of it. The first attempt to restore the ancient line of kings in 1715—" The Fifteen " —in the reign of King George I of Hanover (1714-1727), Sophia's son, was quickly suppressed, owing largely to the incompetence of the Old Chevalier, the son of James VII and II. His nickname of " Old Mr. Melancholy " tells its own tale.

Thirty years later, in 1745, the Young Chevalier, Prince Charles Edward Stewart, the " Bonnie Prince Charlie " of Scottish song and story, shook the throne of George II (1727-1760). Deprived at the last minute of French aid, the Prince landed in the West of Scotland with only seven men to win the crown for his father. It was almost exclusively to Highland chiefs and their clansmen, each clan in theory being descended from a common ancestor, that the daring nature of the enterprise and the charm of the Prince's personality made a stirring appeal. They dwelt in the remote glens of a mountainous country, with only one or two towns and few material resources for industry and trade. Their Gaelic language, their devotion to their chiefs, and their frequent internecine feuds constituted a wholly different way of life from that of the peace-loving Lowlander now beginning to exploit the economic benefits of the Union. The story of the Forty-five, as it is called, has all the elements of romance—the raising of the standard at Glenfinnan—the gathering of the clans—the march towards Edinburgh—the defeat of the Government troops at Prestonpans near Edinburgh—the six weeks' sojourn in the Capital, when once again the halls of Holyrood Palace resounded with royal revelry—the march into England as far as Derby—the apathy of the English Jacobites and the mournful retreat. Caught up by the royal troops under the Duke of Cumberland, the clansmen suffered a disastrous defeat at Culloden Moor near Inverness, the last battle on British soil (16th April 1746). For five months the Prince wandered as a fugitive among the Western Isles. Although a reward of £30,000 was offered for his capture, the faithful Highlanders, poor as they were, refused to betray him, and Flora Macdonald won undying fame by aiding his escape in the disguise of her servant. He reached the Continent and died in Rome in 1788. His brother, Cardinal Henry of York, the last of the Stewarts, spent his declining years in Italy aided by a pension from King George III (1760-1820). Jacobitism became a mere sentiment, enshrined in songs which are to-day the heritage of the whole nation.

Plate 27　Linlithgow Palace and St. Michael's Church, on the shores of Linlithgow Loch

(*Photo : Robert M. Adam*)

Plate 28　The Palace of Holyroodhouse, Edinburgh, the residence of the
Scottish sovereigns and specially associated with Mary Queen of Scots

(Photo : Valentine)

With the suppression of the Rising, the Highlands entered on a period of depression. The chiefs became landlords, intent on profits from sheep runs and, later, from deer forests rented for sport. To such landlords clansmen were now valueless as fighting men. The glens were depopulated and thousands of Highlanders emigrated to the colonies where many distinguished themselves as pioneers and administrators. During this time were first raised those Highland regiments which have gained renown on many a field of battle, not least in the World Wars, while the mercantile marine and British navy have had no finer recruits than the hardy fishermen of the Western Isles. In the late nineteenth century legislation secured fair rents and fixity of tenure for the "crofter," the typical Highland smallholder farmer, often a fisherman as well ; and the post-war hydro-electric installations are designed to harness the latent power of Highland lochs and rivers and so provide a local source of energy possibly for transport and industries hitherto wanting for lack of coal.

The peace which ensued after the Forty-five brought astonishing prosperity to the Lowlands. Wealth derived from the trade with the colonies spread from Glasgow and the west. Agriculture was improved by new methods of farming such as the rotation of crops, the introduction of artificial grasses, and the cultivation of turnips and potatoes. The linen and woollen industries received a new lease of life ; coal and iron mines were opened up ; new roads, canals, and bridges increased the means of communication. To the many inventions and discoveries of this Industrial Revolution, it was a Scot, James Watt, who made perhaps the most important contribution by the development of the steam engine. A renaissance of letters accompanied material progress. Hume in philosophy and history, Robertson in history, Adam Smith in political economy, Reid in philosophy, "Ossian" Macpherson in poetry, Black and Hutton in science, and many others, all won European fame. Robert Burns (1759–1796) in his poems and songs gave such unique expression to the thoughts, the feelings, and the moods of his countrymen that the anniversary of his birth (25th January) is celebrated every year wherever Scots foregather ; while in the next generation the writings of Sir Walter Scott (1771–1832), translated into every civilized tongue, revealed to a delighted world the land of his birth and its people.

During the nineteenth century industry and commerce made unprecedented progress. The results of that development, and of the political and social reforms which accompanied it, are related in subsequent chapters of this book. In these respects the history of Scotland and England is as one. Under modern conditions of intercommunication, and the influence of the radio and the cinema, national characteristics tend to be lost in a featureless uniformity. Scotland, however, like other small countries tenacious of her memories of the past, and of the institutions peculiar to herself, still preserves an alert national consciousness. That consciousness is symbolized in the National War Memorial to the courage and sacrifice of the Scots, erected after the First World War on the summit of Edinburgh Castle rock, and these qualities were equally displayed at home and abroad in the second and greater struggle.

POPULATION

THE population of Scotland at the end of 1945 was about 5,150,000. The exact number is unknown as no census of the whole population has been taken since 1931. The figure mentioned, however, is based on an official estimate, and may be taken as substantially accurate.

The earliest reliable census of the people of Scotland was taken in the year 1755 under the direction of the Reverend Dr. Alexander Webster, Minister of the Tolbooth Church, Edinburgh, and Moderator of the General Assembly of the Church of Scotland. Dr. Webster's enumeration showed that the total population of Scotland in the middle of the eighteenth century was 1,265,380, of whom 253,076 are described by the Reverend Doctor as "fighting men" being men between the ages of 18 and 56 inclusive. Dr. Webster states that those "under 18 years of age were generally too weak to bear the fatigue of war and the weight of arms, and those over 56 too crazy and infirmed, notwithstanding that some instances have appeared to the contrary."

Very little is known about the precise population of Scotland before the middle of the eighteenth century. About the year 1250 in the reign of Alexander III the number of inhabitants in Scotland is supposed to have been about 600,000. This number is not given as a result of an actual enumeration, but as the best estimate that could be formed from contemporary information.

There appears to be little information available in regard to the growth of the population during the next 450 years. In Parliamentary Reports prepared at the time of the Union with England in 1707 the population was estimated at about one million. Some fifty years later Dr. Webster's enumeration indicated an addition of somewhat over a quarter of a million people in the half-century. Since 1801 official decennial censuses have been taken until the year 1931. There was a National Register of the civilian population taken in September 1939.

At the first official census of Scotland in 1801, the population was approximately 1,600,000. Another million was added by 1841, when the total population enumerated was 2,600,000. It would thus appear that the population of Scotland has approximately doubled itself in the last hundred years, and that it is now more than three times as great numerically as it was at the beginning of the last century.

This increase in the population of Scotland has been retarded by reason of the fact that Scotland has suffered great loss by the migration of her people. The progress or retrogression of a country may, in some measure, be assessed by its population trend, and the vitality of a people is evidenced by the excess of births over deaths. In a self-contained country, where the people do not migrate beyond its frontiers, the natural increase of the population, that is, the excess of births over deaths, determines the growth of its numbers, or the diminution of its population where deaths exceed births.

For more than a century Scotland has been an exporter of her people ; her sons and daughters have gone from her shores to build and nourish our Empire, and people of Scots blood are to be found in every corner of the earth. The export of her own sons and daughters, while it is of the greatest value to the Empire and to the world at large, places a strain on the vitality of the Motherland. The law of balancing exports and imports does not apply in the field of population, and the drain of migration has resulted in a constant struggle between the natural excess of births over deaths and the loss by emigration of the flower of Scottish youth.

The following table shows for the five decennial periods ending 1931 the excess of births over deaths and the loss by migration and the resultant increase (or decrease) of the people :

Table showing Increase or Decrease in Population 1881–1931
(The percentages relate to the population at the beginning
of the decennial periods)

	Natural Increase (Excess of Births over Deaths)		Net Loss by Migration		Increase or Decrease of Population	
	Number	Per cent.	Number	Per cent.	Number	Per cent.
1881–1891	507,492	13·6	217,418	5·8	290,074	7·8
1891–1901	499,812	12·4	53,356	1·3	446,456	11·1
1901–1911	542,843	12·2	254,042	5·7	288,801	6·5
1911–1921	360,180	7·6	238,587	5·0	121,593	2·6
1921–1931	352,386	7·2	391,903	8·0	−39,517	−0·8

Plate 29 A township in the Isle of Scarp, off the west coast of Harris,
showing primitive dwellings

(*Photo : Robert M. Adam*)

Plate 30   Skerray, a typical township in north Sutherland

(*Photo : Robert M. Adam*)

The trend of our population figures for the first 30 years of this century gives a clear indication of the severe drain on Scottish manpower which results from the migration of her people. During these 30 years the births in Scotland exceeded the deaths by just over $1\frac{1}{4}$ millions, but during the same period the net outward migration was over 880,000, and the actual increase in our population was approximately 370,000. In these 30 years, therefore, Scotland gave to the world at large nearly 900,000 of her sons and daughters, while in the same period she retained only 370,000 of her natural increase.

One dramatic effect of this loss of young manhood is brought out by an examination of the age distribution of the population in 1901 and in 1931 respectively. While the population as a whole increased by 370,000 there were in fact 219,000 fewer people under the age of 25 in Scotland in 1931 than there were in 1901, and 589,000 more persons over that age at the later date. This ageing of the population, which is the result of the combined effect of a falling birth-rate and a heavy rate of emigration must have a very definite effect on the life and economy of our country. The changing age-distribution of the people of Scotland is clearly shown by the two population pyramids based upon the age distribution of the population of Scotland in 1931 and with 70 years earlier.

The population of Scotland in 1861 was just over 3 millions, and by 1931 it had increased by approximately $1\frac{3}{4}$ millions to 4,843,000. The age distribution at the two dates, however, differs profoundly. It will be observed that in 1861 the numbers living in each quinquennial age-group are greater for each sex than in the next higher age-group, and that the population so expressed forms a nearly perfect pyramid. In the diagram for 1931, it will be observed that the number of children under 5 years of age is actually less than the number living in the next quinquennial period. This is due to the effect of the falling birth-rate, which began to diminish substantially in the latter part of the third decade of the century. The effect of the War of 1914–18 is clearly discernible in the diagram. The immediate post-war boom in births is apparent in the relatively large number living in the age-group 5–9. The depression in the next age-group indicates the fall in the birth-rate during the years of the war, and the depression in the number of males living between 35 and 50 indicates the sacrifices of Scotsmen in the struggle.

Not only have the people of Scotland migrated to other countries,

POPULATION OF SCOTLAND
BY AGE GROUPS

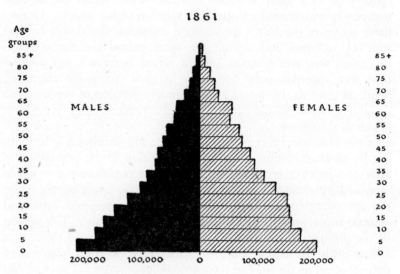

1861

Age groups

MALES   FEMALES

85 +
80
75
70
65
60
55
50
45
40
35
30
25
20
15
10
5
0

200,000   100,000   0   100,000   200,000

Population: Males 1,449,848   Females 1,612,446   Total 3,062,294

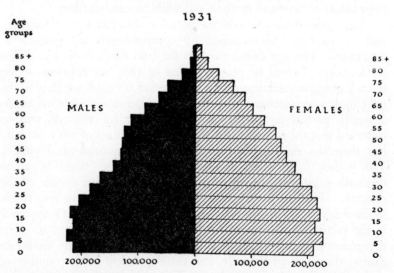

1931

Age groups

MALES   FEMALES

85 +
80
75
70
65
60
55
50
45
40
35
30
25
20
15
10
5
0

200,000   100,000   0   100,000   200,000

Population: Males 2,325,523   Females 2,517,457   Total 4,842,980

POPULATION OF THE COUNTY OF SUTHERLAND: BY AGE GROUPS

1861

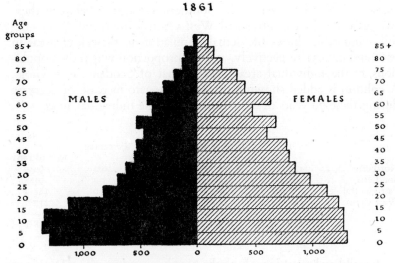

Population: Males 11,058   Females 13,099   Total 24,157

1931

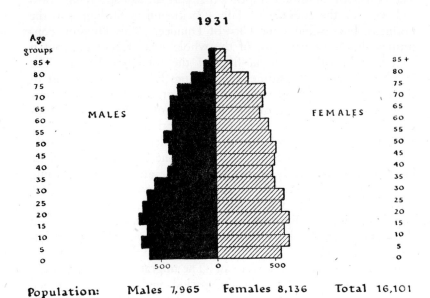

Population: Males 7,965   Females 8,136   Total 16,101

but there has been a very great movement of population within Scotland itself. If we consider the division of Scotland into four areas—the Northern Area, the Southern Area, and between these two areas the East Central and West Central Industrial Areas—the following table shows the actual population in these four areas in 1861 and in 1931 respectively, and the proportion which the populations in the individual areas bear to that of Scotland as a whole. A column is added showing the proportionate increase or decrease during these 70 years of the population in the individual areas.

	1861	Percentage	1931	Percentage	Percentage of 1931 to 1861
Northern . . .	1,020,266	33·3	979,195	20·2	96·0
Southern . . .	273,057	8·9	250,778	5·2	91·8
East Central . .	708,839	23·2	1,305,413	27·0	184·2
West Central . .	1,060,132	34·6	2,307,594	47·6	217·7
	3,062,294	100·0	4,842,980	100·0	158·1

It will be observed that both the Northern and Southern Divisions show decreases in population during the 70 years ending in 1931. The Northern Division comprises that part of Scotland lying north and west of the counties of Fife, Clackmannan, Stirling, and the Lothians, but excludes the City of Dundee. This Division constitutes almost 75 per cent. of the whole area of Scotland, but it contained in 1931 only one-fifth of the total population. The Southern Division constitutes the counties lying south and east of the counties of Dumbarton, Renfrew, Ayr, and Lanark. It comprises about 14 per cent. of the whole area of Scotland, but it contained in 1931 only 5 per cent. of its population.

It will be seen, therefore, that the population is very unevenly distributed throughout Scotland and that one quarter of the people in 1931 occupied nearly 90 per cent. of the area. The remaining 10 per cent. of the area of Scotland has to provide living-room for three-quarters of her whole population. The diminution in the population in the Highland and Border counties mainly arises at the younger ages, and is accounted for partly by a fall in the birth-rate and partly by the migration of the people from these areas to other parts of Britain and overseas. The migration from the Highland and Border counties in the period under review is much greater than the reduction in the populations between 1861 and 1931. In the Northern District the population fell by about 40,000,

Plate 31   The New Town, Edinburgh, built to James Craig's design at the end of the eighteenth century   (*Photo : Aerofilms*)

Plate 32 The Trongate, Glasgow, a view in the industrial capital of Scotland
(*Photo: Alfred Furness; reproduced from 'The Scottish Scene' by permission of George Allen & Unwin Ltd.*)

but during this period the births in this district exceeded the deaths by some 640,000. It therefore follows that no fewer than 680,000 persons left the Northern Division of Scotland to seek their fortune elsewhere. Similarly in the Southern Division the reduction in the population between 1861 and 1931 was about 22,000, but as the excess of births over deaths in this area for that period was 158,000 there must have been a net migration from this part of Scotland of 180,000.

An illustration of the great change which has taken place in the Highland counties is well illustrated by the case of Sutherland, where the population has fallen in the 70 years from 24,000 to 16,000, that is a reduction of 8,000—practically all of which is explained by a reduction in the number of people under the age of 60 years, the number living in the County over that age in 1931 being slightly greater than it was 70 years earlier.

The following population pyramids showing the distribution of the population of this county in 1861 and 1931 give a clear indication of the change in the age constitution of the people.

A typical example of the uneven distribution of the population in Scotland may be obtained by considering the population position of the two counties Sutherland and Renfrew. Sutherland has about nine times the area of Renfrew, but at the last census in 1931 Renfrew County contained eighteen times the population of Sutherland.

The derelict cottages which can be seen on a visit to any of the more remote glens of the Highlands or of the border counties give evidence of the gradual movement of the population from these areas to the gathering centres of population and industry.

The population of the County of Renfrew has increased by some 120,000 in the 70 years up to 1931. A glance at the population pyramid for this county indicates that the increase is fairly general throughout the various age-groups.

The movement of the people of Scotland from the Highlands and the Lowlands to the narrow industrial belt has naturally been accompanied by great changes in the industries followed by the people. To give only two examples which bring these changes into bold relief, it may be stated that in 1861 three out of every ten adult men were employed in agriculture, but in 1931 only one in every ten was so employed. At the earlier date about 400,000 men were following what were called industrial occupations. In 1931 nearly one million were so engaged.

55

POPULATION OF RENFREW COUNTY
(in thousands) BY AGE GROUPS

1861

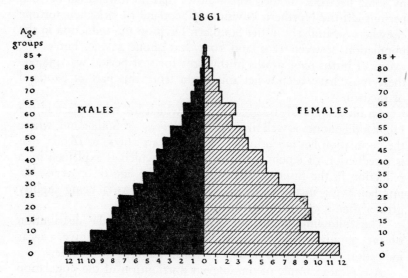

Population: Males 79,380   Females 89,366   Total 168,746

1931

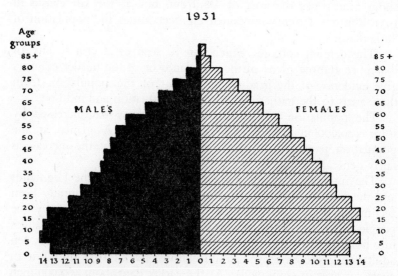

Population: Males 138,320   Females 150,266   Total 288,586

The vital statistics of Scotland show that although the population of Scotland has increased by some half million during this century the annual number of births has fallen from an average of about 130,000 to about 90,000. Scotland is not, however, alone in this fall in the birth-rate. It is satisfactory to find that, although the population had increased, the average annual number of deaths has fallen from about 77,000 at the beginning of this century to about 66,000 at the present time. This fact is evidence of the virility of the Scottish people notwithstanding the drain of their life blood by the emigration of the flower of their youth.

AGRICULTURE

ALTHOUGH it is well known that the bulk of our working population earns its daily bread in factories, shops, or offices rather than in winning the fruits of the soil, it is not so well known that, judged by the numbers employed, agriculture can still rightly be described as our biggest single industry. Judged by the value of the wealth produced, agriculture does not rank so high; but even before the war the estimated value of the net output of Scottish agriculture, *i.e.* the value of what our Scottish farmers sell to the non-farming community, was over £40,000,000 per annum, in spite of the fact that more than two-thirds of the land area of Scotland consists of mountain and heath and deer forests—of land incapable of intensive agricultural development. In 1946 it was estimated at some £70,000,000. It is of course true that, since our agriculture is less highly mechanized than other industries, the value of the output per worker employed is low, but, with developments in farm tractors, combine harvesters, milking machines and so forth, we are witnessing a great acceleration in the application of machinery to farming which should greatly increase the value of the output per worker.

The most striking feature of agriculture in Scotland is the small area of land which is capable of being cultivated intensively. Of the total of 19 million acres no fewer than $10\frac{1}{2}$ million are classified as Rough Grazings, *i.e.* mountain and heath lands, which are generally used for grazing sheep. The actual proportion of the land which is under the plough is a useful index of the intensity of the agriculture of a country. A recent survey carried out under the auspices of the Department of Agriculture for Scotland has divided the land into six groups based on the areas under tillage, rotation grass, and permanent grass. The details of these groups are given as percentages of the total agricultural land in the table on page 59.

The counties which make up the different groups happen to be close together, and the map on page 60 shows this very clearly. The most important figures are the percentages of tillage and rotation grass, and these are added together to show the area which is giving the maximum of agricultural produce per acre. The tillage area includes crops such as the cereals, potatoes and

Distribution of Total Agricultural Land in Scotland
(stated as percentages)

Group	Tillage	Rotation grass	Tillage and Rotation grass	Permanent grass	Total crops and grass	Rough grazing
I	37	17	54	19	73	27
II	33	24	57	4	61	39
III	13	8	21	13	34	66
IV	12	10	22	18	40	60
V	11	9	20	11	31	69
VI	3	2	5	3	8	92
Scotland	13	9	22	8	30	70

other root crops, while the rotation grass is also under the plough. It is sown down for a variable period, which may extend from one year to three or more, and then gives way to a succession of arable crops which may be grown for three to as many as six or more years, in certain very fertile areas, before the land again goes down to grass. This system of agriculture shows clearly the reason for the terms rotation or temporary grass.

Permanent grass does not come under the plough at all and is a very variable crop. In some cases it is highly productive but more usually it does not yield much.

The proportion of rotation in comparison to permanent grass is very much higher in Scotland than in the rest of Great Britain, and the system which is often spoken of as ley farming or alternate husbandry has been practised north of the Border for many years, and is part and parcel of everyday agriculture practice. It should be realized that grass is really the most important crop in Scotland, and on its quality depends the excellence of the main product of our agriculture, our live stock.

The intensive use of all the land which is capable of being ploughed easily is one of the most characteristic features of Scottish agriculture, good temporary grass contributing much to the fertility of the farm. The farming as a whole is of a mixed type and stock loom large in the agricultural picture, another potent factor in maintaining the land in a high state of productiveness, though full use is also made of artificial fertilizers.

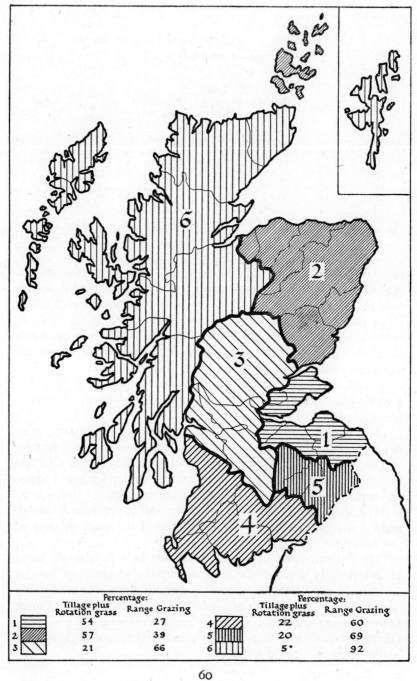

	Percentage:			Percentage:	
	Tillage plus Rotation grass	Range Grazing		Tillage plus Rotation grass	Range Grazing
1	54	27	4	22	60
2	57	39	5	20	69
3	21	66	6	5·	92

If the six groups into which Scotland has been arbitrarily divided are examined, a further simplification is possible. The areas under tillage crops and rotation grass are very similar in the first two groups and the amount of rough grazing land in these groups is also relatively low.

This land stretches from the English border on the east coast right up to the Moray Firth, and is some of the best farmed land in the world. These two groups, which also include the Orkney Islands, have roughly one-third under arable crops, a third under grass, and a third is rough grazing.

The area as a whole is predominantly one of large mixed farms, decreasing somewhat in size as one proceeds northward. In Group I, for example, the average size of holding is about 130 acres, and one farm in every ten is over 300 acres in extent. One-third of the farms exceed 150 acres, whereas in Group II the figure is about one-tenth. The average acreage in Group II is just over 60, and only two out of every hundred farms exceed 300 acres in area. These figures, of course, take no account of the extensive sheep farms with their large acreages of land of low productivity. The agriculture is of a high order, fully mechanized and efficient. This mechanization is clearly seen in the border county of Berwick and extending into the lowland area of Roxburgh along the valley of the Tweed. Here combine harvesters are widely used—large machines which cut the crop and thresh it in one operation leaving the straw behind them on the field. There are more of these machines in these two counties than in the whole of the rest of Scotland, although their number is on the increase elsewhere, and particularly within the area covered by the counties of Group I. The arable farming finds its highest expression in the coastal strip of the Lothians which borders the south coast of the estuary of the Forth. Here is found a narrow belt of early soils which grows very heavy crops of most cereals and of potatoes. At the very edge is a strip which is the seat of an intensive market gardening industry and grows vegetables on a scale paralleled in very few other districts. The produce finds its way on to the market as far south as London.

Incidentally, most of the wheat grown in Scotland comes from Angus, Fife, Perth, and the Lothians.

North of the Forth a similar type of agriculture is general, and in Fife is found the only sugar-beet factory in Scotland, drawing its supplies mainly from that county and those adjoining.

Across the Tay the agriculture is still reminiscent of the intensive farming system of the Lothians and Berwickshire. Good well-managed farms dot the countryside, but as one goes north into Kincardinshire there is one noticeable addition. Whereas in Group I the cattle are mostly purchased for fattening indoors during winter, the more northerly counties in Group II are the seat of a famous livestock breeding industry. In this area the Shorthorn of the beef type and the Aberdeen-Angus black cattle are found, and at Perth an annual sale is held for each of these breeds, attracting buyers from all parts of the world to bid for the bulls. The quality of the stock is reflected in the phenomenal prices which are paid for the best animals.

The growing of seed potatoes for export, principally to England, is a most important feature of the agriculture of Scotland, and the area which has been discussed produces very large tonnages of healthy seed. It should be said that the Department of Agriculture for Scotland has a seed-testing station and a most efficient scheme of certification which guarantees the purity and health of all seed potatoes.

In the Aberdeenshire area the system of agriculture is still of the same general type, though the amount of rotation grass is slightly greater. Wheat is practically unknown and fewer potatoes are grown, but on the other hand cattle of quality are even more numerous.

Though the whole of the land in Groups I and II is characterized by a very high proportion of land under the plough, this is to some extent more concentrated at the coast, and as one proceeds inland the system changes with increasing elevation, giving way finally to smaller farms largely devoted to the raising of stock. There is some really high land which is used primarily for sheep farming and carries either the native Blackface breed or the Cheviot, which was originally imported from the north of England. In normal times large numbers of these sheep were brought down to the lowland farms to be crossed with more rapidly-maturing breeds such as the Oxford Down, the Suffolk, and the Border Leicester for the production of early mutton.

While the main emphasis has been placed upon the high quality beef breeds, the dairying industry is spreading rapidly, and large herds of good milk cows and up-to-date systems of milk production are springing up all over the area to meet the post-war demand for this valuable foodstuff. Before leaving this eastern

Plate 33 Crofts in the West Highlands, with Loch Moidart in the
background

(Photo : Robert M. Adam)

Plate 34 (*Above*) A combined harvester in East Lothian.   (*Below*) A shepherd on a Highland garron (strong pony) driving Blackface sheep in west Perthshire

(*Photos : J. A. More*)

part of Scotland it is of interest to point out that there is a large and important fruit-growing area lying in Angus, in east Perthshire, and in Fife. This is specially suited to soft fruits, particularly raspberries, and the growing of all these fruits is spreading to other areas on the east coast. A great deal of work is being done to establish an industry based on healthy stocks of the soft fruits, for the production of which Scottish conditions are particularly suitable.

The Orkneys are the only part of the Scottish islands which can be classed with the better farmed areas and consist of small mixed farms occupied by progressive farmers. The agriculture is reminiscent of that in the foothills on the mainland, the chief products being sheep, cattle, and eggs. In the years prior to the outbreak of war in 1939 there was a remarkable development of the poultry industry in the Orkneys and large numbers of eggs were exported.

Turning again to the agricultural map of Scotland it will be seen that Groups III, IV, and V could be grouped together. The percentage of the total agricultural area which is under crops and rotation grass is less than half that in the first two groups, whereas the rough grazings have increased to double the amount. Group III is characterized by a preponderance of stock with cattle of the beef type in Perthshire, changing to dairy cattle nearer to Glasgow, where the long-established milk-producing area of Scotland is found in Lanark and Renfrew. There are also large numbers of sheep, particularly in the north-west.

The eastern part of Perthshire and the area of the valleys of the Clyde and the Forth sustain a highly specialized arable farming system, modified for heavier land and higher rainfall.

The Clyde valley is the seat of a valuable fruit-growing industry in which the strawberry was once the most important crop. A very large glasshouse industry has also sprung up with the proximity of the industrial markets, the main crop being the tomato.

This valley was the original home of the breed of horse known as the Clydesdale, which is now spread throughout Scotland and whose popularity is founded on a still wider distribution, ranking as one of the most popular of draught breeds.

In the south-western area, Group IV, dairying is the keystone of the agriculture and the world-famous Ayrshire cow is found here, as in most of the milk-producing areas of Scotland. Throughout Ayrshire, Dumfries, Wigtown, and Kirkcudbrightshire the breed is widespread and a splendid lead has been given to the whole of Great Britain by the dairy farmers of that part of the country. Most of the herds are attested, which means that in them the disease of tuberculosis has been stamped out. The best herds of Ayrshire cattle are a reservoir of healthy, high-yielding dairy cattle which contributes large supplies to Scotland, England and Wales, and countries overseas.

Good mixed farms, on which dairying predominates, are general, and on the sea coast early potatoes are grown with great success. At one time a large amount of farm cheese was made in this area, but of latter years most of the milk has been sold as liquid milk, only the surplus going to cheese.

The higher rainfall of the west coast results in an increase in the area of grass in the farming system and almost one-half of the total permanent grass in Scotland is found here.

In the area there is a good deal of really high land carrying a large sheep stock, and this was the original home of the Blackface sheep, though they have now spread over the greater part of the Highlands of Scotland.

In the Southern Uplands is to be found another native breed of black, hornless cattle—the Galloway. This hardy animal will live and thrive under the most severe conditions and is very popular for crossing with a white Shorthorn bull to give a quicker-maturing, coloured calf called a blue-grey. This is a great favourite with the cattle-feeder on lower ground and is much sought after by the butcher.

The three counties which go to make up Group V are all important sheep-producing areas, the Cheviot making its appearance in the grassy hills which are found here. The sheep sales which are held in this area are justly famed, and large numbers of sheep pass through each autumn, destined both for breeding and feeding. The ubiquity of sheep has given rise to a large woollen-cloth industry in the valley of the River Tweed, with centres at Hawick and Galashiels.

It will be seen that although Groups III, IV, and V are similar in the general distribution of the land the systems of agriculture vary somewhat. Here, as in the other three groups we have discussed, the different forms of agriculture tend to merge into each other imperceptibly, but the main divisions hold true. It will be remembered, for instance, that in the south-east corner of Roxburghshire there is a highly mechanized, arable farming area.

The counties in Group VI form a definite unit which is characterized by an extremely low percentage of tilled land. The outstanding feature is the rough grazings which account for 92 per cent. of the total agricultural land in the area. This group includes the Highlands, the Hebrides, and Shetland and consists almost entirely of sheep walks.

The average size of holding is very small and some of the counties such as Inverness and Ross and Cromarty show an average of under 20 acres, but this excludes the hill land. There are areas of good land, particularly on the east coast of Ross and Cromarty, but on the whole it is an area inhabited only by the sheep farmer. In the glens are to be found the Highland cattle which are native to that part of Scotland. They are hardy, slow-maturing animals which can thrive where it would be almost impossible for other breeds to live, though the Galloway will not be far behind. The Highland cattle are nowadays widely distributed and may be used on hill-land for crossing, the resultant animal still being hardy but maturing at an earlier age.

The sheep found in the Highlands are largely the Blackface breed, although the original importations were the large sheep of the Cheviots, which still predominate in Sutherland and Caithness. It is not always realized that sheep were not the original stock on the hills, but that they displaced cattle, a fact or factor which has resulted in a deterioration of the herbage of this area, since sheep graze much more closely than cattle.

The average size of holding over the whole of the counties and islands in Group VI is greatly reduced by the large number of crofts. This system of holding is a hereditary one, where small patches of tillable land are combined with rights of common grazing on the hill. The crofts really provide part-time employment, and the holders combine it with fishing, weaving, or some similar occupation. The provision of suitable supplementary work for the crofter has been, and still is, the main problem of the Highlands. The system of land tenure, which is general over the rest of Scotland, depends on leases of varying lengths granted by the landowner to the tenant. An appreciable number of the farmers are nowadays owner-occupiers.

Before concluding this survey of Agriculture in Scotland, it is of interest to look at the system whereby the farmer is supplied with the latest technical knowledge, and can obtain advice on his problems. There are three Agricultural Colleges, situated at

Aberdeen, Edinburgh, and Glasgow, which share between them the whole of Scotland. These colleges, in addition to training young men and women who intend to enter agriculture, dairying, or horticulture, are responsible for advising the farmer and providing agricultural education generally. To them are attached agricultural organizers whose duty it is to keep in the closest touch with the farmer and advise him wherever possible. They also carry out experimental work and hold agricultural classes. There are also officers to deal with horticultural work and bee-keeping, while the dairy and poultry industries are not forgotten, their needs being catered for by instructresses specially trained to deal with the problems which arise.

Behind these are specialist advisory officers whose relation to the county organizers is that of the medical specialist to the general practitioner.

These three colleges are in a very suitable position to advise any visitor to Scotland who is specially interested in agriculture.

It is important to note that Scotland is well served in agricultural research. Apart from the facilities for taking degrees and for advanced work in the agricultural sciences provided by the universities of Aberdeen, Edinburgh, and Glasgow, there are a number of well-equipped and specialized research institutes. The dairy industry is served by a well-known dairy school at Auchincruive and by the Hannah Dairy Research Institute at Ayr. Soil science is catered for by the Macaulay Institute for Soil Research at Aberdeen. Aberdeen also covers research into animal nutrition which is conducted at the world-famous Rowett Research Institute. Research in animal breeding is undertaken at the Institute of Animal Genetics, which is a part of Edinburgh University. Another side of the livestock industry is dealt with by the Animal Diseases Research Association station at Gilmerton, near Edinburgh.

Plant breeding has a large place in the research field, and here, too, Scotland keeps her place in the forefront with the Scottish Society for Research in Plant Breeding at Corstorphine, on the outskirts of the capital city.

The story would not be complete without some reference to the work of the Department of Agriculture for Scotland at their Seed Testing and Plant Registration Station near Edinburgh, and the Scottish Agricultural Machinery Testing Station at Mid Calder, which is also under their guidance. The Department of Agriculture, through the Scottish Agricultural Advisory Council, do a great

Plate 35   Ewes and lambs on the banks of the Tweed

(*Photo : ' The Scotsman '*)

Plate 36   Highland cattle

(Photo : Charles Reid)

deal to further the progress of the industry and to correlate research and advisory work generally.

This short summary of the main points of Scottish agriculture can do no more than introduce this important industry. It calls to the mind a picture of farms, varying in size, but all in the hands of capable men with well-planned systems of farming on up-to-date lines. The spirit of enterprise is ever present and during the war period, and to-day, their contribution to the nation's food supply has been unbelievably high. The skill of the Scottish farm worker is traditional and has much to do with the success of the farms. But above all it is the high standard of Scottish livestock which has brought world-wide renown to the farming of Scotland.

With all these assets the industry can face the future with confidence in the sure knowledge of the quality of her exports, whether they be crops, stock, or men.

SEA FISHERIES

BEFORE the War the sea fisheries were much more important to the welfare of Scotland than was the case in England. In proportion to the population they gave employment to seven times as many men. Owing to the tradition of individual or family ownership in vessels and gear which had managed to persist in Scotland, and to the fact that the industry was still spread over a wide area instead of being concentrated in a few large ports, any decline in the fisheries affected a large number of self-contained communities which had made their living from the sea for generations. In England the fisheries have gradually passed into the control of limited companies and have become highly industrialized ; in Scotland they are still, to a great extent, in the hands of seamen or persons on shore directly connected with the sea.

The history of the Scottish fishing industry may be said to begin in the fourteenth century, for very little is recorded regarding it before this date. Then it was that the Government started to encourage fishing, mainly because Flemish, Dutch, and German vessels had already begun to catch herring off our coasts. During the seventeenth and eighteenth centuries several attempts were made to form fishing companies in Scotland, most of which were financed from England, to compete with the Dutch. The latter had an almost complete monopoly of the herring industry for nearly two hundred years. All these fishing companies were a failure and of no direct benefit to Scotland, except in a very small way. The only purely national fisheries were in the Firth of Clyde and Loch Fyne, where herring had always been caught by Scotsmen and was a source of profit. From 1750 to 1829 the so-called Bounty System of payment to fishermen with a view to developing the local fisheries was in force. In 1760 the first attempt was made by Scotsmen to prosecute herring fishing on the East Coast. After the Napoleonic wars herring-curing stations were opened in many places there, and the number of boats and fishermen increased rapidly. The West Coast curing stations date from about the middle of the last century.

White fishing with small open boats had always been carried on, both on the East and West Coasts. The greater part of the catches was used for home consumption. It was either sold fresh or dried for winter use. The Scottish fishermen, unlike those of England, did not venture far from land. Their vessels were smaller and undecked until well on into the nineteenth century. They have always been predominantly "inshore fishermen" until comparatively recent times. Deep-sea trawling, such as had been carried on by English fishermen for nearly a century, did not start in this country until about 1880.

The Scottish fisheries fall into three main categories: (1) Trawling, (2) Herring and Drift-net fishing, (3) Inshore fisheries.

(1) *Trawling.* Before the War about 85 per cent. of the white fish landed in Scotland came from deep-sea trawlers. In England about 99 per cent. of the landings were made from similar vessels. Trawling was started at Aberdeen in 1882. During the next twenty years, after steam had replaced sail, Aberdeen rose to be the third trawling port in Great Britain. This same method of fishing was—and still is—carried on from Leith, Granton, and Dundee, but Aberdeen remains the chief port. Before 1939 it ranked next to Hull and Grimsby in England, both as to the total amount and value of catches. In Scotland, Leith and Granton came next in order.

Aberdeen trawlers normally work off Iceland, the Faroes, Orkneys, Shetlands, and the North-west Coast of Scotland. Other vessels—known locally as "Scratchers"—work round the East Coast and land their fish more often. The Aberdeen steam trawlers have never been large or modern enough to compete with those of Hull and Grimsby. They cannot venture to the far-distant waters of Bear Island or the Barents Sea. They concentrate on the quality rather than on the quantity of fish. Indeed it has always been claimed that Aberdeen sends away the best white fish landed anywhere in Britain. This is because the fish is caught nearer home, owing to the smaller size of the vessels. Yet in the long run quality has proved an economic disadvantage. The rapid development of the fish and chip shops created a demand for cheap, coarse fish, which the Scottish ports have so far been unable to supply. Accordingly the outlook to-day is far from cheerful. What is needed is more capital, larger and better vessels, and better methods of transport if the industry is to hold its own. The chief disadvantage of Aberdeen lies in its distance from the markets; it is not so fortunate as Hull, Grimsby, or Fleetwood in this respect.

The trawling industry has always been fluctuating during the past twenty years. Statistics rise and fall. Before the War there were 320 steam trawlers registered in Scotland as compared with over 1,100 in England and Wales. They had dropped to 95 in 1944, but their number is gradually increasing again. In 1939 over 3,390 men were regularly employed in Scottish steam trawlers, of which about 2,700 belonged to Aberdeen; the rest worked in vessels registered at Dundee, Leith, and Granton. The most important varieties taken are haddock, cod, plaice, and hake. Other fish include whiting, halibut, turbot, lemon-sole, and ling.

A small number of vessels of similar build to steam-trawlers are normally engaged in great-line fishing from Aberdeen. Before the War great-lining was also carried on from Peterhead and some of the Fife ports.

(2) *Herring and Drift-net fishing.* The chief ports in Scotland where herring was landed before 1939 are Lerwick (Shetland), Stornoway, Castlebay (Barra), Mallaig, Stronsay (Orkney), Wick, Fraserburgh, and Peterhead. The number of herring fishermen has seriously declined in recent years, and it is doubtful if the herring industry will ever regain the prosperity it enjoyed when the export trade was at its peak in the early years of this century.

The Scottish herring fishermen have also suffered in the past through individualism and a lack of co-operation. In England most of the drifters are owned by companies, their crews being paid on a wage and share basis. In Scotland the herring fishermen are still at least the nominal owners of their vessels and gear. Unlike the English fishermen, who are concentrated in two or three large ports, they are scattered all along the East Coast. Thus there is little or no co-operative working among either the fishermen themselves or those on shore connected with the industry. A spirit of independence is fostered by the organization of the industry. Many drifters, requisitioned by the Admiralty, were lost during the War. Most of those still in existence are out-of-date, and the cost of replacement is heavy. Stocks of nets have decreased and deteriorated. At the moment new nets are in short supply and their cost high.

Scottish herring are the best in the world, but it is a problem now to find out where to market them. At one time vast quantities of salt herring used to be exported to Russia, Germany, and the Mediterranean countries, but the future significance of these markets is uncertain. The development of refrigeration of herring and the setting up of plant in the chief ports is a hopeful augury.

Plate 37   A fishing village : the harbour, Pittenweem, Fife
(Photo : Crown Copyright)

Plate 38 (*Left*) Mending fishing nets. (*Right*) packing kippered herrings
in boxes for transport

(*Photos : Crown Copyright*)

Herring is also taken by motor boats with ring-nets in the Firth of Clyde and Loch Fyne and the Firth of Forth area. Most of this fish is used for consumption in the home markets.

(3) *Inshore Fisheries.* Until the middle of the last century the majority of Scottish fishermen were " inshore " in the strict meaning of the word, *i.e.* they fished near the coast and landed their catches daily. Even to-day the inshore fisheries in Scotland are of greater importance than in England. In 1935 the total inshore catch of white fish in Scotland amounted to about 355,000 cwt., *i.e.* 15 per cent. of the total landings ; in England and Wales no more than 112,000 cwt., *i.e.* about 1 per cent., was landed by inshore fishermen.

To-day the seine-net method of fishing has almost everywhere replaced the once universal line-fishing, except on the West Coast and in a few small villages elsewhere. In 1930 it was reckoned that there were approximately 10,076 inshore fishermen in Scotland. The number, however, has declined greatly since then.

The Inshore Fisheries are of great diversity. They can be divided into the East Coast, the North Coast (including Orkney and Shetland), and the West Coast. In the two first divisions fishing is usually a whole-time occupation ; in the latter many of the men are crofters as well as fishermen. They only go to sea as a part-time job. Taken as a whole the East Coast inshore fishermen are industrious and enterprizing. Thanks to their initiative, aided by up-to-date motor vessels, generally good harbours, and easy access to markets, they have managed to make a fairly good living in recent years. The chief ports are Eyemouth (Berwickshire), Port Seton (East Lothian), Newhaven (Edinburgh), St. Monans, Pittenweem and Anstruther (Fife), Arbroath (Angus), Peterhead and Fraserburgh (Aberdeenshire), Gardenstown, Macduff, Whitehills, Buckie (Banffshire), Lossiemouth (Morayshire), Avoch (Ross-shire), Helmsdale (Sutherland), and Wick (Caithness). Lossiemouth was the first port to introduce the Danish seine-net about 1920. Since then all the above-mentioned ports have taken to this convenient method of fishing. They benefit by nearness of good fishing-grounds to towns and villages and a reasonably efficient system of road or rail transport to inland markets.

The commercial value of the North and West Coast inshore fisheries (with the exception of those of the Shetlands) has been much less. Creel fishing for lobsters and crabs is, however, carried on fairly extensively, and here the men are badly handicapped by rail and sea transport, and heavy freight charges from the islands. Owing to the poor condition of boats and gear the native fishermen of the Outer Islands and in the Highland lochs have never been able to compete seriously with those from the East Coast, who exploit grounds that are teeming with fish.

In addition to the fisheries for white fish, herrings, and shellfish, fishery stations are to be found off the shores for the capture of salmon by means of nets.

Since the reorganization of the Scottish Departments under the Secretary of State for Scotland in September 1939, the administration of the fisheries has been entrusted to the Scottish Home Department (Fisheries Division) at St. Andrew's House, Edinburgh. The functions of the Fisheries Division include those formerly assigned to the Fishery Board for Scotland (appointed in 1882) whose origins go back to the Board of Fisheries and Manufactures constituted in 1726. In 1809 the Commissioners for the British White Herring Fishery were appointed with jurisdiction extending originally to Great Britain and the Isle of Man ; but the officers of this Board were withdrawn from England in 1849 and from the Isle of Man in 1868, and its functions were thereafter limited to Scotland. The annual reports contain a narrative of the fisheries with summaries of the statistics which extend back to 1809, and are probably unique as a sustained record of a particular industry.

The duties of the Division cover everything relating to the coast and deep-sea fisheries of Scotland, and inland salmon and fresh-water fisheries, and extend to a wide variety of subjects including international relations in fishery matters and domestic conditions affecting all aspects of the fishing industry. The Fisheries Division are assisted by an outdoor staff of Inspectors and Fishery Officers stationed at the principal fishing ports, a marine staff with vessels engaged in enforcing fishery laws in the waters round Scotland, a scientific staff who carry on fishery research from the Marine Laboratory at Aberdeen, a harbour staff who act as technical advisers in connection with applications by harbour authorities for assistance from government funds and supervise work carried out by the aid of such assistance, and a salmon fisheries staff engaged on inspection and research work in connection with the salmon and fresh-water fisheries.

INDUSTRY AND COMMERCE

THE Scot is not by tradition a manufacturer. Although relics of old Scottish trading houses are still to be found in Baltic and other commercial centres in Northern Europe, the quantities of goods which they handled with Aberdeen, Leith, Kirkcaldy, Dundee, and other ports on the East Coast of Scotland were relatively small. It was as a soldier, a scholar, a philosopher, and a poet that the Scot used to be known in Europe, not as a manufacturer.

The industrialization of Scotland began two hundred years ago. The Union with England had opened up for the Scots new markets in the Colonies, and the French wars, which went on intermittently throughout the eighteenth century, frequently closed the " Southern Approaches " to shipping, so diverting the flow of trade to the " Northern Approaches," and thus bringing about a considerable expansion of several small ports on Clydeside, as well as on Mersey-side. The English merchants were not at first disposed to be helpful to the small Scottish traders when they were invading their provinces. For a good many years the Glasgow merchants, who had begun importing tobacco from Virginia, were hampered with vexatious legislation based upon charges that they were evading the payment of the correct import duties. But by 1735 the Glasgow merchants had come out victorious, and for more than forty years—until the War of American Independence—they were most prosperous.

In spite of its rapidly acquired wealth Glasgow was still in 1780 a small city with a population of 43,000, and it was primarily a merchanting rather than a manufacturing place. The colonists' needs, however, led to the founding of many factories in the town. Some were quite large, even by modern standards—a tanning and boot-making factory, for instance, employed 700 people and was said to have been the largest of its kind in Europe—and they filled the holds of the sailing ships with many things, including woollen and linen textiles, clothing, furniture, glassware, and pottery. Most of these undertakings were swept aside after James Watt had invented the practical steam engine and the mechanization of manufacturing processes had got under way. But it should not be forgotten that the industrialization of Clydeside preceded rather than followed the Industrial Revolution.

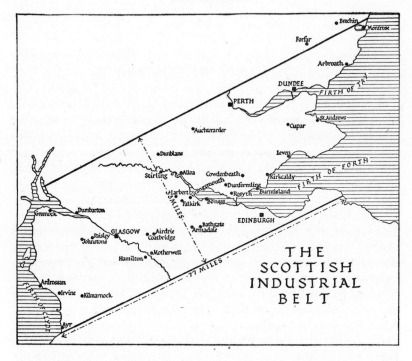

THE
SCOTTISH
INDUSTRIAL
BELT

While Industrial Scotland was coming into being in the west, a remarkable development was taking place in the east, particularly in Fife and in Angus. The traditional fabric of Scotland is linen— just as that of England is woollen—and when the spinners and weavers began to come together to create factories, and to import machinery from Holland, they encountered considerable opposition from the south. Duties were imposed by Parliament, in the interest of the woollen manufacturers, to cripple the Scottish production of linen sheets, handkerchiefs, and tapes. After a stern struggle had taken place, Parliament changed its mind in 1748, and then did its best to foster the Scottish linen industry. Urged on by the British Linen Company, particularly in the days before it restricted its activities to banking, the Scottish linen manufacturers expanded their businesses so rapidly that by 1772 no fewer than 252 linen factories had been opened in the country, most of them being in Angus, Fife, and Perthshire.

And so, in broad outline, the Scottish industrial belt came to be shaped. Its area seems surprisingly small for a country over half the size of England. In width it is little more than 30 miles, and in length it is less than three times that dimension. It runs diagonally across Scotland, to include the coal-fields east of Ayr and those south of Edinburgh, Dumbarton, and the Vale of Leven textile dyeing towns, and the Angus textile manufacturing towns. It includes all five Scottish coal-fields. It includes also much of the finest agricultural land in Scotland, as well as a good deal of practically useless moorland. It is chiefly Lowland, but its northern boundary reaches the fringe of the Highlands. Gleneagles, for example, and a good deal of Loch Lomondside are within it.

One large town lies outside the belt—Aberdeen—but, apart from the people who live there and those engaged in woollen manufacturing in the Borders, in North-east Scotland around Elgin, Keith, and Huntly, and in the Western Highlands and Islands, people who earn their living outside the industrial belt do so by farming or by fishing (or by both). And, relatively speaking, they are not large in number. Between 80 and 90 per cent. of all people in Scotland have their homes in the industrial belt.

Their distribution throughout the belt is, however, far from even. Most of them are crowded into a small area, not much more than 30 miles long, between Greenock and Falkirk, and only a few miles wide. They live in Glasgow and in what may be described as its sphere of influence. Such towns as Greenock, Dumbarton, Johnstone, Paisley, Coatbridge, Airdrie, Motherwell, and Hamilton are essentially parts of Greater Glasgow which, for some geographical or other reason, happened to be located a few miles away from Glasgow Cross. The Ayrshire towns are also closely linked with Glasgow, although the existence of a separate individuality is more discernible. Kilmarnock, for instance, is less like Glasgow in appearance than, say, Greenock and Coatbridge are. Falkirk cannot be considered as a progeny of Glasgow. Lying mid-way between Glasgow and Edinburgh, it has affinities with both cities, besides having a distinct existence in its own right.

Glasgow

With this definition of what is implied by the generic term "Glasgow," its remarkable history over the last two hundred years can be the better understood. Few districts in the world have experienced such vicissitudes. Even at the beginning of the eighteenth century, before Glasgow had achieved any standing as a commercial place—it was still a small ecclesiastical and academic

75

city—it suffered heavily in the ill-fated Darien Scheme, in which many lives and most of the capital of Scotland were lost. Then came the first wave of great prosperity, consequent on the growth of the tobacco trade with Virginia and the sugar trade with Jamaica, and in the seventeen-seventies the money market in Glasgow was quite glutted. Apart from the purchase of land locally, most of the profits were invested in the Colonies, and when the War of American Independence was lost—and few fought harder to prevent its being lost than the Glasgow merchants and their families—everything was confiscated by the victors. For a few years the West Indian markets brought some succour, but when in 1793 these were cut off at the outbreak of the Napoleonic Wars, the old Glasgow trading world disappeared in a turmoil of bankruptcies.

Yet, although 1793 was one of the blackest years in Glasgow's history, it also saw the beginnings of another wave of fortune-making—only this time the wealth was acquired by manufacturers rather than by traders. Indeed, the red-cloaked "tobacco lord" disappeared from the city's streets, and his place was taken by a grim, stern-faced factory owner, wearing a "hard hat" and dressed in drab grey.

Although the linen industry had been located in the East of Scotland rather than in the West, many small spinning, weaving, bleaching, and dyeing factories had sprung up in Glasgow. In them during the seventeen-eighties the way was discovered of weaving muslins purely of cotton. The cotton industry had already been established in Lancashire, where such famous inventors as Arkwright, Hargreaves, and Crompton had made their notable achievements. It is not generally realized, however, that the next generation of textile engineers flourished chiefly in the West of Scotland, and that they were the men who put the management and operation of cotton factories on a really practical foundation—men, for instance, like Robert Kelly, who was the first to operate a spinning mule by water power, John Snodgrass, who devised the first scutching machine for cleaning cotton fibres, and Archibald Buchanan, who gave Glasgow a lead of almost twenty years in adopting the power loom.

The existence of many swiftly flowing rivers and streams in the West of Scotland—then of primary importance in supplying power—and the humid atmosphere also tended to foster the cotton boom. Within fifty years no fewer than 134 cotton factories, almost all of considerable size, were built in Scotland—

usually in the Glasgow district—and in the eighteen-thirties an estimate was made that, including hand-loom weavers working in their homes, almost 200,000 people were engaged in the Scottish cotton industry.

The multitudes poured into Glasgow, from the Highlands and the Lowlands, from the North and South of Ireland, from the North of England—as is shown in this table giving the population figures of Glasgow :

1781 . . .	43,000
1791 . . .	67,000
1801 . . .	77,000
1811 . . .	101,000
1821 . . .	147,000
1831 . . .	202,000
1841 . . .	283,000

A thousand dreadful social problems followed this prodigious expansion, for the old city of closes and vennels could not accommodate a fraction of these people decently. Yet the industry went on growing and also creating many other ancillary industries.

As late as 1840 it still seemed that Glasgow rather than Manchester was going to be the centre of the cotton industry, especially in its finer lines. Then followed a period of stalemate. The number of cotton factories in 1850 was 150. It was the same in 1860. The boom was over, but the cotton industry remained the principal employer of labour in Glasgow. Just as one American war signalled the end of Glasgow's first great special line of business, so another American war—this time, the Civil War—did so for the second. Glasgow's financial investments were in the Southern States. Again the losses were severe. But worse was the cutting off of supplies of raw cotton for several years. Other districts, notably Lancashire, came through the inevitable depression. But many of the Glasgow cotton manufacturers seemed to have lost interest in their trade. The heavy industries, shipbuilding, and engineering attracted them, not only because excellent profits were being made at that time, but also because, to the younger generations, they appeared more like " men's work " than spinning and weaving cotton. And so the money which should have been used in the textile factories to make —and to keep—buildings, plant, and equipment up-to-date was invested elsewhere. Soon the Glasgow cotton industry was obsolescent, and although as late as the eighteen-eighties there were still

114 cotton factories in Lanarkshire and Renfrewshire, the owners of many did not care much about what happened to them. Wages were low and did not attract young people. Machinery was not repaired, was "run to death," and when it could work no more was sent to the scrap heap.

There are a few notable survivors in the industry to-day—the great Paisley thread mills, for instance, the Glasgow factory which makes the finest shirtings in the world and which is said to have done more in Central Europe to establish the reputation of "Scottish Quality" then any other factory, the muslin factories which still make the flowing head-dresses for the Sheikhs of Araby, and the window "hollands" factories which weave some of the sturdiest blinds. But few people think of Scotland as a producer of cotton textiles nowadays. Like the Paisley shawl, the industry is, unfortunately, now a thing of the past.

In woollens the position is better. Carpets are a Glasgow specialty—indeed, the largest carpet manufacturing firm in the Empire, with 5,000 employees, is in Glasgow. Hosiery, particularly women's outerwear, is another feature, and some of the world's fashions, mistakenly thought to come from Paris, are actually created in Glasgow. Large quantities of knitting wools too are spun and dyed. So Glasgow has remained an important textile centre. Indeed, most fibres are still handled there—linen thread is an example, for Glasgow is a large manufacturer of boot-laces and thread for shoes. Silk, rayon, even a little jute are woven in Glasgow, and recently the city has become a leading producer of fibre-glass.

But it is not of these things that people think when Clydeside is mentioned. It is of ships, locomotives, engineering, iron and steel, coal—these to the world are Glasgow's specialties. They are creations of comparatively recent times. The records of Glasgow's trades as late as the 1750 period show that there were few mill-wrights—as engineers were then known—in the district, and almost all of the machinery used in the factories established at that time was imported, most of it, incidentally, from the Low Countries. James Watt in his younger days set up one of the first engineering works in Scotland, his company of "mechanicians" having at one time as many as sixteen employees. Then he joined Dr. John Roebuck at the Carron Works, near Falkirk, which, at the time of their foundation in 1760, represented the beginnings of the Scottish iron industries. But after another ten years he went to Birmingham, and that city probably benefited more from his genius than Glasgow

Plate 39   The Harbour, Aberdeen, the largest trawling port in Scotland

(*Photo : Valentine*)

Plate 40   The *Queen Elizabeth* on the stocks at Clydebank   *(Photo : E N.A.)*

did. So with William Murdoch, the other great Scottish engineer of the eighteenth century, who also went to Birmingham and had few contacts with Scotland during the most active years of his life. They were followed by several young men from South-west Scotland, particularly Kirkcudbright, who chose to go, however, to Lancashire instead of to the Midlands. Of the five great Lancashire cotton spinning houses of the early eighteen-hundreds, no fewer than three were controlled by men who had gone south as young millwrights from South-west Scotland.

The first really important engineering works built in Scotland was that of James Cook and Co. (1805) in the street in Tradeston, Glasgow, now named after them. Cook was the founder of one of Glasgow's special lines, that of making machinery for the sugar and other plantations. Almost all of this work is still carried out in Glasgow, nowadays by eight engineering firms of quite considerable size. Shortly after Cook had founded his factory, Glasgow became greatly interested in the coming of marine engineering. Henry Bell had just built the *Comet*, the first practical steamship to travel in European waters, and in a comparatively short time several firms came into being to design and build ships' engines. Some eventually grew to be very important concerns, and it is interesting to note that every important shipbuilding undertaking established on the Clyde during the Victorian period was founded by a marine engineer, after he had decided to expand his business by building the ships themselves as well as their engines. By 1880 the Clyde had become a river of shipyards. In the 1840 period another of Glasgow's great engineering industries came into being. It was the construction of locomotives, and it grew so extensively that, in the years before the First World War, Glasgow was the principal centre in Europe for making locomotives for the world.

The outstanding branch of engineering on Clydeside is, however, shipbuilding. Although the construction of small wooden ships is a very old industry in the West of Scotland—a Greenock firm is over 200 years old—the rise of the industry followed the replacement of wood in shipbuilding by iron and steel. Three men were perhaps outstanding in creating the Clyde shipbuilding industry—David Napier, Robert Napier, and John Elder—but a great many others contributed in making the West of Scotland the chief centre in the world for building ships. It would be unfair to claim that every important development in the industry had its origin on Clydeside —the Tyne, in particular, made notable contributions—but it would be true to say that most of the developments in the design of ships and in increasing the efficiency of marine engines, boilers, and their ancillary equipment came from Clydeside. During the twentieth century the industry continued expanding and, as recently as 1929, the Clyde was building more than 20 per cent. of the world ships. Increasing competition from abroad has since tended to reduce this percentage, but during the Second World War there were still almost thirty shipyards on the Clyde, working throughout the daylight hours to construct ships with which to ward off the enemy's attacks. Victory in the Second World War, no less than that in the First World War, was won at sea. Every type and size of ship is built on Clydeside, ranging from battleships, like the *Vanguard*, and liners, like the *Queen Elizabeth*, down to tramp steamers, dredgers, tugs, fishing boats, and yachts.

In recent years Glasgow's specialization in the heavier branches of engineering has been criticized, current trends being towards the lighter side of engineering, and particularly towards those lending themselves to mass production. Even though Glasgow's activities are too much concentrated on the heavier side of engineering, the lighter branches are much more thoroughly established on Clydeside than is commonly realized, for the products of Clydeside engineering works include aircraft, air-conditioning plant, automobiles, clocks, conveyors, electrical appliances, lifts, machine tools, oil engines, pumps, refrigerators, radio receivers and equipment, scientific instruments, textile machinery and a great range of domestic appliances, including three specialties—sewing machines, wringers, and vacuum cleaners. In addition, Clydeside is one of the chief centres in Europe of the structural engineering industry.

Glasgow's place in heavy engineering has a direct relationship to the growth of the heavy industries, particularly in Lanarkshire. The first iron works to be established in Scotland were, as already mentioned, those of the Carron Company, near Falkirk, in 1760. The Clyde Works, on the outskirts of Glasgow, were founded in 1786. But it was not until the first decade of the nineteenth century that the remarkable properties of the blackband iron-ore, found abundantly in Lanarkshire, were properly realized. With plentiful coal supplies available, the County of Lanarkshire, which had formerly been the fruit garden of the West of Scotland, was dug up and turned over in quest of its mineral wealth. Bings and slag heaps went up on all sides, iron and steel works were erected in profusion, and the fresh air was filled with grime and smoke. After

1835 the annual production of pig iron in Lanarkshire began to reach astonishing proportions, and by the eighteen-sixties Clydeside had become the principal producer of pig iron in the British Isles. Here too the progress of the industry was advanced by the inventiveness of local engineers. For instance, it was J. B. Neilson, of Glasgow, who invented the hot blast system for furnaces in 1828, thus greatly increasing their efficiency, and it was James Nasmyth, of Edinburgh, who invented the steam hammer in 1842. Subsequently other famous inventors, such as Henry Bessemer of London, came to Clydeside to carry out their experiments in steel-making. The industry expanded throughout the nineteenth century, but it has since been greatly handicapped, first by the exhaustion of the native iron-ore which can be economically mined in Lanarkshire, and more recently by the fear that the coal resources of Lanarkshire will also soon be gone. Clydeside, the home of such firms as Baird's, Beardmore's, Colville's, and Stewarts and Lloyds', will not give up its place in the heavy industry readily, and Lanarkshire will, no doubt, continue throughout the twentieth century to be one of the chief British centres of this industry. But, having to import so much of its raw material, probably its greatest days are past.

The statement often read in the press about Glasgow having its eggs in one basket (the heavy industries, including shipbuilding) has to be treated with caution, for Glasgow has on the other hand probably a greater variety of industries than any other town—not excluding London—in the British Commonwealth. One of the advantages derived from possessing shipbuilding as a major industry is that, as ships have to be self-contained when at sea, they must carry almost all of the things required to meet their passengers' needs. Accordingly, an incentive was given to manufacturers to provide this infinite variety of things locally. Some, it must be admitted, failed to do business in anything more than a small way, but others—such as, for instance, some manufacturers of sanitary appliances and of air-conditioning plant—went ahead from this local market, to build up a much bigger one.

Bearing this in mind, and also the changes which have occurred in Glasgow's chief manufacturing lines, the following points—selected at random—about some of Glasgow's lighter industries may be the better appreciated. A Glasgow firm has the largest export market of bottled beer in the British Isles. One of the largest book-producing and publishing firms in Great Britain, and perhaps in the world, has its works in Glasgow. Some of the leading proprietary foodstuffs and other victuals, such as jams and biscuits, are made in large quantities on Clydeside. A Glasgow firm has pioneered the use of aluminium foil for wrapping and other purposes. The largest manufacturers of rag blotting-papers in the world have their mills in Lanarkshire. Glasgow is the leading centre in the country for printing Christmas cards. The printing of automatically numbered tickets was first developed in Glasgow. Most of the clay tobacco pipes used in the world are made in Glasgow. Many of the best leather footballs are produced in Glasgow. The manufacture of wood-pulp containers is another local specialty. Large quantities of Glasgow-made sweets are exported. Glasgow is one of the leading places in the country for garment-making. Much of the high-quality chrome leather for the " uppers " of shoes is tanned in Glasgow. Considerable volumes of Lancashire and Yorkshire cloths are conveyed to Glasgow every day to be dyed and finished. The Glasgow district exports its firebricks to all parts of the industrial world—even to Japan. A great many of the " bright " bolts and nuts used throughout the country are manufactured in Glasgow. No fewer than 57 firms in the Glasgow district make paints and oils. The principal hydraulic engineering firm in the country is in Kilmarnock. Ayrshire is the chief centre in Great Britain for manufacturing explosives. And so on—the range of Glasgow's industrial products is, indeed, tremendous.

It is not, however, only as a manufacturing place that Glasgow is important. It is one of the country's chief ports and one of the leading distributing centres, both in the wholesale and the retail branches. Even before the Napoleonic Wars were over the adventurous spirit of the Glasgow merchants had reasserted itself, and they were among the leaders, not only in breaking the blockade of Europe, but also in challenging the exclusive rights of the East India Company to trade with the Orient. The Glasgow traders were particularly active in opening up trade for themselves—and for others—with India and later with China.

As an example, their temporary monopoly of the tea trade may be mentioned. The China Clippers—themselves usually Clyde-built—raced to Glasgow, not to London, and at the appropriate seasons most of the buyers from Mincing Lane descended on Glasgow. In making their city one of the world's leading ports, the Glasgow people dredged the River Clyde so thoroughly that, instead of being a salmon river, largely choked with silt, it became a really great artificial waterway. From the eighteen-sixties onwards they built dock after dock, and have continued to do so ever since. Many of the ships which steam up the Clyde are Glasgow-owned, and the part Glasgow shipping lines played in conveying emigrants to the Colonies should be noted. The high proportion of Scottish names in Canada, New Zealand, Australia, and South Africa is in itself an indication of how much the Scots did to create the British Common-wealth. The nationalist who said that the British Empire should really be known as the Scottish Empire knew he was exaggerating, but he had some justification for his claim.

The tea business, while it was focused on Glasgow, brought into being two of Britain's leading companies of British retail grocers and had a considerable influence on the rise of a third. Throughout much of the Victorian age Glasgow and Manchester had a keen rivalry about which would become the leading distributing centre outside London. In consequence Glasgow now has several streets of really excellent shops. Manchester still has an advantage over Glasgow in having the many neighbouring Lancashire manu-facturing towns to draw on. But Glasgow has become not only the chief shopping centre for Scotland, but also for Ireland and even for part of the northern fringe of England. During the Victorian era too the Glasgow wholesalers built up a tremendous business, supplying food, clothing, furniture, and other necessities to the Empire. Indeed, during the eighteen-nineties it was said that if one Glasgow firm chose to call in all the money it was owed in Canada and another all it was owed in South Africa, the financial stability of those two countries would have been much affected.

And so Glasgow has gone on growing. As early as 1830 it was describing itself as the Second City of the Empire. It still does, and can state good reasons for doing so. Certainly Calcutta and Bombay have passed it, but with native populations only. Montreal and Sydney have also asserted their right to the title, but in doing so they use the figures of what might be described as Greater Montreal and Greater Sydney. By comparison Greater Glasgow remains the larger place.

In the eighteen-nineties Glasgow was actually the Sixth City of Europe, but since then its growth has slowed down. To-day the population within the city boundaries is probably about 1,100,000 and within the boundaries in which continuous development has taken place, 1,500,000. Estimates have put the size of Greater Glasgow as high as almost two millions.

EDINBURGH

Edinburgh's sphere of influence is scattered and less densely peopled than Glasgow's. It extends from Falkirk and Stirling in the west, to the Fife manufacturing towns in the north, and well down into the Borders to Hawick and perhaps as far west as Dumfries.

Falkirk is, however, in many ways, particularly industrially, linked with Glasgow rather than with Edinburgh, Lying almost midway between the two cities, it sometimes speaks of itself as the Hub of Industrial Scotland. Accordingly, before discussing how Edinburgh makes its living, reference should be made to Falkirk and the towns near it, such as Larbert, Grangemouth, and Bo'ness, Stirling and Alloa, Bathgate and Armadale.

The Industrial Revolution began in Falkirk in the middle of the eighteenth century with the construction of the Carron Ironworks. The availability in the district of coal and iron, as well as water power, was responsible for the choice of Falkirk, and although local iron-ore is no longer used, coal is still mined extensively in what is known as the Stirlingshire coal-field. Near at hand, too, and particularly immediately south of Edinburgh, is the Lothian field, in which considerable developments are likely to be made. Incidentally, it should be said that, if oil is ever found in Scotland in quantities justifying the sinking of wells commercially, this is perhaps the most likely district in which it will be achieved.

The major industry of Falkirk to-day is making light castings, and foundries of all ages and efficiency, from the most up-to-date to the not-so-up-to-date, produce cookers and stoves, baths, grates, and " rain-water goods." Falkirk was fortunate during the war in being selected as the site for very extensive aluminium rolling mills, so it has an important place in what seems to be one of the industries of the future.

The industries of the adjacent towns of Larbert and Bonny-bridge closely resemble those of Falkirk, but the industries of Grange-mouth are quite different. Founded in 1777, at the Forth end of the Forth and Clyde Canal, Grangemouth has had a new lease of life in recent times, and has risen to be, according to quantities handled, the third port of Scotland—it is actually second in size—by dealing particularly with Baltic wood, oil and spirits. Several industries, including shipbuilding and soap making, are carried on in Grange-mouth, while in recent years a factory making dyestuffs and pharmaceutical chemicals has been extended on an impressive scale.

The south shore of the Forth, from Grangemouth, past Bo'ness, to Leith, has been described as the Scottish Zuider Zee. Already quite considerable reclamation schemes for slob land have been carried out, and more are likely to be begun in the next few years. On the north bank of the river, and rather closer to its source, is the industrial district running from Alloa to Stirling. In addition to coal-mining it has several industries. Indeed, three very well-known firms have their works in Alloa, and are engaged in woollen spinning, electrical engineering, and brewing. Several firms in the district knit and weave woollen garments, while yet another industry, also related originally to the good supply of water, is paper-making. As in most parts of Scotland, industries are met with rather unexpectedly. For instance, a cotton factory at Dunblane makes the finest linings for suits in the country, a Menstrie furniture-making firm specializes in office desks, and a Stirling firm is engaged in the rubber industry.

Bathgate and Armadale are both best known for their steel castings, and quite near them is the shale oil district which has had a remarkable history over the last eighty years. In a small triangular area, running for about six miles along the Forth, ending just west of the Forth Bridge, and with a depth of about 16 miles, the world's use of mineral oils were pioneered by "Paraffin" Young and his colleagues. The shale is mined and dry-distilled, to produce oils which are used as illuminants and lubricants. The shale resources are still great, and as new uses for the oils are being discovered—for instance, as heavy Diesel oil—the prospects seem reasonably promising. Some of the older small towns in the district have, however, been selected for the location of new industries, and the recent construction of two factories at Broxburn for manufacturing vacuum cleaners and immersion heaters is noteworthy.

Edinburgh is a larger town than is commonly realized. Its population is over half a million—implying that it is highly industrialized. Before the middle of the eighteenth century Edinburgh was, except for Aberdeen, the only town in Scotland with any pretensions to size. Besides being the political and military capital, it had a small but busy trading community in the adjacent port at Leith, and it was itself the centre of Scottish craftsmanship. Many of the traditions of that craftsmanship have been retained, and some of the exhibits at two recent Industrial Exhibitions in Edinburgh revealed fine skill in design as well as in manual ability. These exhibitions were held in 1936 (Exhibition of Scottish Everyday Art) and 1944 (Exhibition of the Industries of Edinburgh and Leith). Among the articles which merited the appellation "quality" were : furniture, glass and cut crystal, leather goods, printed books, printed household fabrics, silverware, stoneware and hand-made pottery, surgical instruments, tapestry, toys, woven and knitted woollen goods, and wrought-iron.

Some of the Edinburgh firms engaged in making these things are of quite considerable size. For instance, a company employing several hundred workers is engaged in the woollen industry, and a company which specializes in cutting crystal glass has almost 300 workers. Of all the Edinburgh crafts, the one outstanding is probably printing. Although Glasgow rather than Edinburgh was first responsible for gaining a European reputation for Scottish printing —through the Wilson type-founding works and the Foulis Press— the Edinburgh typographers and colour printers were held in high esteem by the late decades of the eighteenth century. So too were the publishers. The *Encyclopaedia Britannica* and *Who's Who* are only two of many famous works which had their origin in Edinburgh, while some distinguished periodicals have borne the Edinburgh imprint since their foundation—for instance, *Blackwood's Magazine*, first published in 1817.

An unusual and pleasing feature of the Edinburgh printing industry has been the survival of family traditions, but the industry has also been progressive. Several new factories were built and extensive alterations made to existing factories in the nineteen-thirties, and the largest firm, employing almost 1,000 workers, has equipped itself to design and build most of its own plant. Colour printing, including cartography, is an Edinburgh specialty, but the range of products is considerable, including stationery and card-board cartons, both of which are made in very large quantities.

Closely associated with the printing industry is the paper-making industry. The earliest known mill was situated at Dalry, on the Water of Leith, about 1591. To-day a dozen paper-mills, located south and west of Edinburgh, are engaged in making various grades of paper, but particularly good quality paper. As much as 75 per cent. of the esparto grass—from which many of the best papers are made—is imported through the Edinburgh harbours, chiefly Granton, and more fine paper is made within 20 miles of Edinburgh than anywhere else in Great Britain.

Edinburgh's industries fall less readily into a pattern than those of Glasgow. Some are clearly traditional, while others are no less

Plate 41   Industrial Scotland : factories at Clydebank

(*Photo : Valentine*)

Plate 42   Woollen industry in Southern Scotland : Innerleithen

(Photo : Robert M. Adam)

clearly importations. In the former category come beer and biscuits. One of the least known points about Edinburgh is that it is probably the second largest brewing centre in Great Britain. The gay old gentleman with pointed beard, of popular advertisements, is an Edinburgh man. Altogether, however, Edinburgh has many brands, some known throughout the world, others known perhaps to a comparatively few connoisseurs. There are twenty-three breweries in Edinburgh, brought there by plentiful water supply, pure atmosphere, and proximity to agricultural districts. Edinburgh ale is usually heavy, and until recently was supplied only in casks. Nowadays many other kinds of beer come from Edinburgh, including some of the finest lagers obtainable in Great Britain. Two of Scotland's largest whisky distilleries and several smaller ones are in Edinburgh. In addition, a great deal of blending is done in Leith, the port always associated with the import and export of wines and spirits from and to the continent.

The foodstuffs manufacturing industry in Edinburgh is chiefly concerned with biscuits, although it should be noted in passing that there are several other branches engaged in blending tea, making sweets, and baking oatcakes, and that one of the largest margarine factories in the country is located at Craigmillar on the outskirts of the city. A dozen factories make biscuits, including some which are very large and well known. No doubt, the industry began when some of the bakers found that their biscuits were in greater demand than their bread, and gradually turned their whole business over to this one line. Those Edinburgh bakers, however, who kept to their original kind of production have also distinguished themselves, and no other city in Great Britain can show such a delightful variety of beautifully made cakes as are to be seen in Princes Street.

The most important of the industries brought to Edinburgh are rubber manufacturing and engineering. The second largest British company in the rubber industry has its main works in Edinburgh, while three smaller companies are also engaged in the industry within the city's boundaries. Among Edinburgh's specialties are footwear, floor covering, tyres, golf balls, and various industrial rubber articles. The industry was founded in Edinburgh in 1855 by an American syndicate, who saw a loophole in some patents which had been registered in terms of England instead of Great Britain—as had no doubt been intended.

To a certain extent the Edinburgh engineering trades are directly descended from those of the millwrights, 150 years ago—for instance, the type founders, the heating engineers, the makers of bakery appliances, and the manufacturers of printing and paper-mill machinery. Except, however, for the last of these, the older branches of engineering have not attained substantial size. On the other hand the larger of the two manufacturers of paper-mill machinery has grown steadily since its foundation in 1821, and is perhaps the principal firm engaged in this branch of engineering in the country.

The newer engineering concerns—and in some instances the reference to newness is only relative—include the largest electrical engineering firm in Scotland, one of the leading structural engineering firms in Great Britain, several manufacturers of gas meters, a well-known manufacturer of marine auxiliaries and hydraulic machinery, and the chief manufacturer of high-strained and other special wires in the country. During the Second World War several English engineering companies opened branch factories in Edinburgh. Some are carrying on these factories, and, in consequence, Edinburgh is adding to her products such things as radio and radio components and several high precision articles.

Although, to most visitors, the High Street, Princes Street, and the New Town are the centres of attraction in Edinburgh, those interested in how people earn their livings find the ancient port of Leith —still the second port in Scotland—quite absorbing. It contains not only a modern shipyard, large docks, and works supplying nautical equipment of various kinds, but a remarkable diversity of factories. Its products include : bed settees, biscuits, boilers, chemicals, coffee essence, fertilizers, fish, flour, gas meters, gin, ham, hosiery, leather, oatmeal, paint and varnish, proprietary foodstuffs, rope, rubber, seeds, stationery, sugar, tea, timber, tobacco, and many other things. Those who see Edinburgh without seeing Leith are, indeed, missing much that is fascinating about Scotland's Capital City.

Going south from Edinburgh, through the district associated with two such apparently incongruous industries as coal-mining and paper-making, factories are soon encountered engaged in making woollen textiles. From Bonnyrigg and Haddington, down to Galashiels, Selkirk, and Hawick, at first individual factories and then groups of factories are encountered. Galashiels is perhaps the chief of the Border woollen manufacturing towns—the technical college for the industry is located there—but the towns are so widely separated that it is really impossible to draw lines of demarcation. Jedburgh, the nearest Scottish town to Newcastle, should be included, although its principal industry nowadays is connected with rayon, and, going south-west, Langholm. Peebles to the north-west has the largest tweed mill in the Borders. Indeed, Dumfries and Annan, just north of Carlisle, are also Border woollen towns and, it can be maintained, so are the southern Ayrshire towns, such as Irvine and Stewarton, with their large hosiery factories, and Kilmarnock and Ayr, with their carpet interests.

The traditional branch of the woollen industry is the weaving of tweeds, the wool having come from the local Cheviot sheep. Tweeds differ from Yorkshire worsteds principally in the way the yarn is prepared. In worsteds it is combed—the process is comparable to combing hair—the longer fibres being disentangled and laid parallel to one another. For tweeds it is carded—the fibres are deliberately tangled and mixed in every way. This fundamental difference runs right through the resultant cloths. Tweed is heavier and warmer than worsted. It looks rougher and glazes less readily.

Scotch tweed is usually associated with sports wear and with men's suits rather than women's suits. It is one of the most sought-after of all British exports, particularly in the United States and in Central Europe. Tweed is expensive, however, and the prosperity of the industry is to no small extent linked with Europe's purchasing power. The hosiery industry, focused particularly on Hawick and Dumfries, is to a relatively greater degree concerned with the home market, and it was on the whole in a flourishing condition between the wars. Much of the finest hosiery in Great Britain is made in these towns, and it is in Hawick that many of the fashions in women's outerwear are set each year.

At the present time it is not possible to evaluate the importance of the road bridge shortly to be built across the Forth, and linking the outskirts of Edinburgh with the industrial south of Fife. The significance of this bridge is psychological as well as economic. Indeed, it will almost convert Rosyth, with its great naval dockyard, into a suburb of Edinburgh.

It was in Fife—formerly a kingdom instead of a county—that industry was first established in Scotland, largely because it had the advantage of being protected against invading hordes by the Firths of Forth and Tay, and by substantial hills on its western boundaries. Many fanciful stories are told about how the people of Dunfermline learned to weave fine linen, and about how smuggling and other strange practices were carried on in the small seaports on the coast. The linen industry is still one of the principal industries of Fife, and although the Dunfermline manufacturers have been inclined to give up flax in favour of natural and artificial silk, the parts of the county, including Kirkcaldy, which have specialized in heavier fabrics, for use, for instance, as towels, canvas, bags, and twine, have continued to take an active part in the industry. The linen industry —as well as the paper industry—is well distributed throughout the county, but most of the other industrial undertakings are in the south, following the coast as far as Leven.

It is in this district that the great Scottish coal-mining developments of the next few decades are likely to be made. To what extent and in what ways they will affect other industrial developments cannot be forecast, but already there is considerable diversification in the products of Fife. There are very large linoleum works in Kirkcaldy and elsewhere in the county, a highly successful shipyard at Burntisland, one of the leading chemical engineering firms in Great Britain at Leven, the chief plastics works in Scotland at Leslie, several well-known paper mills and distilleries, a sugarbeet factory at Cupar, and many rather smaller undertakings, making a variety of things, ranging from yachts and aircraft, to fountain pens, golf clubs, iron and steel castings, textile machinery, textile printing-sheets, carpets, hosiery, and oilskins.

DUNDEE

Dundee used to describe itself as Scotland's Second Commercial City. Edinburgh has become relatively more important commercially since then, but so many new industrial ventures are being planned for Dundee, that a distinct improvement in its status is to be looked for. During the nineteen-thirties suggestions were made that Dundee had even been replaced by Aberdeen as the third of the Scottish cities in size. Here, too, Dundee may be destined to regain its position—if, indeed, it was ever lost.

The Dundee sphere of influence extends across the Tay to the north of Fife. The University College of St. Andrews University is, for instance, situated in Dundee. But, although the linoleum industry of Newburgh and the textile accessories industry of Tayport are closely linked with Dundee, the towns of the north of Fife are really residential rather than manufacturing suburbs of the city.

Dundee has perhaps the best site of the four large Scottish towns, and has, on the whole, the best weather. But it is the least well known. English people, when asked to give the names of some Scottish towns, never miss Edinburgh, Glasgow, and Aberdeen. But they are quite as likely to mention, say, Perth, Stirling, Ayr, or Inverness as Dundee. A possible explanation is that Dundee people, bearing in mind the way their native city was industrialized during the nineteenth century, and the rather exaggerated Victorian embellishments to be seen on so many of the leading buildings, hesitate before proclaiming where they hail from. Yet the city, with its neighbourhood, possesses many amenities, and it is these which have recently proved so attractive to certain American industrialists.

The manufacturing towns associated with Dundee include : Arbroath, with its three large engineering works making air-conditioning plant, textile machinery and lawn mowers ; Perth, with its laboratory glass manufacturing works, distilleries, laundries and dye works, fine linen works, and printing establishments ; Brechin, with its new engineering works ; Forfar, Montrose, and perhaps also Auchterarder, with its woollen weaving factories.

Dundee is popularly known as the city of jute, jam, and journalists, and that gives an indication of how its people make their living, although it does not give proper recognition to its shipyard—the largest in Scotland apart from the Clyde—and its textile engineering works—one of which is much the most important engaged in that branch of engineering in Scotland.

When the linen industry spread throughout Fife and Angus during the later decades of the eighteenth century, Dundee became the centre for the manufacture of canvases and other heavy linen sheets. Shortly afterwards some of the manufacturers became interested in jute, an Indian fibre which was very cheap and plentiful, but which, because of its coarseness, had never been spun economically. They succeeded in overcoming many of the mechanical difficulties, and when the application of power to spinning and weaving had been successfully achieved they realized the possibility of producing a new kind of fabric which, because of its low cost, would replace all other cloths used for bags, sacks, and other kinds of containers, as well as for twines and ropes. The change over from flax began in the eighteen-thirties and reached its peak in 1855.

In more recent times, as factories were established in Calcutta to spin and weave jute, the weakness of the position became increasingly apparent, for the low level of Asiatic wages inevitably brought down the prices of jute cloth. Nevertheless, the industry has so far maintained its position fairly well, and in the years before the outbreak of the Second World War roughly 40 per cent. of the registered workers in Dundee were engaged in it. Its size is indicated by there being at that time no fewer than seventy-four factories in the Dundee district engaged in the industry.

One line of development has been that of finding new uses for jute—and, incidentally, spinning and weaving finer qualities of jute. It has nowadays many applications, not only as the backing for carpets and linoleum, but, suitably bleached and dyed, as rugs and wall covering. It is also being combined successfully with other fibres, such as wool and rayon. The people of Dundee perceive, however, that although jute will long remain their principal industry, it is likely to give less employment in years to come.

Linen has continued to be an important Dundee industry, and a good many of the textile factories in the district are still engaged in making heavy linen instead of jute fabrics. The "jam" side of Dundee's commercial activities had its origin in the magnificent fruit farms of the Carse of Gowrie and elsewhere in the Dundee district. The Victorian manufacturers took advantage, however, of the splendid deep-water harbours at their doorsteps to make use also of imported fruit, and in consequence the two most famous Dundee foodstuffs, Dundee marmalade and Dundee cake, are made largely from the produce not of Scotland but of far-off sunny lands.

In some respects Dundee comes next to London as a publishing centre for periodicals, and the proportion of Fleet Street journalists who began their careers by the Tay is surprisingly high. In this field, too, Dundee postcards—the adhesive postage stamp, as well as the postcard itself, were Dundee inventions—calendars, greeting cards, and cardboard boxes are well known. One Dundee firm is the principal publisher of postcards in Great Britain.

ABERDEEN

The industrial belt ends a little north of Montrose with two small towns, Johnshaven and Inverbervie, in which linen weaving has been carried on for many years ; but whether the journey north is taken by the coast or inland through Forfar and Brechin, the fact that industrial Scotland has been left behind becomes increasingly apparent. The farmland is magnificent and extensive, and the coastal villages clearly make their living by fishing. North of the plain the Grampian Mountains dominate the horizon.

Forty miles on from Montrose, however, a great city is almost suddenly encountered, its silver granite buildings glistening in the sun. It is Aberdeen. It has a university and a cathedral, and it is obviously an important agricultural and fishing centre. But it is no less obviously something more than that, for Aberdeen is a large town which has grown up independently—or, in the main, independently—of the Scottish industrial belt.

When Aberdeen emerged into history it was already a trading community of some size. Its business was with the Baltic countries. Indeed, the town, like its citizens, has quite a Scandinavian appearance. It was for a long time the largest town in Scotland, and was not replaced by Edinburgh until 1350. A great many of the Scots whose memories survive in the Hanseatic towns were Aberdonians.

One of the traditional industries is shipbuilding—the already-mentioned China Clippers, for instance, were first built in Aberdeen —and the coming of the iron ship was a heavy blow to the city, for it is far away from the Lanarkshire coal-mines and iron works. Three shipyards have survived the change, each employing between 500 and 1,000 workers, but compensation was chiefly found in paper-making and in woollen manufacturing. To-day five paper mills, including the largest in Scotland, are located in the Aberdeen district. The city has a splendid weaving factory, one of the most important in the country, in which the best "overcoatings" are made, and several hosiery mills, which share with Dumfries in the production of most of the woollen gloves made in Great Britain. Its most impressively immense textile factory is, however, engaged in the linen industry and makes, among other things, a great many of the fire hoses used in the country.

It has a surprisingly large engineering industry, which constructs mechanical handling appliances, plantation machinery, oil engines, stone-working machinery, and marine accessories. Recently an agricultural implements engineering works of considerable size has been located in the city, but pride of place among the engineering companies of the north-east must be given to an undertaking in the neighbouring town of Fraserburgh, which makes pneumatic tools for a world market.

Apart from one or two unexpected industries, such as comb-making, most of the other Aberdeen industries—canning, making chemicals, manufacturing confectionery, and fish curing—are related to fishing and agriculture. The most important exception is the indigenous granite industry.

Where the Aberdeen sphere of influence ends is a matter of some controversy. It sweeps around the coast, skirting the Highlands, and includes Peterhead and Fraserburgh—with their own canning industries—besides most of the Moray Firth herring ports. It includes Huntly, with its hosiery works, but does it also include Keith and Elgin, with their woollen weaving works, famous for their fine scarves ? And the great Speyside whisky distilling industry ? Certainly, some of these places, notably Elgin, are nearer to Inverness than Aberdeen. But the people of Aberdeen are basically of Scandinavian stock, as are most of the people of these other towns. When Inverness is reached, so is the Highlands.

THE NORTH-WEST

Inverness is, in fact, one of the towns calling itself the Capital of the Highlands, and the business men of Inverness have a habit of looking to Glasgow—not much more than five hours away by some trains—rather than to Aberdeen—never less than four hours away. Like Fraserburgh, Inverness has a well-known engineering works, this one specializing in welding. The other industries of the town are what might be expected—distilling, woollen weaving, canning. Except for the aluminium works centred around the hydro-electric stations in the Fort William district, the industries of the north-west, other than those associated with fishing and agriculture, are two in number—woollen weaving, including the famous Harris tweeds, and distilling. Whether the new hydro-electric schemes will lead to the industrialization of the Western Highlands, and whether, if they do, the people who go to work in those factories will be Highlanders—that remains to be seen. Public opinion is, in any case, divided on the point, some seeing the problems of poverty in the Highlands best solved by building factories, some deploring the thought.

One point about the Western Highlands which is often forgotten. They lead the surveyor back to Glasgow, for, industrially at least, Glasgow is the Capital of the Highlands. And in bringing this account of the industries of Scotland to its close, the point should again be made that it is on Glasgow that industrial life in Scotland is focused. The diversification of Scotland's industries, as described in this chapter, may surprise the visitor, but he should remember that—with a few exceptions, such as jute, linoleum, and some specialized branches of engineering—everything that is made elsewhere in Scotland is also made in Glasgow.

Plate 43   Comrie mine, Fife, the most modern coal-mine in Scotland

(Photo : Crown Copyright)

Plate 44   (*Above*) Dundee and the Law hill seen from the Firth of Tay
(*Below*) The Tay Bridge and Dundee
(*Photos : J. B. White*)

HYDRO-ELECTRICITY

THE first hydro-electric station in Britain was opened more than fifty years ago, in 1896, at Foyers in Inverness-shire, by the British Aluminium Company. In 1909 the same Company built a second station in Inverness-shire at Kinlochleven, and in 1924 they carried out a further large development in that district, known as the Lochaber Power Scheme. Also in 1924 there was a small scheme on the Clyde at Bonnington and Stonebyres under the Lanarkshire Hydro-Electric Act. In 1930 and 1934 the Grampian Company's schemes, which had been authorized in 1922, came into operation, and two years later the Galloway Power Company's chain of hydro-electric stations in southern Scotland, authorized in 1929, had commenced production. During the next ten years there was no further development of Scotland's water-power.

Scarcely any part of Scotland is more than fifty miles from the sea, and although much of the country is mountainous there are no extensive high plateaux. Consequently, in spite of some areas of relatively high rainfall, with an annual average exceeding 125 inches, Scotland does not possess rivers of the size and gradient associated with large-scale Continental hydro-electric works. Nevertheless, taken collectively the water-power of the Scottish river systems is an asset of considerable national importance.

It seems hard to understand why hydro-electric development should have been delayed in Scotland at a time when similar developments in other countries throughout the world were being pushed ahead, and in many cases planned and executed by Scottish engineers. Perhaps the chief factor was superabundance of coal, which for over a hundred years has formed the basis for Scottish industry. At first when coal was cheap and plentiful there seemed little need to develop the water-power as well. Later, hydro-electric schemes were opposed by the coal industry, presumably from a fear that the hydro-electric competition might lead to curtailment of employment for mine workers and a depreciation of the returns on capital invested in the coal-mining industry.

Strong opposition to hydro-electric development in the High-lands also arose from exaggerated fears as to the damage which would be done to the very valuable salmon and trout fishings in the lochs and rivers concerned, and to destruction of beautiful scenery. These attract many visitors, and are thus a valuable source of revenue in the employment which they give and the rates which they yield to local authorities. It was feared that these assets might be destroyed without any proportionate compensation to the Highlands, from which the electric power might be exported to supply industries already established in the south, or be used for electro-metallurgical processes giving small employment in proportion to the quantities of electricity consumed.

For one reason or another the fact remains that hydro-electric development in Scotland was held up. From 1922 to 1943 Parliament sanctioned no scheme for hydro-electric development in northern Scotland, although it is there that the great bulk of the undeveloped water-power resources of the United Kingdom are situated. Even in 1941, when the need for additional supplies of electricity was clamant, a scheme which had received the favourable report of a Parliamentary Committee failed to obtain Parliamentary approval.

The then Secretary of State, Mr. Thomas Johnston, therefore set up a special committee, under the Chairmanship of Lord Cooper, "to consider the practicability and the desirability of further development in the use of water-power resources in Scotland for the generation of electricity, and by what type of authority or body such development, if any, should be undertaken."

Much has been heard about the depopulation of the Highlands. It is not sufficiently realized that the decrease is continuing and is becoming more rapid in some districts than ever before. The Cooper Committee felt unanimously that electricity could become an important factor, if not indeed the major factor, in the arrest of this decline. Electric light, electric power for cooking, heating, and all the modern labour-saving devices of the home ; electricity to help the expansion of existing industries and to encourage the formation of new ones, and in every Highland village at least some of the electrical advantages of urban life, from X-ray and electro-therapy apparatus to cinemas—these things might mean a complete change in the Highland economic outlook. It must be remembered that many Highland communities are still dependent upon paraffin and peat for light and warmth, and water has often to be carried by hand from a well where a small electric pump could save endless drudgery.

Unfortunately, Highland depopulation has already proceeded far. Even if the electric power could be generated free, the cost of transmission and distribution to the scattered crofts and hamlets would prevent the electricity being sold at a price which the inhabitants or small industrial users could afford without a substantial subsidy. On the other hand, the potential water-power of the Highlands is so great that local demands cannot, within any predictable period, absorb more than an insignificant fraction of the total resources. Outside the Highland area there is an acute shortage of electric power.

The Cooper Committee, with these facts before them, considered that if part of the surplus Highland power were exported to the Lowlands, it could earn revenue to meet the inevitable deficit on distributing electricity in the remote and isolated districts.

On 5th August 1943 the Hydro-Electric Development (Scotland) Act became law, having been passed by both Houses of Parliament without a division. That Act gave effect to all the main recommendations of the Cooper Committee. It established the North of Scotland Hydro-Electric Board as the public authority responsible for all further hydro-electric development in, roughly, the north-western two-thirds of Scotland.

In order to safeguard the fisheries and to ensure that the Board's works should not conflict with Highland scenery, the Act set up a Fisheries Committee and an Amenity Committee to advise the Secretary of State for Scotland and the Board. In addition, the Board also retains the expert advice of a former Chief Inspector of Salmon Fisheries and of a panel of eminent Scottish architects.

The Board is planning the co-ordinated full development of all Highland water-power. A survey already completed estimates a potential annual output of over 6,000 million units. The Highlands and Islands, in fact all that area known as the North of Scotland, have first claim on the electricity produced within it. The Board have also to make available, at the lowest practicable cost, bulk supplies of electricity suitable for the needs of large electro industries, in the hopes that by this means new industrial enterprises may be attracted to commence operations in the Highlands. The electricity surplus to these needs is exported to an assured market in Central and South Scotland. The price paid for this exported electricity is the price of electricity produced by the most economical coal-powered station in Britain. At present the cost of production is more in favour of hydro-electric plant than a coal-fired steam station, and the Board can therefore earn revenue with which to finance the uneconomic distribution schemes in sparsely populated districts.

Three of the Board's first major projects, in the districts of Loch Sloy in Dumbartonshire, Tummel-Garry in Central Perthshire, and Mullardoch-Fasnakyle-Affric in north-west Inverness-shire, will earn sufficient revenue to balance the loss on about a dozen uneconomic schemes in the western Highlands and Islands. In some remote districts the electricity is being supplied without delay by Diesel plant, until the hydro-electric stations are completed.

At Loch Sloy there is an admirable site for a storage reservoir created by a dam 1,160 feet long and 165 feet high in a narrow part of the glen. The water is taken from the reservoir by tunnel and pipeline to a power station some 900 feet below on the shore of Loch Lomond.

The annual rainfall at Loch Sloy exceeds 110 inches, and the natural catchment area of the loch has been materially increased by the diversion of other waters. Many schemes in Scotland require the artificial enlargement of their catchment areas by the diversion of other head streams, because few Scottish rivers possess sufficiently extensive high-level catchment areas, and in many parts of the country glacial moraine, or the agricultural value of the land which would be flooded, make it difficult to find suitable sites for the large storage reservoirs necessitated by the unpredictable variations of seasonal rainfall.

Much of the beauty of Scottish scenery lies in its remarkable diversity. In hydro-electric work this diversity means that almost every scheme requires special treatment and individual planning. This is illustrated by the main project in the Board's Second Constructional Scheme. It covers a large catchment area in the Tummel-Garry district of Central Perthshire. There are three generating stations : Errochty, with a catchment area of 86 square miles ; Clunie, with a catchment area of 515 square miles, and Pitlochry, with a catchment area of 706 square miles. In addition to collecting, by means of 17 miles of diversion tunnels, much water previously undeveloped, this scheme also re-uses the flow in the River Tummel already largely controlled by the operations of the Grampian Electricity Supply Company.

The Tummel contains one of the principal salmon runs of the River Tay, world famous for its angling. A special feature of this scheme is therefore the large salmon passes to enable these fish to surmount the dams at Pitlochry and at Clunie below Loch Tummel. The ladders are the result of extensive scientific research and embody a new type of orifice between pools and other original details. It is hoped to record the ascent of fish by automatic electrical counting equipment, and there will be observation chambers with under-water windows for studying, in a manner not previously attempted, the movements and behaviour of the fish in passes and reservoirs.

Just as the Tummel-Garry project required special consideration to safeguard the salmon fisheries, the Mullardoch-Fasnakyle-Affric project called for special care to preserve the scenery, for Glen Affric, and particularly Loch Affric, is one of the most beautiful valleys in Britain. The Board's scheme leaves Loch Affric unaffected and will raise the level of the lower loch, Benevean, by only twenty-five feet, restricting fluctuation of the water level within natural limits. The main power station will be located in another valley, at Fasnakyle in Strath Glass, and the plan arranges for the water to be conveyed to the power stations by tunnels without visible pipelines. A flow will always be maintained in the River Affric, with its famous waterfalls, by "compensation water" discharged from the Benevean Dam.

Within the next ten years the Board expect to construct a considerable number of power stations, and they have already prepared plans to distribute electricity throughout almost the whole of their distribution area, within which electricity may thus become available to all but the remotest crofts.

The North of Scotland Hydro-Electric Board are not only producers and distributors of electricity. Their Act requires that " the Board shall, so far as their powers and duties permit, col-laborate in the carrying out of any measures for the economic development and social improvement of the North of Scotland district or any part thereof." The Board are therefore in consulta-tion with other public and private bodies and individuals who are also contemplating developments in the northern area, and already new activities of widely different sorts are profiting from this collaboration.

Indirectly, as for example through the great contribution which the hydro-electric works will make to county rates, and, to a greater degree, directly by the provision of electricity, the Board are bring-ing fresh hope of regeneration to many districts. Electricity is not the only need which must be met if the Highland glens are to be repopulated, but it has now become perhaps the greatest need. The operations of the North of Scotland Hydro-Electric Board will have effects upon the whole economy of the Highlands which cannot fail to be profound and may well prove revolutionary.

LEGAL AND LAND SYSTEMS

THE LEGAL SYSTEM

THE Act of Union of 1707 which consummated the parliamentary union of the sister kingdoms of England and Scotland preserved entire " in all Time coming " the existing legal system of Scotland, and to-day the civil and criminal jurisdiction of the Scottish courts still remain separate and distinct from those of England. By this means, as well as by its native vigour, the law of Scotland retained and still retains its own peculiar characteristics, modified though these have been by legislation of the British Parliament and adaptation to meet the changing needs of modern life.

The supreme civil court of Scotland known as the Court of Session is of respectable antiquity, dating as it does from 1532 in the reign of King James V of Scotland. It was set up to provide a permanent continuous court with a fixed seat or habitation, whence its name " Court of Session." Originally consisting of fifteen judges—the " Auld Feiftein "—its numbers are now reduced to thirteen and it sits in Edinburgh in the old Parliament House of Scotland. Its jurisdiction, both original and appellate, is of the widest character : the ancient division between law and equity familiar to the English law and perpetuated in the Chancery and King's Bench Divisions of the High Court of Justice, finds no place either in the jurisprudence or courts of Scotland, and hence a visitor to-day to the supreme court of Scotland may find in a single day the same judge disposing of actions of divorce, intricate questions of trust administration, and claims of damages for personal injury. The court itself is divided into what is known as the Outer and the Inner House, the former composed of the five junior judges sitting alone, and the latter of two divisions of four judges, each sitting as a court of appeal of co-ordinate jurisdiction, presided over by the Lord President and the Lord Justice-Clerk respectively. From the decision of the Court of Session a right of appeal lies to the House of Lords.

Before this supreme court the privilege of audience is enjoyed by the Faculty of Advocates, the Bar of Scotland, from whose ranks are recruited the bench not only of the supreme court but in large measure the bench of the inferior or Sheriff Courts. The barrister, or advocate, to use the Scottish term, is, as the word implies, primarily a pleader. By the law of Scotland the legal profession is divided into two parts, the advocates, alone privileged to plead before the supreme civil and criminal courts, and still wearing the ancient wig and gown, and the law agents, a term applied to all those, other than members of the Faculty of Advocates, entitled to practise in a court of law. The term law agent, which is self-explanatory, is practically synonymous with " solicitor." There are numerous societies or associations of law agents, many of great antiquity ; and it is the initials of membership of some of these societies which account for the mysterious lettering, such as " W.S. " (Writer to His Majesty's Signet) and " S.S.C." (Solicitor before the Supreme Courts), on brass plates in Edinburgh and elsewhere throughout Scotland. All such law agents have the same legal status.

The supreme criminal court of Scotland, known as the High Court of Justiciary, derives historically from the ancient office of the Justiciar, formerly one of the great royal officers. Its judges, known as Commissioners of Justiciary, are the same as those of the Court of Session, and it is presided over by the Lord Justice-General who is also Lord President of the Court of Session. Unlike the Court of Session, the High Court holds sittings not only in Edinburgh but also on " circuit " in certain cities and burghs of Scotland. In addition to its original and privative jurisdiction in certain grave crimes such as murder, rape, and wilful fire-raising, the High Court exercises an appellate jurisdiction from the decisions and sentences of the courts of summary criminal jurisdiction. Trials before the High Court are always trials by jury. Since 1926 there has been in Scotland a Court of Criminal Appeal, composed of members of the High Court, to hear appeals in all cases tried by jury either in the High Court or in the Sheriff Court. No appeal lies from the decisions of the High Court of Justiciary or the Court of Criminal Appeal, except to the exercise of the Royal Clemency. The High Court possesses extremely wide powers of punishment ; it alone can inflict the capital penalty. It also possesses at common law an inherent but sparely exercised power of declaring new common law crimes and offences.

Prosecutions in the High Court, as in the lower Sheriff Court, are instituted at the instances of the Lord Advocate or his subordinates. The right of private prosecution, however, still exists in Scotland, but it is only exercised on the rarest occasion. The Lord Advocate, or King's Advocate as he was formerly known, is a high officer of State, corresponding in some measure to the Attorney-General in England. He is a member of the government of the day, and as his is a political appointment, he changes with a change of administration. In the discharge of his duty as public prosecutor in the High Court the Lord Advocate has the assistance of the Solicitor-General for Scotland and of four subordinate officials known as Advocates-Depute; it is only in comparatively rare cases that the Lord Advocate prosecutes in person. Through his local and subordinate official known as the Procurator-Fiscal he also conducts public prosecutions in the Sheriff courts, both in summary proceedings and in trials before the Sheriff and a jury. The decision whether to prosecute or not, and if so, before what court, rests finally with the Lord Advocate, who thus exercises a very wide and responsible jurisdiction. By this means the investigation and prosecution of crime is centralized and public justice vindicated by a public officer. In Scotland there are no coroners, any necessary inquiries being privately conducted by the Procurator-Fiscal, and no preliminary public hearing before trial.

The inferior civil and criminal courts of Scotland, apart from the burgh or magistrates' courts of limited local jurisdiction, are known as the Sheriff Courts. The office of Sheriff is of great antiquity and outdates both the Court of Session and the High Court of Justiciary. Formerly the Sheriff was also an important administrative and judicial officer, and was introduced into Scotland at least as early as the twelfth century. To-day the Sheriff is primarily a judicial officer, though he still has certain local administrative duties to discharge, and administers justice in local courts known as the Sheriff Court. Each county in Scotland has one or more of these Sheriff Courts presided over by a resident judge known as the Sheriff-Substitute. The civil and criminal jurisdiction of their court is wide, though not co-extensive with that of the supreme courts. Thus although a decree of separation can be obtained in the Sheriff Court, a decree of divorce cannot, jurisdiction in divorce being restricted to the Court of Session; and though a charge of culpable homicide or manslaughter can be tried and punished by the Sheriff, a charge of murder can only be competently tried before the High Court of Justiciary. The Sheriff, as opposed to the Sheriff-Substitute, is not necessarily resident in his jurisdiction and is almost invariably appointed from among senior practising members of the bar. His jurisdiction generally includes two or more counties, and he is responsible for the proper admini-

Plate 45   Parliament Hall, Edinburgh, where the Parliament of
Scotland met till the Union of the Parliaments in 1707

(Photo : F. C. Inglis)

Plate 46   Judges of the Court of Session

(Photo : ' The Scotsman ')

stration of the Sheriff Court within those counties ; he also exercises an appellate jurisdiction from the decisions of the Sheriff-Substitute in civil matters. As already indicated, all decisions of the Sheriff Courts both in civil and criminal matters may be subjected on appeal either to the Court of Session or to the High Court of Justiciary according to their nature.

Before leaving the Sheriff Court notice should be taken of the Procurator-Fiscal. Originally the Procurator-Fiscal was the Sheriff's own officer, dating from the distant day when the Sheriff was both prosecutor and judge in his own court. To-day he is the subordinate of the Lord Advocate, whom he represents in the Sheriff Court, in which he prosecutes for the public interest. He is also responsible for the investigation of crime within his district, and reporting the result of his investigations to the Lord Advocate.

Mention should also be made of the Justices of the Peace. These are unpaid lay magistrates appointed by the Lord Chancellor on the recommendation of the Lords-Lieutenant of the counties in which they reside. Their functions and jurisdictions are strictly limited to matters of minor administration and civil and criminal causes of trivial value and importance. Their most important duties, however, lie in the licensing of premises for the sale and consumption of excisable liquors. Their judicial decisions are subject to review by the Court of Session and the High Court of Justiciary in civil and criminal matters respectively.

The burgh or magistrates' courts already mentioned are local police courts of limited jurisdiction. Their powers of punishment are restricted by statute to fines or short terms of imprisonment, and only minor police offences are disposed of by them. The bench in their courts is manned by unpaid magistrates—with one exception in Glasgow—elected from the town council of the burgh or city, while prosecutions are conducted by a locally appointed prosecutor. The judgments of these local law-givers are subject to review by the High Court of Justiciary.

The appointment of judges in the supreme and inferior courts, other than the burgh or police courts, rests with the Crown. This means that the bench is normally recruited from practising members of the Bar who are usually political supporters of the party in power. This custom has on the whole worked equitably, and as merit is not usually overlooked it may be said that the system of political selection has produced no worse results than any other. By invariable and rigid custom, all political activities must cease on acceptance of a full-time appointment to the Bench. By statute appointees are required to be of at least six years' standing in their profession ; in fact they are invariably of much greater seniority. Tenure of office is secure *quamdiu se bene gesserit*—during good behaviour.

Modern legislation and the close community of interest between England and Scotland have both tended to assimilate the two systems in many respects, but there still remains much in which the domestic jurisprudence of Scotland is a native growth. The common law of Scotland derives in large measure from the civil and canon law of Rome. A knowledge of Roman law is still, if not essential, at least a valued part of the equipment of every Scots lawyer, and it has been said that the civil law " as explained and in some respects amended by the Dutch and French commentators of the sixteenth and seventeenth centuries is the basis of the Scots law of contract and of property, apart from feudal conveyancing." The Dutch law schools of Leyden and Utrecht were the training ground of many Scots lawyers of the seventeenth and eighteenth centuries, while even to-day citations from Dutch and French " civilians " may be heard quoted in the courts.

There is perhaps one respect in which the Scottish legal system was for long in advance of its time. The law's delays are proverbial, so also unfortunately are its costs. By statute of 1424 the Scottish Parliament ordained that " gif there be ony pure [poor] creature, " for fault of cunning [knowledge] or expenses that cannot nor may " not follow his cause, the King for the love of God, sall ordain " the judge, before quhom the cause suld be determined, to purwey " and get a leill and wise advocate to follow sik pure creature's " cause." That statute has been observed both in the spirit and in the letter.

THE LAND SYSTEM

The land system of Scotland is peculiarly its own : for over eight centuries this has been governed by the rules of the feudal system, modified to meet economic, political, and social changes. Under this system the Sovereign is the source of all land rights in the kingdom, and those who hold from the Crown—Crown vassals as they are called—give off or " feu " to sub-vassals, to whom they stand in the position of overlords or " superiors," portions of the land which they themselves hold from the Crown. This process, of course, is capable of infinite extension. The return that the vassal made to his superior formerly consisted of various types of service, most usually military. To-day the return is almost invariably an annual money payment known as a " feu duty." This in brief is the foundation on which the modern land system of Scotland is built and still in large measure rests.

The development of such a contractual system of land rights as grew from feudal principles could only have led to confusion, uncertainty, and chaos had it not been linked with a system of registration and publication of titles. This was finally achieved by a Scottish statute of 1617 which provided for the registration of titles to land and of deeds of security affecting land. By this means order, certainty, and security were achieved in a matter vital to the community, and with certain amendments in detail this system of registration still operates to-day, and is now housed in the Register House, Edinburgh, erected towards the close of the eighteenth century to the designs of Robert Adam, Scotland's most famous architect.

Although the foundation of the Scottish land system is feudal it must not be supposed that leasehold rights are not available, or that a complete leasehold code of law does not exist. A Scottish lease has for long been protected as a real right and not merely a personal contract. This was settled so far back as 1449 by statutes couched in the quaint and crabbed Scots of the day, bearing to be enacted " for the safetie and favour of the puir people that labouris the grund." The vassal in possession of land, known as the feuar, is fully entitled to sell or lease his lands on any terms that are not at variance with his contract or charter from his superior. His rights as feuar can only be terminated by such a fundamental breach of his contract as entitles his superior to bring the contract to an end— to " irritate the feu "—and to resume possession of the land. The succession to land in Scotland is, as might be expected in a system erected on the feudal principle, governed by the law of primogeniture.

The legal and land system of Scotland in their salient and peculiarly Scottish features reflect alike the history and life of Scotland : originating in antiquity they have grown up with the nation, shared the storm and stress of its story, and still retain to-day a strength and vigour to face new needs and new conditions. And so may be accomplished the command laid upon all judges by King James I in the words of the Act of 1424, " that alsweil to pure as to rich, bot [without] fraud or favour, they do full law and justice."

ADMINISTRATION—LOCAL AND CENTRAL

THE local administration of Scotland, unlike that of many continental countries, is in the hands of popularly elected bodies of a purely local character and composition. The direction they receive from the Central Government comes in somewhat indirect ways to be described later.

These local authorities are the councils of counties, towns, and districts. Scotland is divided into thirty-three counties of very different sizes and densities in population. In two instances, counties have amalgamated to provide local services, so that there are thirty-one administrative counties, each having its county council. Within each county lie several towns which, either by ancient Charter or by virtue of an Act of Parliament, have been created burghs, and have therefore town councils of their own. But historical distinctions having been swept away, there are now, from the administrative point of view, only two types of burgh, namely, Large Burghs and Small Burghs. The Large Burghs run all their own services except education, and in several instances police, both of which are provided by the county. Small Burghs run only minor services for themselves; and the county attends to their education, police, major health services, public assistance, classified roads, and a variety of other matters. Each burgh sends one or more councillors to represent it in the county council. The other county councillors are elected from the various divisions of the rural or landward area of the county. There are four Large Burghs which are in an exceptional position. They are Edinburgh, Glasgow, Dundee, and Aberdeen, each of which bears the title of county of the city, and is completely independent of the county within which it happens to be situated.

Midlothian, to take an example, has its county council. Edinburgh is within Midlothian, but apart from it. Within Midlothian are five Small Burghs, each having its own town council and minor services, but having also representation on the county council, and receiving services for which the burgh makes annual payment to the county. Finally, the landward area of Midlothian, as of all counties, is divided into several districts each having a district council, exercising minor functions of a narrowly local character. They sometimes have other work delegated to them by the county.

Who are the councillors ? The qualifications are few and simple. They must be British subjects of full age and resident in the council's area for a short qualifying period. Disqualifications are few and apply to fairly exceptional circumstances. There is no preliminary training. Although a council, as originally conceived, has no connection with politics, there is an increasing tendency for the candidates to be nominees of the various political parties. The councillors are popularly elected, and hold office for three years. Town councillors retire in rotation, one-third each year ; in counties all retire together every third year. All councillors are eligible for re-election. They receive no salary. The chairman of the town council, the Provost, holds his position for three years. The council nominates senior members to be magistrates in the local police courts. They are Bailies, and like the Provost and others are unpaid. The chairman of the county council is the Convener.

How does the council perform its task ? Each council has regular fixed meetings, but it is impossible for a general meeting to deal with ordinary routine work in detail. This is delegated to committees. These committees are presided over by conveners who are experienced councillors familiar with the work involved.

A council is required by law to set up certain committees : apart from these, it may have as many additional committees as it pleases. The conveners of such committees report regularly to the full council. They are guided in their administration by permanent officials, appointed and paid by the council, who have received a professional training and are the executive. Thus the Public Health Committee works along with the Medical Officer of Health, the Education Committee with the Director of Education, and so on. The council frames policy and the official carries out their instructions.

In addition to the two permanent officials of the council already mentioned there are many others : the Town or County Clerk, who occupies a position analogous to that of secretary to a large company ; the Surveyor, who in towns is concerned with the upkeep of streets and in counties with the roads ; the Chief Constable, who is head of the local police force ; the Sanitary Inspector, who enforces cleanliness of streets and buildings ; the Assistance Officer, who relieves the poor ; the Medical Officer of Health who, along with the Veterinary Surgeon, the Sanitary Inspector, and the Analyst and the Sampling Officers, ensures proper conditions in dairies and slaughterhouses, prevents diseased meat or infected milk from reaching the public, and secures purity in the food and drugs offered for sale ; the

Assessor, who values all land and buildings in the area for taxation purposes ; and the managers of the various municipal trading undertakings, such as transport, gas, and electricity.

Who pays for the local services ? The cost is met partly by a grant annually voted in the Budget by the British Parliament and based on the estimates for each Department of State, but chiefly by the ratepayers who are the owners and occupiers of property within the council's area of administration. In counties, rates are paid by owners and occupiers in equal proportions ; in burghs the larger share falls on the occupier. This division of payment is peculiar to Scotland. (In England the occupier pays, but the landlord makes no contribution.) Payment in Scotland is based on the annual value of the house, shop, factory, or other heritable property, calculated according to definite rules. This assessment of value of all property in the district is made by the Assessor, from whose decision the ratepayer may appeal, first to the Valuation Committee of the council, and thence, if desired, to three judges of the Court of Session, sitting as the Lands Valuation Appeal Court.

The government grant is distributed by the central departments according to a formula evolved by the British Treasury, the amount being subject to revision at intervals of five years. So it will be seen that rates are based not on income or profit but on the yearly value of the property the ratepayer happens to own or occupy in the region. The Finance Committee of the council looks after the council's expenditure and frames its budget. It is assisted by the permanent paid financial officials.

What part does the central government play in relation to local activity ? There are government departments intimately concerned to supervise and guide. The four main Scottish departments have offices in Edinburgh. These are the Scottish Home Department, and the Departments of Health, Education, and Agriculture. Other departments, such as the Ministry of Labour and the Ministry of Transport, are common to the United Kingdom. They are administered from London but have offices in Scotland.

The central Scottish departments act in the name of the minister who is at the head of them, the Secretary of State for Scotland. The office is an old one dating back before the Union with England, but in years of unrest it was frequently left unfilled. Growing Scottish national feeling caused the office to be instituted afresh some sixty years ago, and many new powers were then conferred on the Secretary for Scotland which his predecessors did not possess. His appointment is political, changing with the government. He is answerable to Parliament for the entire Scottish administration. He carries out his great responsibility through the central departments which all work at his direction to ensure general efficiency. He has to speak for Scotland in Parliament.

So we may picture Scottish administration as a pyramid having as its base the local councils, entrenched in their native soil, in close contact with local conditions. Resting on this solid base are the walls formed by the central departments, giving unity to the structure and leading up to the apex of the whole edifice which is represented by the Secretary of State.

SOCIAL AND INDUSTRIAL WELFARE

THE PATTERN OF SOCIAL WELFARE

Philanthropy

THE Scottish people have built up a great variety of institutions, each contributing to some aspect of social welfare. Voluntary hospitals and District Nursing Associations care for people when they are ill, and Friendly Societies and State Health Insurance provide them with weekly payments. Public Assistance Committees, often called Social Welfare Committees, have built up a successful system for boarding out orphan children. Community Centres, Miners' Welfare Institutes, and Boys' Clubs provide for the leisure time of many people. The old established Scottish system of free legal aid for the poor, and the modern network of Citizens' Advice Bureaux bring guidance and advice to the citizen perplexed by the intricate society in which he lives. These are only a few of the institutions. They appear to have no relation to one another and to have grown up without a plan. Is it possible to discern any kind of pattern in this apparently chaotic growth of unrelated societies, authorities, and services ? If we trace out some of the threads that are woven into the texture of Scotland's social welfare we shall discover that it is not without a pattern. Some of these threads are philanthropy, mutual aid, the voluntary association, the local authority, and last, but not least, the State.

Let us examine philanthropy. The Scots are a religious people. For centuries they have argued and quarrelled about religion. The consciences of many have been troubled by the demands of Christianity for the care of the poor, the orphaned, the widowed, and the broken-hearted. This has led to a widespread sense of social responsibility even among those who would not claim to be Christian. This, too, has led to the foundation of institutions as different and as distinctive as the Orphan Homes of Scotland, the Missions to the Deaf, the Boys' Brigade, and the Eventide Homes of the Church of Scotland. The nineteenth century saw a great development of this philanthropy. The great voluntary hospitals, under the leadership of men like Lister and Simpson, were built up with funds provided voluntarily. Surgeons and doctors gave their services freely. Innumerable charities, Nursing Associations, Missions

Plate 47   The Lord Lyon King of Arms making a Royal Proclamation
at the Mercat Cross, Edinburgh

(Photo : ' The Scotsman ')

Plate 48   The Town Council of Edinburgh : the Lord Provost making
a public announcement

(*Photo : Dunlop*)

to the Blind, Societies for the Prevention of Cruelty to Children, coal funds, and soup kitchens came into being. At the ports societies concerned with the welfare of seamen were formed to provide hostels and institutes. At first local in character, in many cases these societies formed federations which became such well-known national organizations as the Queen's Institute of District Nursing, the Scottish National Federation for the Welfare of the Blind, and the Royal Scottish Society for the Prevention of Cruelty to Children. To-day philanthropy is less concerned with material needs—with the provision of clothes and coal, shelter and soup, now more and more the province of the State—than it is with supplementing State action by providing libraries and playing fields, boys' clubs and community centres, public parks and welfare clinics.

The Carnegie Trusts

Early in the century Andrew Carnegie founded in Scotland a number of philanthropic trusts which have had far-reaching influence on this tendency of social welfare to broaden its field from material to non-material needs. In founding the Carnegie Dunfermline Trust, Carnegie asked his trustees to spend their annual revenue of £25,000 (it has since risen to £48,000) in attempts to bring into the monotonous lives of the toiling masses of Dunfermline more of sweetness and light. The trustees have provided swimming baths and gymnasia, community centres and playing fields, a craft school and a music institute, and a delightful public park. In 1906 the Trust inaugurated a system of School Medical Inspection three years before it became permissible for local authorities to do so.

The Carnegie United Kingdom Trust with an annual income of £122,000 has been able to influence local authorities and the State in certain fields of social welfare. The shape of the county library service has been determined by the Trust's library policy initiated in 1915. The Trust provided the initial capital and the running costs for five years for nineteen authorities in Great Britain. This large-scale experiment led to the legislation which permitted County Councils to maintain County Library Schemes. In the field of Maternity and Child Welfare the trustees made an extensive inquiry which was reported in 1917, and financed the building of six model Maternity and Child Welfare Clinics, one of which was built in Scotland at Motherwell.

For some years the National Council of Social Service has

administered a fund provided by the Trust to make grants towards the cost of building new village halls. At the same time it has administered a loan fund for the same purpose provided by the Development Commission, a body set up by Act of Parliament to develop the rural areas. For example, a village with a population of 1,200 people wishes to build a hall costing £3,000. A grant of £500 can be obtained from the Trust fund and a loan of £1,500 through the Development Commission from the State. The loan is interest free and repayable over seven years. Eighty-three village halls have been built or improved in Scotland with the help of this scheme.

The Trust has been behind such voluntary movements as the Scottish Community Drama Association, the Scottish Youth Hostels Association, the Scottish Women's Rural Institutes, the Scottish Association of Young Farmers' Clubs, and the Scottish Council of Social Service. Music and drama, adult education, and land settlement are other fields of social welfare which have been influenced by the policies of the Trust, the latest venture of which has been the establishment in 1946 of the Bureau of Current Affairs. This has been set up by the Trust to provide accurate up-to-date information for discussion groups. The experiment is on a large scale and may have very far-reaching results on adult education.

MUTUAL AID AND THE VOLUNTARY ASSOCIATION

The Voluntary Association

Voluntary associations are free associations in two senses. In the first place the purposes of the association are freely chosen and in the second place the members are free to join the association or to abstain from joining. A voluntary association usually has a constitution setting out the objects of the association ; who are entitled to be members ; what the obligations and rights of these members are and how its affairs are to be managed. It assumes the willingness of members to give voluntary service as members of committees and as office-bearers. Without this kind of unpaid service the great network of Friendly Societies, Nursing Associations, Youth Organizations, Recreational Clubs, Cripple Aid Societies, Citizens' Advice Bureaux, Trade Unions, and Church Organizations could not exist. They have often arisen in the face of popular disapproval. A few people have recognized a need and have endeavoured to meet it. The voluntary association has enabled minority movements to experiment and to make new ideas palatable to a conservative majority. Voluntary associations are important for what they have done, for the institutions they have built up, and the wider opportunities they have made possible. They are also important because as well as showing new social needs they have demonstrated how they could be met.

Like the other threads in the pattern of social welfare the voluntary association continues in the twentieth century to be important. Indeed, the century has witnessed the growth of newly recognized needs. A variety of Women's organizations is evidence of the new status of women in public affairs. Among them the Women's Rural Institutes, started during the 1914–18 war, have made notable progress. In 1946 there were 1,000 institutes with 50,000 members. Closely associated with the co-operative movement are the Women's Co-operative Guilds. In 1943 these two national movements, along with other women's organizations including the National Council of Women, the Women Citizens' Association, the Soroptimists, and the Hospital Almoners Association, set up the Scottish Women's Group on Public Welfare. This Group has enabled these organizations to consult together on social matters of special interest to women.

The Scottish Youth Hostels Association, started in 1931, has been a popular movement initiated by groups of keen young people who, recognizing a need, set about meeting it. In 1946 it had seventy-two Youth Hostels, property worth £92,600, and a membership of 34,000.

Among the new voluntary associations of a national character which have grown up in the past twenty-five years, are the Scottish Community Drama Association, the British Legion (Scotland), the Scottish Association of Boys' Clubs, the Association for the Preservation of Rural Scotland, the Scottish Association of Girls' Clubs, the Saltire Society, and the Scottish Orthopaedic Council. In 1943 the Scottish Council of Social Service was instituted. Associated with it are no fewer than seventy-four national voluntary associations.

Friendly Societies

Closely related to the idea of the voluntary association is that of mutual aid. Scotland in the eighteenth century had societies which consisted of about fifty members and were called Penny or Halfpenny Societies. The society had no funds, but when a member was confined to bed by sickness every member paid him a penny weekly, and if he was able to go about, though not to work, a half-penny. It was from such simple forms of mutual aid that the Friendly Societies in Scotland grew. In 1944 there were 135 societies having 161,997 members and £17,103,161 of accumulated funds. They familiarized large numbers of working-class people with the idea of sickness and burial insurance. To be buried in a pauper's grave was regarded as the greatest degradation anyone could suffer. Funeral benefit was therefore one of the most important for which people joined friendly societies. Originally local in character, the local "lodges" and "tents" combined to form the great friendly orders, the Foresters, the Shepherds, the Gardeners, and the Rechabites. They familiarized working men with the means of combining to secure better wages and better working conditions, and were often the nucleus of the trade union.

Co-operative Societies

Another form of mutual aid which has met with great success in Scotland is the Co-operative Society. The Co-operative Society is a voluntary association of consumers who join together to run their own shops. Each member owns at least a minimum number of shares, but cannot have more than £200 worth, this being the legal limit. He receives a fixed rate of interest on his shares and a dividend on the amount of his purchases. The dividend varies from society to society and from year to year. It may be as low as one shilling per £ of purchases or as high as 3s. 6d. If a member purchases £40 worth of goods during a year from a society paying a dividend at the rate of 2s. 6d. in the £ she will receive £5. The average purchases of members of all 234 societies in Scotland in 1944 was £57, 19s. This represented a total trade of £62,416,707 among 1,077,221 members. While the Co-operative Society is a trading concern and the material benefits of the "store," as it is popularly called, loom large, it has brought social as well as material benefits. There has always been some idealism about the co-operative movement. During the nineteenth century when ideas of competition predominated it kept alive the older idea of mutual aid and community of interest. Associated with the movement are three voluntary organizations which propagate the co-operative ideal. These are the Women's Co-operative Guilds, the Men's Guilds, and the Co-operative Youth Movement.

Plate 49 His Majesty the King knighting the Lord Provost of Edinburgh

(*Photo : ' The Scotsman '*)

Plate 50 St. Andrews House, the administrative centre of Scotland,
on the Calton Hill, Edinburgh

(*Photo : Valentine*)

MUTUAL AID IN INDUSTRY

Trade Unions

Trade Unions have come to play a large part in the industrial life of Scotland. At the beginning of this century the Scottish Trade Unions had 175,000 members. By 1939 this number had risen to 570,000, about 40 per cent. of all workers over sixteen years of age. The number increased still more during the war, so that in 1945 there were 613,000 members connected with the seventy-nine Trade Unions affiliated to the Scottish Trades Union Congress. The following table shows how the members were distributed between the main industries and trades.

Membership of Scottish Trade Unions in 1945

Industries and Trades	Number of Members of Trade Unions
Mining and Quarrying	65,700
Railways and Transport	155,730
Shipbuilding, Engineering, and Metal Industries . . .	169,051
Food, Distributive Trades, Textiles, Clothing, and Leather .	107,767
Building, Vehicle Building, Woodworking, and Furnishing .	61,719
Public Employees, General Workers, Printing and Paper .	53,210
	613,177

The Scottish Trades Union Congress has become a powerful influence in industrial affairs in Scotland. It secures co-operation and co-ordination between Trade Unions and watches over all legislative measures affecting the interests of trade unionists. It is consulted by Government Departments on all questions relating to industry. Through it the Trades Unions are related to other bodies concerned with social welfare. For example, the Congress appoints representatives to the National Playing Fields Association, the Scottish Savings Committee, and the Scottish Council of Social Service.

Employers' Organizations

There is no employers' organization in Scotland corresponding to the Scottish Trades Union Congress. There is the British Employers' Confederation, whose membership comprises the national federations of employers throughout the whole of Great Britain. Its main purpose is to secure the co-operation of those federations in dealing with all questions arising out of the relations between employers and their workpeople. In 1936 there were 270 national federations in Great Britain and 1,550 employers' organizations of a local or regional character.

Relations between Worker and Employer

Between the Trade Unions and the Employers' Organizations there has grown up a highly complex system for the regulation of wages and conditions of employment and the settlement of disputes. Formerly negotiations were conducted locally, but gradually the area of negotiation has extended till in many cases there is national machinery for achieving national agreements. In many industries there have been set up Joint Industrial Councils on which there are representatives of Trade Unions and Employers' Organizations. They are voluntary associations, that is to say, they have been set up by agreement without any kind of compulsion on the part of the Government. An example of this is the Scottish National Joint Council for the Building Industry on which are representatives of the Scottish National Building Trades Federation (Employers) and the National Federation of Building Trades Operatives. As well as machinery of a voluntary character for negotiating wages questions there have grown up voluntary joint agreements to enable disputes to be settled by reference to Boards of Conciliation and Arbitration. As long ago as 1890 there was such a Board for the Steel Trades in the West of Scotland. The joint agreements under which these Boards are set up usually provide that in the event of agreement not being reached in a dispute the decision of a mutually acceptable umpire will be adopted. Although the Boards of Conciliation and Arbitration have no State sanction to enforce their decisions they have an almost unbroken record of acceptance and loyal observance.

While wages and conditions are for the most part settled by the voluntary methods just described, there are a number of trades in which minimum remuneration is fixed by Wages Councils (known till 1945 as Trade Boards) set up under the Trade Boards Acts and the Wages Councils Act of 1945. They are mostly in trades where organization on both sides is weak or there is a section of the trade in which wages and conditions are less favourable than those agreed upon between organized employers and workers. In 1944 there were forty Trade Boards covering trades throughout Great Britain, and six which operated in Scotland alone.

The Local Authority

Kinds of Local Authority

A local authority is a body set up by Act of Parliament to administer certain services within a defined area. It can only administer services which Parliament has given it " powers " to administer. There are five kinds of local authorities in Scotland : (1) Town Councils of Cities which administer all local authority services within their areas. (2) County Councils which administer (a) Education throughout the whole of their areas and (b) Public Health and Public Assistance Services throughout the whole of their areas except in (3) Large Burghs, where Town Councils administer all local authority services except Education. (4) Town Councils of Small Burghs which administer Housing, Refuse Collection and Street Cleaning, Water Supply, and a number of minor services. (5) District Councils which administer Recreational Services and Burial Grounds in areas outside the Burghs. In the areas outside the Burghs the County Councils are also responsible for Housing, Water Supply, and a great variety of services. The local authorities finance the services they provide partly from Government grants and partly out of rates levied both on owners and occupiers of property within their areas.

Functions

The local authority is an old thread in the pattern of social welfare. Since 1579 Scotland has had a Poor Law providing maintenance out of public funds for poor, aged or infirm persons, and for all these centuries it has been administered by a local authority of one kind or another. Unpopular with the working classes because of its emphasis on deterrence and inquiry into means, it is nearing the end of its long history. There began in 1908 a process which has been called the " break up of the Poor Law." In that year the Old Age Pensions Act enabled people on reaching the age of seventy to obtain a pension, subject to a means test carried out by officers, not of the local authority, but of a central authority. This was the first of a series of measures passed by successive governments which enabled people to obtain a benefit on a particular contingency arising. While the local authority services of assistance to poor, aged or infirm persons have declined in importance, other local authority services have developed. There has been a great development of maternity and child welfare services by the County Councils and the Town Councils of Large Burghs. In each Council area there is a Medical Officer of Health to whom every birth must be notified within thirty-six hours. This ensures that every new baby is visited by a Health Visitor who can give advice to the mother, and make known to her the services available to her. Many prospective mothers find their way to the ante-natal clinics provided by the local authorities. There doctors and nurses give advice and training in the care of babies. After the birth of the baby many mothers continue to attend the Maternity and Child Welfare Clinic to have the baby weighed regularly, to obtain special foods, sunlight treatment, and the support and guidance the confident expert can give the timid mother. The local authorities also maintain a public service of certified midwives. The Maternity Services (Scotland) Act, 1937, requires local authorities to make available the services of a midwife and a doctor to all expectant mothers who apply for them. Many local authorities maintain Maternity Homes or Maternity Hospitals. These are particularly important where housing standards are low and the dangers of infection are high. The Medical Officer of Health, the Health Visitor, the Certified Midwife, and the General Practitioner have co-operated in the building up of a Maternity and Child Welfare service which is paying dividends in improved health and happiness for thousands of mothers and babies.

Infectious Diseases

The local authorities are responsible for the prevention and cure of infectious diseases. There is a list of those such as smallpox, scarlet fever, and diphtheria which must be notified to the Medical Officer of Health. This enables anyone suffering from one of these diseases to be removed to the local authority's Infectious Diseases Hospital and for steps to be taken to trace the source of infection and to prevent its spread. In recent years a great deal has been done to make known to mothers the advantages of immunization against diphtheria. Local authorities have a special responsibility for the

Plate 51   Social Welfare.   (*Above*) A Carnegie Institute Lounge, Dunfermline
(*Below*) Children getting sun-ray treatment at a Children's Country Home
near Dunfermline   (*Photos : Norval*)

Plate 52 Social Welfare. (*Above*) Elgin Hostel, Portree, founded by the Carnegie U.K. Trust for boys attending secondary schools. (*Below*) Buses conveying workers from Comrie coal-mine, Fife, to their homes in the surrounding country (*Photo : ' Illustrated '*)

care of those suffering from tuberculosis. Each authority has a tuberculosis officer to care for those who remain in their homes. Many authorities maintain a sanatorium.

Recreation

It has long been recognized that disease and ill-health are related to bad housing and to the lack of opportunities for recreation and social life. This has led to the building of houses being one of the most important of the social services. Closely related to this is the provision of playing fields, bowling greens, tennis courts, and community centres where people may engage in health-giving activities. Many local authorities have public parks, golf courses, and swimming baths. The Burgh of Coatbridge has a public park with a lake which is kept stocked with trout so that the citizen may enjoy angling.

THE STATE SOCIAL SERVICES

In 1946 the State Social Services were extended, simplified, and co-ordinated. They may be conveniently divided into (1) Insurance Services, (2) Assistance Services, and (3) Other Services. Of course these services are common to the whole of Britain.

Insurance Services

Social Insurance is a form of compulsory mutual aid whereby large numbers of citizens are compelled to make weekly contributions to a fund from which benefits are paid, on certain contingencies arising, to those who contribute. Friendly Societies and Trade Unions had made large numbers familiar with this idea in relation to the contingencies of sickness, death, and unemployment before the State schemes of health insurance and unemployment insurance began in the second decade of this century. Although the need for insurance to pay for a decent funeral has played a large part among the concerns of working-class folk it was only in 1946 that a death grant (of £20) was included among the State social insurances. The essential features of the social insurance scheme are (1) A weekly compulsory contribution deducted from the insured person's wages. (2) A weekly compulsory contribution paid by the insured person's employer. (3) A contribution card for each insured person to which are affixed stamps to the value of the joint contribution of worker and employer. (4) The insured person has a right to the various benefits and grants when he satisfies certain well-defined conditions. (5) The contributions of the workers and the employers along with contributions made by the State are paid into a National Insurance Fund out of which all benefits, grants, and administration are paid. Sickness benefit is at the rate of 26s. per week. In addition a married man will receive 18s. for his wife and 7s. 6d. for his eldest child. Unemployment benefit is at the same rate. When a new baby arrives a maternity grant of £4 will be paid and an attendance allowance of £1 per week for four weeks. A widow receives £1, 16s. for thirteen weeks and, under certain conditions, a pension of £1, 6s. There is a retirement pension for a married couple of £2, 2s. For these benefits he contributes 3s. 9d. per week. In addition he will contribute fivepence per week for Industrial Injuries Insurance and tenpence per week towards the Health Service. That is to say a married man pays five shillings per week towards the cost of Insurance and Health Services. His employer contributes three shillings and tenpence.

National Insurance has been exceedingly popular with the working-classes compared with social assistance. When the Beveridge Report on Social and Allied Services was published during the war, civilian and serviceman alike welcomed it with an enthusiasm seldom given to a government paper. The National Insurance Act of 1946 extended the scope of social insurance so that " Every person . . . being over school-leaving age and under pensionable age . . . shall become insured under this Act and thereafter continue throughout his life to be so insured." It extended insurance to persons working under contract of service however large their incomes. Self-employed persons, shopkeepers, and professional men were brought into social insurance for the first time.

Assistance Services

The Assistance Services provided by the State began in 1908 with the non-contributory Old Age Pension. The next big step took place in 1935, when the Unemployment Assistance Board (in 1940 shortened to Assistance Board) was set up to deal with the assistance of unemployed persons who had suffered long unemployment and were no longer entitled to unemployment insurance benefit. In 1940 Old Age Pensioners who formerly supplemented their pensions by means of Public Assistance were transferred to the care of the Board, another step in the " break up of the Poor Law." It is the policy of the Government to reduce as far as possible the number of people who will need assistance, by bringing them within the scope of insurance for all contingencies and to make the benefits such that they will meet minimum needs. It is the intention of the Government that those who still need assistance will receive it from the Assistance Board and not from the local authority Public Assistance Committee.

An important feature of both Public Assistance and Assistance Board administration in recent years has been the emphasis on " welfare." The officers of both services have increasingly concerned themselves with constructive family case work rather than the mere giving of relief.

Other Services

The National Health Service Act of 1946 extended to everyone the medical benefits which till then had been available to insured persons. Every man, woman, and child has the right to a complete range of medical services without qualifying contributions. These include a doctor of the patient's own choice, medicines, specialist's services, hospital and dental treatment services. The Health Service co-ordinates the hospital system throughout the country, bringing the voluntary hospitals and the local authority hospitals into an integrated system. From August 1946 every family with two or more children is entitled to a family allowance of five shillings a week for each child except the first.

OTHER RECENT DEVELOPMENTS

Two of the most important developments of recent years have been (1) Organizations for facilitating consultation and co-operation between voluntary bodies and those set up by Act of Parliament, and (2) Organizations for providing the citizen with a service of advice and information on the services which have been established for this benefit.

Scottish Council of Social Service

In 1943 the Scottish Council of Social Service was set up in succession to the former regional organization of the National

Council of Social Service, to provide a common centre of consultation and co-operation for the voluntary associations. Associated with the Council are some eighty bodies, including the Churches, the Scottish Trades Union Congress, the Educational Institute of Scotland, and the four Universities. The principal Government Departments appoint assessors to the Council. Reference has already been made to the Women's Group on Public Welfare which is associated with the Council. Groups of a similar kind are the Standing Conference of Voluntary Youth Organizations, to which is affiliated seventeen national youth organizations, and the Committee on the Welfare of the Disabled, which has associated with it the societies concerned with handicapped people.

Citizens' Advice Bureaux

Citizens' Advice Bureaux grew up during the war. They are managed by a voluntary association on which are representatives of both voluntary and statutory bodies. They are wholly concerned with advice and information. When any inquirer needs specialized help, say, legal advice or money, the Citizens' Advice Bureaux directs the inquirer to the person or authority capable of giving it. In most cases Citizens' Advice Bureaux have received financial assistance from the local authority, so they are an example of the interweaving of the voluntary and the statutory authority.

The pattern of Social Welfare, with its strands of philanthropy, mutual aid, the voluntary association, the local authority, and the State, is a complex one. Life is a complex business with many aspects ; the institutions for social welfare in Scotland have grown up in response to the needs of these many aspects.

THE CHURCH

THE Church of Scotland is a democratic church. It acknowledges no head but Jesus Christ, and its system of government is based on the claim of the people to choose their own pastors. Since the Reformation, and particularly since the Scottish Parliament finally established Presbyterianism in 1690 by ratifying the Westminster Confession of Faith as the national standard of belief in Scotland, the Church has suffered many divisions and secessions, almost all of which have been due to a jealous eagerness in defence of its basic principle—the spiritual independence of the Church in its relations with the State.

It may be said that every member of the Church of Scotland has some share in governing it. The administration of each parish, apart from the conduct of public worship over which the parish minister has sole authority, is in the hands of the *kirk session*, composed of *ruling elders*, and these are nominated by the *congregation*, consisting of all in the parish who are full members of the Church. Any layman may be ordained as an elder, and as such officiates at the Sacrament of the Lord's Supper, which is celebrated from two to four times a year : for it is the part of the elders to distribute the sacred elements from the communion table to the congregation. Any elder may also be elected by the kirk session to represent it at meetings of the *presbytery*, which has authority over a district of parishes, or by the presbytery to represent it in the *General Assembly of the Church of Scotland*, the supreme body which meets annually. Membership of a presbytery carries with it membership of the *Synod*, which exercises supervision in certain matters over a group of presbyteries. A *Moderator* is elected to preside over each of these bodies, and even a parish minister is addressed as " Moderator " when presiding at a meeting of his kirk session. By the General Assembly an elder may be appointed to serve on one of its numerous committees, and so may come to make his influence felt in the affairs of the national Church.

Women are not eligible for the eldership or the ministry. They may serve as deacons and on congregational boards, and even on General Assembly committees ; and they play an important part in the Church's social work, partly through the Woman's Guild, which has nearly 120,000 members.

The other members of a presbytery or of the General Assembly are the ministers. A candidate for the ministry, having completed his prescribed course of education at a university or theological college, and been ordained and licensed to preach by the presbytery, must be " called " to the charge of a congregation. A committee elected by the congregation seeks out and nominates suitable candidates for the vacant charge, and if the congregation is not unanimous, a vote is taken. The " call " to the approved candidate must be endorsed by the presbytery, which finally inducts him to his charge ; but the actual choice is the congregation's alone. A Church of Scotland minister is paid his stipend out of funds administered by the General Trustees, and this is generally supplemented by a fixed annual payment from his congregation according to their means.

The " call " is so earnestly treasured that in a sense its history is the history of the Church of Scotland itself during the last 250 years. By the Act of Parliament of 1690 the right of patrons to nominate ministers to benefices was abolished. At the Union of the Parliaments of England and Scotland in 1707 a special statute was passed for the security of the Protestant religion and of Presbyterian church government in Scotland ; and to this day the very first act of the Sovereign on his accession to the throne of Great Britain is to take a solemn oath to maintain this settlement inviolably. Yet within five years of the Union the British Parliament passed an Act restoring patronage in the Church of Scotland, and this ill-considered step led to a long sequel of strife and dissension.

For some years the right of patronage was not pressed, but through it at length the structure of the Established Church suffered its first major damage in 1733, when the first Seceders formed the *Associate Synod*. In 1743 the rigid sect known as the Cameronians constituted themselves as the *Reformed Presbytery*; and another split in the Established Church, again due to the vexed question of patronage, resulted in the *Relief Presbytery*, formed in 1761. It was about this date that the hero of John Galt's novel *Annals of the Parish*, was "presented" to the charge of "Dalmailing," and found the church door nailed up by the people to forbid his entry. The biggest secession of all took place in 1843, and is known as " The Disruption." The highest legal authority in the land, the Court of Session, had overturned the Veto Act, passed by the General Assembly of 1834, which maintained that no minister could be " intruded " on a congregation against its wishes. At the General Assembly of 1843 the Moderator, after reading a solemn protest from the chair, walked out of the hall, followed by a great number of ministers and elders. Four hundred and seventy-four ministers gave up their churches and their manses (their official residences) and formed the *Free Church of Scotland*. Within four years they had raised £1,254,000 and built 654 new churches. "No other religious body within the dominions of the Crown," writes a recent English historian, "showed such energy and self-sacrifice during the Victorian age."

There were thus two main churches in Scotland from 1843, but thereafter the tide turned from secession towards reunion. The majority of the Associate Synod joined with the Relief Church in 1847 to form the *United Presbyterian Church*, and in 1852 some smaller bodies of earlier seceders joined the Free Church. In 1874 the British Parliament belatedly repealed the Patronage Act of 1712. It was not, however, till 1900 that the Free Church and the "U.P.'s" joined to form the *United Free Church*, leaving outside only a few objectors, who were nicknamed the "Wee Frees." The reunion of the Established and United Free Churches was finally achieved in 1929, thus bringing the majority of Presbyterians in Scotland within one fold.

With every reunion there had been a few congregations who had adhered to their original principles and declined to compromise. Even in 1929 some congregations of the United Free Church held aloof. There are several other churches to-day, each a memorial to what may be called either the stubbornness or the conscientious steadfastness of a minority. Besides the nine presbyteries of the United Free Church (Continuing), there are still fourteen presbyteries of the old Free Church; four of the *Free Presbyterian Church* which seceded from it in 1893; three presbyteries of the United Original Seceders which contain the remains of the Associate Presbytery and some other minorities; and the joint presbytery of the Reformed Presbyterians, the spiritual descendants of the Covenanters of 1638, who may claim to be the senior of all these bodies and the most uncompromising. The Church of Scotland itself comprises 66 presbyteries, containing 2,426 charges. In addition it has 10 charges and 13 chaplains in England, 21 charges and 2 other ministers in Continental presbyteries, and 175 in overseas presbyteries, making a total of 3,158. In the General Assembly of 1946 there were 816 representative ministers and an equal number of elders.

The most influential of the presbyterian minorities in Scotland is the Free Church, which is still strong in parts of the west and

north-west Highlands, where it took firm root after 1843, although
the earlier secessions had had little effect there. The Free Church
maintains an austerity of doctrine, a strict discipline, an uncompromising attitude on the observance of Sunday, and a " puritan "
outlook on worldly pleasures such as music and dancing, none of
which is to-day characteristic of the Church of Scotland. The
foreign visitor, unless he travels in the remote Highlands, is unlikely to encounter the type of minister depicted in Neil Gunn's
novels, or in James Bridie's play, *Mr. Bolfry*.

Of the non-Presbyterian bodies in Scotland, the largest is that
of the *Roman Catholics*. With four episcopal and two archiepiscopal
sees, the Church of Rome numbers well over 600,000 members in
Scotland, principally in Glasgow and the neighbouring towns,
where there is a large Irish population ; but there are also many
small Roman Catholic communities in parts of the Highlands and
in the Hebrides, whom the tide of the Reformation never reached.

The *Episcopal Church in Scotland*, nearly 60,000 strong, resembles
the Church of England in its doctrine and worship, but is a distinct
and independent body which has continued, through many vicissitudes and even persecutions, ever since episcopacy ceased to be
the official religion in Scotland. It is the parent of the Episcopal
Church in the United States of America. Strongest in Aberdeenshire and Banffshire, it also counts many adherents elsewhere amongst
the landed gentry, whose forebears joined it in the last century,
perhaps in consequence of the general anglicization of speech and
manners which followed the fashion of sending their sons to school
in England. This Church has seven episcopal sees in Scotland. One
bishop, chosen by the rest to preside at their conferences, is known as
the Primus; but he does not exercise the authority of an archbishop.

The Baptists, the Methodists, and the Congregational Union are
all established in Scotland. There is a Jewish community of about
18,000, almost entirely in Glasgow. But, even adding all the fore-
going to the Church of Scotland's membership of about 1,260,000,
it is likely that nearly half of Scotland's population of five millions
does not profess membership of any religious community at all.

These figures are at variance with the general conception of the
Scots as an extremely devout and church-going people, a notion
which was much truer fifty years ago than it is to-day. Many
reasons have been advanced for this decline. As in other countries,
there has been a general lowering of the spiritual temperature. But
undoubtedly an eloquent preacher can still " fill his church " : for

Plate 53 (*Above*) St. Monans Church, Fife (Decorated Gothic)
(*Below*) Reay Kirk, Caithness (post-Reformation church architecture)

(*Photos : A. Reiach*)

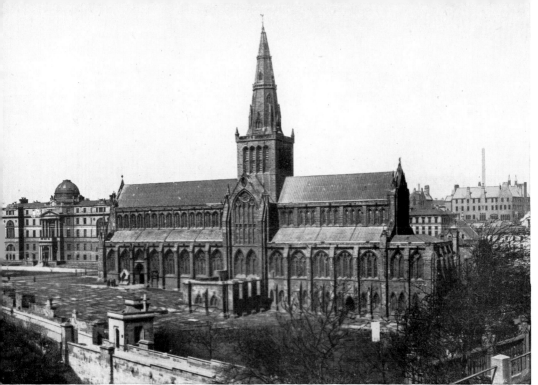

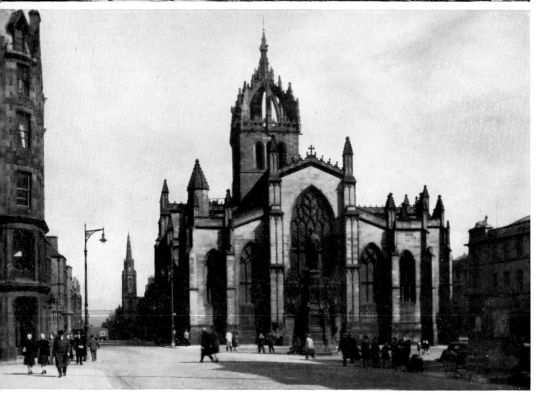

Plate 54 (*Above*) Glasgow Cathedral. (*Below*) St. Giles' Cathedral, Edinburgh
(*Photos : Valentine*)

the tradition persists that the centre and crown of presbyterian wor-
worship is the sermon.

There is one occasion in the year when the Church of Scotland
shows something of its ancient power and prestige. This is the
meeting in May in Edinburgh of the General Assembly. Its
Moderator, who is elected annually, takes rank for his year of office
next after the Lord Chancellor of Great Britain, above whom in
Scotland none ranks but the Sovereign, the Royal Family, and the
Sovereign's representatives in the counties. That expresses the importance of the General Assembly, though its Moderator, before and
after his year of office, may be only a humble country minister. The
sitting of the Assembly is attended by a Lord High Commissioner
representing the King, who lives during these few days in the Palace
of Holyroodhouse, and is treated with all the deference due to the
Sovereign's personal representative. It is his duty to watch over the
Assembly's deliberations on the King's behalf, and see that it does not
encroach on temporal matters; but otherwise he has no authority
over it. There was an occasion, in 1743, when the Lord High Commissioner arrived in Edinburgh without the usual message of Royal
greeting. The Assembly vindicated its right to meet without the
Sovereign's permission, and at the same time avoided jeopardizing
the validity of its acts by proceeding to elect its Moderator and other
officials and then adjourning till the Commissioner's letter duly arrived.

To the spectator the meeting of the General Assembly must
always be impressive as a democratic and representative sample of
the Scottish people, for it discusses not only points of theology or
church government, but a wide range of social problems. Though
women cannot sit as members of it, several are invited each year
to witness certain of its debates and to address it; it is then seen
how large and important a part they take in the Church's actitivies
—at home in its care for the aged and the sick, and its social work
for young people and for the armed forces; abroad in its notable
and far-spread missions in India, China, Manchuria, and many parts
of Africa.

When the General Assembly meets, when sentries pace before the
palace, flags fly from public buildings, and Edinburgh is filled with
many distinguished men and women from all parts of Scotland,
then the ancient city regains the air of a capital. "Assembly Week" is
the chief event of the year in Edinburgh, and the fact that it centres
in the meeting of the supreme court of the Church of Scotland sym-
bolizes the place which that Church still holds in the nation's life.

EDUCATION

THE chief characteristics of Scottish education are its age and its simplicity. Since the time of the religious revolution known as the Reformation it was the ideal of John Knox and his followers that poverty should be no barrier to the highest education which the country could afford. In the famous Book of Discipline (1561) they laid down a scheme of what would now be primary, secondary, and university education, which, though not realized for many years, remained the guiding principle of Scottish education.

The history of the country is full of stories of men who, from the humblest origins, won their way to the universities, and from them to the highest posts in the Church, in Law, Medicine, Colonial Administration, and Teaching. For centuries while England had only two universities, Scotland had five—one at St. Andrews (founded 1412), one at Glasgow (1451), two at Aberdeen (King's College (1494) and Marischal College (1593), amalgamated in 1858), and one at Edinburgh (1582). The two English universities were the resort of men mostly well endowed with this world's goods ; the Scottish universities, on the other hand, were open to rich and poor alike. Thus, even to-day, there is an intimacy in Scotland about the universities in their relationship to the general public that is not found south of the border. Recent statistics show that the proportions attending the universities are, in Scotland, 1 out of 473 of the population, in England 1 out of 1,018, and in Wales 1 out of 1,473.

Figures such as these serve to emphasize the great influence which the universities in Scotland have had on the whole conception and trend of educational ideal and practice until quite recent times. For lads (and latterly girls) bent on making their way in life, the university was the goal, and thus there was imposed on Scotland an academic outlook that, with the passage of the centuries, became traditional. Secondary education (*i.e.* from 12 to 18 years) was largely moulded on university require-ments, and elementary education, the forerunner to the secondary course, was tinged with preparation for the secondary course. It was an education prevailingly bookish, and nothing in Scottish education is more interesting than the gradual emergence of a broader general culture. It was slow to develop. To read the stories of life in the earlier Scottish schools in which pupils were being prepared for the universities is to be made aware of a grim business, especially in the north of Scotland, in which the arts, the study of nature, and the physical needs of the body played only a very small part.

How great is the change to-day ! The process has been un-spectacular ; but it is true to say that, little by little, this severe academic régime has given place to a new ideal which, paramountly, aims at fitting every individual child to do the work in after life for which he is best suited, and at making him a worthy citizen, intellectually and physically, of a country which has long sustained, through good times and bad, that strong democratic attitude of mind and spirit which is the hallmark of the Scot whether at home or abroad. Nevertheless it is not to be implied that Scotland has abandoned its standards of achievement in the Classics or in Language and the Sciences. Nor has the desire for university education become less ardent. It is the accent and emphasis that have altered. Sheer bookishness is at a discount. We seek an ampler air.

Before describing the actual system of Scottish education from the nursery school to the university or technical college there is one more general point of interest towards the understanding of the Scottish frame of mind. In England, in spite of all social changes, the " public school," *i.e.* the school not under State control, has a very great influence, and parents, anxious for the future careers of their offspring, make substantial sacrifices to procure residential education at one or other of these institutions, many of them ancient, others nineteenth-century growths. But in Scotland there is no corresponding urge. It is true that there is a tendency on the part of prosperous Scotsmen to send their sons and daughters to English public schools, but this affects only a tiny part of the popu-lace. In Scotland itself there are some five or six public schools which, while playing an honourable part in Scottish education, are not fundamental to it. It cannot, in fact, be too strongly emphasized, by way of contrast with England, that the Scottish tradition is founded on the day school, and that the very large proportion of men and women in the public life of Scotland are educated in non-residential schools, many of them co-educational, with effects that have a pronounced influence on Scottish character and ways of thinking.

The frame-work of the system in Scotland is readily grasped.

It proceeds from the nursery school (3–5 years) to the Infants' Department (5–7 years), and thence to the Primary School (7 to approximately 12 years), at which point there is a break. At about 12 years the pupil is tested in various ways—oral, written, psychological —and proceeds either to a Junior Secondary School (12–15 years) or to the Senior Secondary School (12–18 years). The distinction between Junior and Senior Secondary schools is not, in all cases, quite clear-cut, but, essentially, the former is intended for the pupil leaving school at the statutory school-leaving age, the latter for those intending to go into the professions or the higher branches of commerce and industry.

When the statutory age is reached and the pupil goes to work, he may add to his attainments by attendance at well-organized evening Continuation Schools where a wide variety of subjects is offered, suitable either for the right use of leisure or for technical or commercial advancement. Thereafter he may attend the evening classes organized at technical schools and colleges or at commercial colleges. The developments in these directions have been very great in the present century, and, with the increase of positive interest in the claims of youth which the 1939–45 war helped to advance, the possibilities are very considerable.

Pupils remaining at school for the full Senior Secondary course take, as a rule, the examinations conducted on a national scale by the Scottish Education Department. The examinations are intended to test the pupil's progress through a five years' curriculum, and if success is obtained the pupil is awarded a Group Leaving Certificate, which is regarded as the passport to the universities and the technical colleges, where day study is intended, and is recognized as the usual requirement for entry on a career in banking, insurance, and the like. An interesting feature of this certificate is contained in the word " Group," since it illustrates one of the main tendencies of Scottish education, which is to avoid any premature specialization and rather to give a sound all-round education on the basis of which to build further study. In the universities the same tendency is reflected in the open competition for entrance bursaries which are held annually. The range of subjects selected by the candidate must needs be fairly wide. These competitions are to be contrasted with the examinations for Scholarships and Exhibitions at the Colleges of Oxford and Cambridge where high specialization in one subject is required.

The structure, then, of Scottish education is simple. But what

Plate 55   Thistle Chapel, St. Giles' Cathedral, Edinburgh.   Designed
by Sir Robert Lorimer, 1909, for the use of the Knights of the Thistle

(Photo : ' Country Life ')

Plate 56   Meeting of the Moderators of the Established Church and
of the United Free Church at the Union of the Churches in 1929

(*Photo : ' The Scotsman '*)

must be noted is that, within the structure, great changes of emphasis are now proceeding. No-one can read the latest Act, passed by Parliament in 1945, without commenting on the manifest desire to develop the child in all its aspects. There is thus a degree of attention to physical education, health services, school meals, playing fields, out of school corporate activity that was, comparatively speaking, unknown even thirty years ago ; and one of the major problems of the modern teacher is to give adequate attention to his or her enlarged duties without loss of the fundamental drilling in the basic subjects.

The cost of education in Scotland is met partly from funds obtained from the central Government and partly from the rates levied in each locality. Each year Parliament votes to Scotland a sum which is called the Education (Scotland) Fund, and which is based on a proportion of the sum voted for England and Wales. This Fund is administered by the Scottish Education Department under the Secretary of State for Scotland, and is distributed mainly in accordance with the number of teachers and the number of pupils in each area. The remainder of the total sum required is met from the rates levied on all householders in each area. For educational purposes Scotland is divided into the four main cities—Edinburgh, Glasgow, Aberdeen, and Dundee—and thirty-one counties. Each of these divisions has its City or County Council, and each in its turn elects an Education Committee which is given very wide powers in the expenditure of the sums to be devoted to education, derived on the one hand from the central Government and on the other from the local rates.

It is to be noted here that while these Education Committees are required to conform to regulations issued by the Scottish Education Department under the Secretary of State for Scotland, in virtue of the powers granted him by Act of Parliament, they are not in any marked degree hampered by the intrusion of the central Government authority. They are, in fact, encouraged to develop their educational resources in such a way as to meet the particular needs of the area, whether industrial or rural, and in all the most active areas in Scotland a nice balance is kept by the Education Committee between what is demanded of them by the Central Authority and what they themselves may find it proper to foster.

With regard to the teachers themselves it is significant of the strength of the academic tradition to observe that, since 1924, all males entering the profession of teacher, excepting those dealing with art, handwork, music, or physical education, must be university graduates, and all must have undergone at least one year's training at a College under a body set up for the purpose, called the National Committee for the Training of Teachers. Graduation is not essential for women teachers, but a very large proportion of women take a university degree before proceeding to a Training College for Teachers. On a broad general survey it may fairly be said that the Scottish standard of requirement, academically and professionally, is as high as anywhere in Europe. But, once again, let it be emphasized that, to the academic standard, there is now being added in ever-increasing measure the demand that the teacher shall be the guide and leader in good citizenship, and much of his success is measured by those extra school activities which in earlier times he was not called upon to undertake. To say this is not to imply that the teacher of an older generation shut his school door at four in the afternoon and departed to his own concerns. That would give a completely misleading picture of the power and influence which the " dominie " exercised in school and church and in the whole society of the place in which he spent his life. Yet it must be reiterated that, in the enormously complex civilization of the twentieth century, the burdens laid upon the teachers are substantially different from those which his predecessors had to face. Upon the child of to-day are borne influences—the cinema, radio, sport, the changed circumstances of much of home life—that make the work of the teacher, as guide, philosopher, and friend, infinitely arduous and exacting. That this is well realized is to be seen in the kind of discussion frequently found at the meetings of the organized body of teachers—the Educational Institute of Scotland—which, among many other activities, has found time to initiate and carry on successfully, in co-operation with the Education Committee, invaluable research into the impact on the individual child of those influences to which reference is made above.

In view of the difficulties encountered in other countries on the score of the teaching of religion in schools, it is worthy of note that Scotland, once the home of fierce sectarian strife, has become tolerant to the point of magnanimity. The large body of the populace is Protestant, Roman Catholics being a minority except in the west of Scotland. Scottish Episcopalians, too, are relatively small in number. Up to 1918 the schools of the smaller denominations had a struggling existence, but by an Act passed in that year the denominational schools were made transferable by sale or lease from the religious community to the local Education Authority on terms highly advantageous to the minority. By 1920 nearly all the schools had been transferred, and except in very isolated instances the relations between the local Education Authorities and the denominational authorities have been prevailingly harmonious. Subject to the approval of the denominational body as regards religious belief, the teachers in these schools are appointed by the Education Authority. The salaries of these teachers are exactly the same as in the non-denominational schools. Religious observance in the denominational schools proceeds according to "use and wont" under a supervisor appointed by the Education Authority. The concordat thus arrived at is a genuine example of religious toleration, and there is no sign that what has worked so well now for nearly thirty years will be easily overturned.

We turn now, for a little, to examine the Scottish position in respect of adult education. It has been noted earlier in this article that there are the Continuation Schools for young men and women anxious to improve themselves. But how has Scotland progressed in the great schemes which, early in the present century, were set afoot by certain English pioneers? It must be admitted straightway that Scotland has not developed any system of adult education comparable with what has been evolved in England. Why this should have been so in a country so devoted to education is a little difficult to explain. The main reason, one feels, for the comparative slowness of growth is the fact that the universities themselves absorbed a large part of the population interested in higher study. Within the past twenty years, however, considerable progress has been made by the joint efforts of the Universities, the Education Authorities adjacent to each university, and the Workers' Educational Association. There are, nevertheless, still very few, if any, tutorial classes covering a two or three years' course. Practically all the courses are single year, and, as a rule, are confined to such subjects as Political Science, Philosophy, English Literature, and Languages, though, before the outbreak of war in 1939, demands were being made in Music and the Arts, which betokened a welcome change of outlook from the somewhat rigid régime of the earlier years of the century. A fresh spur to effort was found when in 1935 the late Marquess of Lothian, ambassador to the United States of America, whose premature death in the early stages of the war was a profound loss to both Britain and America, gave one of his estates, at Newbattle near Edinburgh, as a residential college of adult education. It was opened for students in 1937, and by the end of the third year thereafter had made a fair degree of headway. It must, of course, be admitted that the early stages were not easy, nor were the ideals of Lord Lothian truly understood. There was a fear that it might become the breeding ground of " left-wing " politicians. Moreover, Scotland, a country which educates with a very definite purpose in mind, did not readily assimilate the founder's ideal, that men and women who have had no opportunities in their youth for the cultivation of their intellectual and artistic interests, might, at Newbattle, amid its beautiful surroundings, find peace for a period and be free to pursue intensively what, in their workaday life, they could only snatch at intervals. The first reception of Lord Lothian's gift was not altogether to Scotland's credit. The strong utilitarian element in Scottish educational thought scouted the idea that men and women, once having been to Newbattle, would gladly and willingly return to their former avocations, and a chilly realism attended the opening of this quite new venture in the Scottish educational world. It is too soon to pass judgment or to assess probable developments, but the conjecture may be made that it will become the training ground of men and women whose main interest is in one or other form of social service, and that, as adult education generally extends its boundaries, it will become the rallying place for a wealth of informal cultural activitity which will enable it to fill a unique place in the Scottish educational framework.

This survey started with reference to the Scottish universities, the crown of the educational edifice, and with this it must end. It would be impossible within short limits adequately to describe their immense development since those early days in pre-Reformation Scotland when those at St. Andrews, Glasgow, and Aberdeen were founded ; or in the post-Reformation period when the Town's College of Edinburgh grew into a university. What one must needs remember is that for centuries they were, in effect, the real home of what we now call secondary education. Their studies were simple, and in breadth and extent bore no relationship to the standards demanded to-day. Early in the nineteenth century when a University Commission visited them at the instance of the Government, they were quiet places where men of distinction who were actively inclined produced their works in philosophy, political economy, and the classics in the peace of a long vacation, and where those less actively inclined pursued their leisurely ways.

Plate 57   (*Above*) St. Andrews University, United College
(*Below*) George Heriot's School, Edinburgh
(*Photos : Valentine*)

Plate 58   Glasgow University

(Photo : Alfred Furness ; reproduced from ' The Scottish Scene ' by permission of George Allen & Unwin Ltd)

To examine the courses of study detailed in a *Calendar* of any of the universities a hundred years ago, and compare them with those in a current volume, is to be made aware of the gigantic strides that have been taken in every department of intellectual activity. For centuries the Faculties of Arts and Divinity, with Law as a minor third, held the field. But with the advance of Science throughout the nineteenth century the pre-eminence of these Faculties was threatened. Medical studies developed in every direction ; so did Science, not only in the domain of the older studies in Mathematics and Natural Philosophy, but in Chemistry, Zoology, Botany, Geology, Geography, Agriculture, Forestry, Pharmacy, and Engineering. At the beginning of the present century the teaching of these subjects had reached a high pitch. There was, however, comparatively little sustained research of any kind. Much work, indeed great individual work, had been accomplished. But modern research, whether of the individual or the team as we know it to-day, was lacking. It was at this point that Andrew Carnegie, the Dunfermline-born lad who made his millions in the iron and steel industry in America, founded in 1901 the Carnegie Trust for the Universities of Scotland, partly to help the poor student with his fees, but partly also to aid the universities in their major projects and to foster research in Science, Medicine, History, Economics, Languages, and Literature. The annual income of this Trust was, and is, about £120,000 per annum, £20,000 of which is devoted to the stimulation of higher university studies. No aspect of Carnegie's great benefaction has been more fruitful than this, and there can be no doubt that the volume and variety of post-graduate study in the Scottish Universities, and in the Technical Colleges which are also aided by the Trust, is directly attributable to the unique opportunity afforded by this gift.

This research side of university activity is well worth stressing since it helps to illustrate the change in attitude that has gradually come upon the whole university scene. In earlier times they were, fundamentally, teaching institutions, and the fame of a professor, while resting, no doubt, on his published contributions to learning, was won chiefly through his ability to hold and engross the attention of the mass of students who composed the pass or ordinary classes. The legends that have gathered round an older generation of the professoriate are those of the great teacher. To-day, legends will be made less easily. It is not to be inferred that the professors do not continue to teach the mass of the students. Most of them are no less assiduous than their predecessors. But they have much more to do. They have large numbers of students studying for an " honours " degree—of higher standard than the " ordinary "—for whom a definite measure of individual attention is needful ; they have, it may be, post-graduates working for the higher degrees, of whose interests they must take heed ; they have their own particular studies to promote in books and in papers contributed to learned societies and journals, and thus their academic lives are singularly different in scope and emphasis from those of more peaceful days. Whether all this is for the ultimate good of the universities some older critics may venture to doubt. But there can be no going back. To match the demands of the twentieth century the universities must be given resources in money, material, and staffs, which will permit of that continued development whereby the boundaries of knowledge may be enlarged and the intellectual life of the nation kept flourishing and healthy. Great as were the functions of the Scottish universities in past days in keeping alive the flame of learning, they are to-day still greater. From the State they require and, it is expected, will obtain, subsidies which, along with their private funds, will make their widespread advancement possible. But with these subsidies there must be no limitation of that essential freedom which they have, prevailingly, enjoyed, and it is to the credit of all concerned with them that no such limitation is being contemplated. In that freedom lies their peculiar strength and their responsibility.

It has been said that the spirit of sacrifice made by past generations of Scottish parents in order to give their children the highest education which the country has to offer has declined. The assertion is without true foundation. There still exist in ample, and indeed oppressive measure, serious and humble folks in all walks of life who, despite the necessary rise in the cost of university and technical education, are determined to give to their children the same chances as were afforded their elders in more settled times. Scottish education has been described as utilitarian and, indeed, the charge, if it be a charge, is not unfounded. But in a comparatively poor country like Scotland could it be other than very directly concerned, in the first instance, with getting on in life ? The truth is that only in the most exceptionally favourable circumstances can education be entirely divorced from the pressure exercised by the preparation for a career. And though, indeed, the career be the immediate objective, there is, nevertheless, that persisting belief in the sovereign qualities of a thorough education which, all thought of gain apart, animates the large proportion of the people. Education is an integral part of a great Scottish heritage ; and, whatever be the fresh facets of thought and ideal which this changing world may reveal, there is no fear that the Scottish people will lose hold upon the virtues of that astringent scholarship on which their reputation is well founded. They will not readily forfeit the claim made for them by the historian and critic Macaulay, a writer by no means prone to compliments, when he said of the Scots that they are " a people whose education and habits are such that, in every quarter of the world, they rise above the mass of those with whom they mix, as surely as oil rises to the top of water."

THE SCIENCES—PHYSICAL AND NATURAL

SCOTLAND's contribution to scientific progress is, like her scotch-broth, a concoction of many ingredients, for her scientific men have made striking additions to knowledge in many diverse fields. Their merit certainly impressed Sir Francis Galton, for in his attempt in 1874 to estimate scientific ability in the British Isles, he stated that " owing to my list not being exhaustive I hardly like to attempt conclusions as to the precise productiveness of scientific ability of the Scotch, English, and Irish, but there cannot be a shadow of doubt that its degrees are in the order I have named." An analysis of over a thousand outstanding personalities selected from the *Dictionary of National Biography*, led Havelock Ellis in 1904 to a similar conclusion —" we probably have to recognize that intellectual aptitudes are especially marked among the Scotch " and " in science Scotland stands very high."

This pre-eminence has been attributed to the Scottish educational system, but it is clear that, apart from schooling, natural genius has often forced its way to the surface in spite of poverty and other hindrances. How else can we account for the accomplishments of such men as James Ferguson (1710–76), a Banffshire herd boy whose formal education was limited to three months at Keith Grammar School, and who became a noted astronomer, " a very uncommon genius, especially in mechanical contrivances and executions " ; Alexander Wilson (1776–1813), originally a Paisley weaver, poet, and pedlar, who at infinite sacrifice wrote the first great account of American birds ; Thomas Henderson (1798–1844), a Dundee lawyer's clerk, who as government astronomer at Cape Town made the first real determination of the distance of any star ; Hugh Miller (1802–56), of Cromarty, the geologist, who began work as a stone-mason ; James Young (1811–83), a Glasgow cabinet-maker who originated the shale-oil industry ; and James Croll (1821–90) and James Bennie (1821–1901), a Perthshire wheelwright and a weaver, both geologists whose discoveries added to our conception of the Ice Age.

The natural genius of these men and the genius of Scottish science bears a characteristic stamp—it is a faculty for minute detailed observation, for accuracy in small things, leading on the one hand to the reasoning of the mathematician, and on the other to the interpretation of the concrete facts of nature. Its strength lies in exactness and close argument. Frequently it goes a step further and applies its new knowledge to the development of devices or contrivances which ease the labour or add to the pleasure of mankind. Scottish science has been strong on the practical and inventive side.

Some Scottish Scientific Discoveries

The first of our historical men of science was born about the year of Magna Carta, and became famous enough to be pilloried by Boccaccio and by Dante in his *Inferno*, but Michael Scott " the Wizard" (*c.* 1214–92) was a true scholar, international in his interests, a student at Oxford and Paris, at Padua and Toledo, a chemist and mathematician, a mediciner of high repute, an astronomer and astrologer to the Emperor Frederick II. He stands alone ; for a couple of centuries and more Scotland was rent by war with England and by internal strife, and although the fifteenth century saw the founding of three of her universities it produced no scientific men of note.

Then after a long interval appeared, in 1614, one of the great discoveries of all time, the " wonderful rule of logarithms " of the versatile laird of Merchiston in Edinburgh, John Napier (1550–1617), which made possible computations hitherto undreamed of, and placed in the hands of calculators an instrument which has had a profound influence upon the progress of science even to our own day. The mathematical tradition continued strongly ; it was well served by a family which showed a strain of scientific heredity almost unique. James Gregory (1638–75), born in Aberdeen, was the first (if we exclude his mother, Janet Anderson, and her father David Anderson, both mathematicians) of a family which for two centuries almost monopolized the university chairs of Mathematics and Medicine in Scotland, and in five generations provided British universities with sixteen professors. He himself became Professor of Mathematics first at St. Andrews and then in Edinburgh, and is remembered for his work on quadrature of curves and on series, which prepared the way for Newton's fluxions, for his invention of the first or " Gregorian " reflecting telescope which, modified by Newton and Herschel, held the astronomical field for two centuries, and for his original suggestions that the distance of the sun might be measured by observation of the transits of Venus or

Mercury across the sun's face, and the distance of the stars by comparing their brightness with that of the sun.

Mathematical knowledge was further advanced by men like Colin Maclaurin (1698–1746) and James Stirling (1693–1770), both particularly interested in analysis and the geometry of curves, both of European fame, the latter a Jacobite out in the '45, the former the designer of Edinburgh's fortifications against Prince Charlie's army, and both good friends.

Meantime interest was converging upon experimental science. Light was the special study of Sir David Brewster (1781–1868), Principal first of St. Andrews and later of Edinburgh University. He investigated double refraction and resolved the problem of polarized light in a way that later confirmed the wave theory of light, but many will remember him rather for his invention in 1817 of that beautiful toy (which also has its serious uses), the kaleidoscope, for the modern stereoscope, in which he used lenses for the first time, and for his suggestion that in lighthouse illumination diatropic lenses and zones refracting the beams of a single lamp should replace reflectors, a discovery repeated later and independently by the French physicist, Fresnel.

Of William Thomson, Lord Kelvin (1824–1907), Professor of Natural Philosophy in the University of Glasgow, it might be said that he took all physics for his playground. With his colleague and collaborator, Professor Macquorn Rankine (1820–72), and, with Clausius and Carnot, he founded present-day thermodynamics. The dynamics of heat, of fluids, of electricity, of light, each yielded new fundamental ideas to his keen investigation; between 1851 and 1854 he formulated the two great laws of thermodynamics—equivalence and transformation; " potential " and " kinetic " energy were his terms; he made submarine telegraphy a possibility. From abstruse mathematical calculations his mind could switch to practical devices, so that his inventions may be reckoned by the score; to mention a few—the mirror galvanometer, deep-sea sounding apparatus, pressure- and tide-gauges, a tide-predictor, a water-tap that did not leak, a vastly improved mariner's compass. Equally brilliant was the Edinburgh scholar, James Clerk Maxwell (1831–79), whose kinetic theory of gases and theory of the electro-magnetic field blazed the trail for all future investigation on these and related matters. " The direct results of Maxwell's grand comprehensive theory of electricity and light are, on the practical side, wireless telegraphy; on the theoretical side, the modern doctrine of Relativity."

Scottish inventions of the period, which are still appreciated, were the drawing and copying instruments—pantograph and eidograph—devised by Professor William Wallace (1768–1843) of Edinburgh ; William Nicol's polarizing prism (1829), indispensible in the study of rocks and in other kinds of optical work ; the modern telephone, invented (1876) by Alexander Graham Bell ; the vacuum flask by Sir James Dewar.

In a country credited with a severely practical outlook it was natural that the results of scientific discovery should be turned to the service of industry, and Scotland took its full share in the mechanical transformation of the eighteenth and nineteenth centuries. At once a great scientist and a great engineer, James Watt (1736–1819), a Greenock man, turned to practical use, in his improvement of the steam-engine, Black's new discovery of latent heat. He not only replaced atmospheric pressure upon the pistons, as employed in earlier steam-engines, by steam pressure (1768–69) and utilized the expansive work of the steam upon the pistons (1776), but also devised the double-acting engine, parallel motion, the throttle valve, the speed-regulating governor (all in 1784) and many other devices which make the modern steam-engine fundamentally his invention. The first engines effectively to propel a ship were designed by William Symington (1763–1831), who in 1787 had patented a steam-engine with rotary motion, by chains and ratchets, for a mechanical road-carriage, and who in 1801 designed engines, working paddle-wheels by a crank, for the tugboat *Charlotte Dundas*, the parent of all paddle-wheel vessels. In recent days the largest ocean-going vessels have been vastly improved in steering and propelling machinery by the many inventions of A. B. Brown of Edinburgh.

The steam-hammer was devised in 1839–40 by James Nasmyth (1808–90) to undertake heavy forging, although the first steam-hammer in Britain was not set up until 1843 ; but at the age of nineteen this ingenious engineer had already designed a new steam-carriage which in 1827 and 1828 was to be seen on the roads about Edinburgh.

Lighthouse construction and illumination owe much to the skill of the Stevenson family : Robert (the grandfather of R.L.S.) who built the Bell Rock Lighthouse, completed in 1812, and his sons Alan (*b.* 1807) who designed the Skerryvore Lighthouse, and Thomas (*b.* 1818) who made a reformation in the lighting systems.

The practical purpose to which Watt turned the latent heat of steam recalls the great discovery of " latent heat " itself, made in 1762 by Professor Joseph Black (1728–99) of Edinburgh University. Black was aware also of the existence of specific heat, and the greatest credit belongs to his pioneering work in experimental chemistry, when by consistent use of the balance and meticulous quantative analysis he determined changes due to chemical action. Thus he discovered " fixed air " or carbonic acid gas (1754) and the relationship of the " mild " to the " caustic " alkalis. To the same period belong Daniel Rutherford's discovery (1772) of " malignant air," or as it is now called, nitrogen, and Thomas Charles Hope's discovery of a new mineral, strontia (1792). In another direction the investigations of Thomas Graham (1805–69), afterwards Master of the Mint, and his enunciation of the laws of the diffusion of gases and liquids laid the foundations of colloid chemistry.

Far-reaching influences upon human affairs may also be claimed for industrial applications of chemical knowledge, first made in Scotland. There was the resounding invention of Rev. Alexander John Forsyth of Belhelvie near Aberdeen, who doomed the old flint-lock gun by using fulminate of mercury in his new device, the percussion lock (1806), as a means of igniting the charge of gun-powder. Wholly beneficial were the constructive discoveries of James Young (1811–83), originally a working cabinet-maker in Glasgow, for he furnished the people for the first time with a cheap and brilliant light—the light of the paraffin lamp and the paraffin candle. He started what was probably the forerunner of all petroleum refining works in 1848 in a Derbyshire coal pit ; in 1850 he patented and commenced the low-temperature distillation of coal, the beginning of the shale-oil industry, and his patent, worked in America, not only gave the people there the new " coal-oil " light, but stimulated the exploration which resulted in 1859 in Drake's striking oil. A chemical industry of quite a different type of which Edinburgh long held a practical monopoly in the United Kingdom was the manufacture of certain drugs, such as strychnine and morphine, and similar alkaloids. Pharmaceutical chemistry was undoubtedly encouraged by the demands of the pre-eminent medical school of Edinburgh ; here, in 1847, chloro-form was first successfully made and used as an anaesthetic, and Edinburgh still remains one of the chief manufacturing centres of the drug.

While the physical sciences were thus fashioning new ideas of matter and releasing hidden energies for man's service, the natural

Plate 59   The Peatery in the Royal Botanic Garden, Edinburgh

(*Photo : Robert M. Adam*)

Plate 60   Fingal's Cave, Staffa, a magnificent example of basaltic
columnar formation

(*Photo : E.N.A.*)

sciences were sketching new pictures of the earth itself and of its products. To the earth story Scotland made great contributions. In his *Theory of the Earth* James Hutton (1726–97) recognized the great part played by heat in the formation of the earth's crust, discovered that granite was an igneous rock, and interpreted surface features as due to elevation, flexure, erosion, subsidence, and deposition. He was the "father of modern geology," who inspired John Playfair, and through him Lyell, whose *Principles* so stimulated Charles Darwin and many another. Hutton had also some notion of the powerful influence of glacial action, and thus initiated in Scotland an inquiry into glaciation, followed up with great effect by Playfair, James and Archibald Geikie, Benjamin Peach, John Horne, and others. The two last geologists also took a leading part in that brilliant interpretation of a most complicated system of foldings and overthrusts which has made the North-west Highlands of Scotland a set-piece for geologists the world over.

Since Sir Robert Sibbald (1641–1722), the founder of the Botanic Garden in Edinburgh and of the Edinburgh Medical School, first essayed to describe the plants and animals of his country in his *Scotia Illustrata* (1684), Scotland has not lacked for naturalists. One of the greatest was Dr. Robert Brown (1773–1858), a Montrose man, dubbed by Humboldt "*botanicorum facile princeps*," friend of Sir Joseph Banks and of Captain Flinders, with whom he sailed to New Holland in 1801. He was a great traveller and collector, and made important contributions to the science of plant classification and the structure and life-activities of plants. Two of his interesting discoveries were Brownian movement and the incessant circulation of protoplasm in plant cells.

To the science of the seas Scotland gave a splendid lead through two alumni of the University of Edinburgh who eventually succeeded to its Chair of Natural History : Edward Forbes (1815–54), "the most original, brilliant, and inspiring naturalist of his day," who by his description of life-zones in the sea founded the science of oceanography, and Sir Wyville Thomson (1830–82), who planned and carried out the Challenger expedition, the greatest scientific exploration of the seas the world has ever known. Within the bounds of Scotland herself, the Bathymetrical Survey (1897–1909) of Sir John Murray and Laurence Pullar is perhaps the most thorough investigation of the fresh-water lakes of any country. The story of Scottish naturalists cannot be told even in summary here, but behind it we discern a spirit of adventure and of sacrifice which led men like Sir John Richardson to share most worthily in the Franklin expeditions to the Arctic and in many of the exploring voyages of the nineteenth century, which impelled travellers like James Bruce, Mungo Park, Alexander Gordon Laing, Walter Oudney, David Livingstone, John Kirk, and Joseph Thomson to become pioneers in the revelation of Africa's dark continent, and others of our sons to venture and discover in India, Australia, and America.

Science in Scotland To-day

No country can continue to thrive by contemplation of the achievements of its past, and the science is dead which does not keep accumulating facts and extracting from them vital truths. How does Scotland stand to-day in relation to scientific progress ?

In the past her performance has been dependent upon the native genius, reinforced by direction mainly in her four ancient universities (St. Andrews founded in 1412, by modern reckoning, Glasgow 1451, Aberdeen 1494, and Edinburgh 1582). These have followed the universal drift by developing highly specialized teaching and research in the different branches of science, and progress here continues with increasing vigour. But new knowledge gained in the laboratories is barren unless it reaches its scientific public, and this has been provided for by the great printing and publishing houses for which Scotland has long been famous, and especially by the learned societies through their meetings and publications, notably by the Royal Society of Edinburgh (established by Royal Charter in 1783) and by others devoted to special branches of study, mathematical, chemical, geological, geographical, botanical, zoo-logical, and so on.

All these long-established institutions will continue to play their part in Scotland's scientific endeavour, but it is noticeable that new trends are showing themselves. The scientific advance of a country depends not only upon the discovery of new knowledge, but also upon the effectiveness with which new knowledge is brought to heel for the well-being of the people. In recent years there has been a growing realization of the practical value in industry of a scientific background, and this has led to greater demands for the training of youth in the universities and in schools of applied science. With the latter, as with the former, Scotland is well served. Technical colleges in Glasgow, Edinburgh, Aberdeen, and

Dundee and a special school for woollen textiles at Galashiels back their practical training for industrial work with an education in scientific principles. Agricultural colleges in Edinburgh, Glasgow, and Aberdeen serve their own region, and in each area are developing a closer contact between the student and the practice of farming on lines approved by experience and experiment. There are Veterinary Colleges in Edinburgh and Glasgow, the former of which, the Royal (Dick) Veterinary College, beginning humbly in 1823, was granted a Royal Charter in 1844, and is affiliated to the University of Edinburgh; but the likelihood is that before long veterinary education in Scotland will come fully under the wings of the universities of Edinburgh and Glasgow.

As notable as the urge towards developing industry by incorporating new knowledge, is a new trend observable in the pursuit of knowledge itself. Broadly speaking, in the past, scientific discoveries have been individualistic and have been encouraged in great part in the scientific departments of universities. But with the greater demand for the rapid application of discoveries to ordinary affairs, and with the specialization which makes it impossible for one person to be a scientific know-all, planned or organized research by teams of scientific workers has become imperative. Team work involves co-ordinated individual efforts, and it implies a goal towards which the separate investigations move. Although it is a common practice in university departments, its most notable growth has been in industry, on the one hand, where the larger commercial firms find it essential to employ scientific staffs to synthesize or devise new products and to test their commercial possibilities; and, on the other hand, in the creation of special research institutes.

The research institutes, in some cases founded and supported by private individuals or by associations of interested persons, are in all cases backed by Government grants. They have been created for the purpose of discovering or following up lines of investigation which promise to benefit the basic industries of the country, particularly agriculture and fisheries. Each institute is independent and has its own specific interest. The agricultural institutes include, in the neighbourhood of Aberdeen, the Rowett Research Institute for Animal Nutrition and the Macaulay Institute for Soil Research; in the neighbourhood of Glasgow, the Hannah Institute for Dairy Research; in the neighbourhood of Edinburgh, the Animal Diseases Research Institute, the Institute of Animal Genetics, the

Scottish Plant-breeding Station, the Seed-testing and Plant Registration Station, and the Agricultural Machinery Station, the two last being directly under the Department of Agriculture for Scotland. Fishery research is concentrated in Aberdeen in two institutions : in the long-established laboratory of the Fisheries Branch of the Scottish Home Department, specially interested in the natural history and statistics of Scottish fisheries ; and in the Torry Fishery Research Station of the Department of Scientific and Industrial Research, which investigates methods of preserving, curing, processing, and transporting fish catches. In 1945 a branch of the Wool Industries Research Association was established at Galashiels. In a somewhat different category falls the Millport Marine Station, for its interests are not predominantly economic, but the investigations, both fundamental and applied, of its staff, and its visiting naturalists make a notable contribution to marine scientific research.

If any doubt still exists about the practical value of scientific work in the affairs of life it must be banished by the record of the research institutions during their brief period of service. To take one as an example—the scientific workers at the Animal Diseases Research Station at Moredun near Edinburgh, in discovering the causes and means for the prevention of three important infective diseases of sheep : braxy, louping-ill, and lamb-dysentery; in counteracting cobalt-deficiency in sheep and cattle pastures, and in relating milk-fever in cattle to acute calcium deficiency for which they devised a calcium treatment now adopted throughout the world, have saved for farmers and the people hundreds of thousands of sheep and cattle, the value of which Dr. Russell Greig conservatively estimates at over £300,000 a year.

The future for scientific work in Scotland is bright. Increased facilities at the universities for the training of research workers, the greater inducements being given for the prosecution of applied as well as fundamental research, and the stimulus of the practical efforts of the Research Institutes and of the scientific staffs of commercial firms, all point to a steady accumulation of knowledge and to its application for the welfare of mankind—" Knowledge directeth practice and practice increaseth knowledge."

Plate 61   Skerryvore Lighthouse, near the island of Tiree, designed by
Alan Stevenson and built in 1844
(*Photo : 'The Scotsman'*)

Plate 62   The Forth Bridge, a famous cantilever bridge, opened in 1890

(*Photo : Valentine*)

MEDICINE AND PUBLIC HEALTH

SCOTTISH medicine has an honoured place not only in the sphere of scientific progress, but in the development and organization of medical services in many parts of the world and in the services of the Crown : as early as 1644 four surgeons were appointed to the army " presently sent from this kingdom into England, each to have charge of two regiments," fifteen pounds sterling to be paid to each of them for the furnishing of their chests, with 5s. daily allowance to each surgeon and 4s. to his mates. Alexander Carlyle, the well-known Scottish divine, recorded that in the second half of the eighteenth century there used to be a club in London which met once a week in the British Coffee House at eight in the evening. The members were Scottish physicians from the city and court end of the town, and one of the most famous of them, William Hunter (1718–83), the celebrated teacher of anatomy and founder of the Hunterian collection in the University of Glasgow, was credited with the toast : " May no English nobleman venture out of the world without a Scottish physician, as I am sure there are none who venture in."

Through time it came to be realized that, with advances in medical science, treatment in hospital offered to the patient the best prospect of recovery. The Royal Infirmary of Edinburgh made a humble start in 1729, with accommodation for six patients in a small house at the head of Robertson's Close in the Cowgate. The hospital in Aberdeen, also with six beds, was ready for occupation in 1742, and the Royal Infirmary of Glasgow was opened in 1795. Along with this early hospital development there came the growth of dispensaries in many Scottish towns for the provision of out-patient medical care for the sick poor, and with the growth of hospitals and dispensaries Scottish medicine forged ahead under the stimulus of such great masters as Syme (1799–1870) and Lister (1827–1912). With the passing of the Poor Law Amendment Act in 1845, the newly created Parochial Boards were required to appoint a medical man to care for the sick poor in their area. This new medical provision was not introduced without difficulty, for many of the more rural parts of the country had no resident medical man. In the negotiations involved in setting up the poor law service

Professor Sir J. Y. Simpson (1811–70) took a leading part. He was one of the great medical figures of his day, discoverer of the anaesthetic effects of chloroform, eminent medical historian, and always in the forefront of the medical politics of his time.

The teaching of medicine evolved very gradually in Scotland. In Glasgow the Faculty of Physicians and Surgeons was established in 1599, mainly through the efforts of Peter Lowe, and regulated the practice of medicine, surgery, and pharmacy in the West of Scotland. The course of events was somewhat similar in Edinburgh, where, in 1681, the Royal College of Physicians was erected by patent from King Charles II. at a time when the struggles between physicians and surgeon-apothecaries were still at their height. To-day each of the four universities has an important medical school, and there are in addition extra-mural schools of medicine in Edinburgh and Glasgow. The number of full-time undergraduate medical students attending the Scottish universities in 1938–39 was 2,881— 438 at Aberdeen, 1,107 at Edinburgh, 1,064 at Glasgow, and 272 at St. Andrews. The number of students attending the extra-mural schools in Glasgow and Edinburgh during the same academic year was 1,375, of whom 560 were students in the School of Medicine of the Royal Colleges at Edinburgh. The number of entrants to the extra-mural schools varied widely in the twenty years between the wars. In 1926 it was about 80, but during the period 1931–38 the number increased enormously : in 1936 it was 281.

By long tradition Scottish schools have provided facilities for the medical education of students drawn from far beyond the country, and though nowadays pressure of accommodation is such as to make it impossible for the schools to accept more than a fraction of the students who seek admission, some places are still reserved for men from overseas, and an effort is made to allocate these places, so far as possible, to students from parts of the world where facilities for medical education are not available. It is not surprising that in a country that has produced so many brilliant clinicians much of the emphasis in Scottish medical teaching should have been directed to the clinical approach. Already before the war there had been considerable development of post-graduate teaching in Scotland, and with the return from the Services of many doctors this side of medical education has received a great impetus, and is now a prominent part of the work of the Scottish medical schools.

For long Scotland has been a doctor-exporting country. To-day the tendency of Scottish graduates to roam is still apparent, though perhaps not to the same extent as formerly. The Medical Register of 1943 contained information about the place of residence of 2,277 Scottish graduates: of these 1,125, less than 50 per cent., were resident in Scotland, 683 in England and Wales, 6 in Ireland, 350 abroad, while 113 held permanent commissions in His Majesty's Services. The proportion of Scottish graduates who remained in their home country was lower than in the case of England and Wales or Ireland, and the proportion of Scottish graduates resident overseas was correspondingly higher. It used to be said that in the military services the proportion of Scottish and Irish doctors was very high, but in this sphere Scotland seems rather to have lagged of recent years.

The general organization of health services in Scotland is similar to that in England. The Secretary of State for Scotland is responsible to Parliament for the work of the Scottish Department of Health (the counterpart of the Ministry of Health in England), as he is for the other Scottish Departments. Local health services are administered by some fifty-five major health authorities, the councils of counties and of towns having a population of over fifty thousand. Some health services are provided on a United Kingdom basis—by the Ministry of Labour and National Service, the Ministry of Fuel and Power, the Ministry of Pensions, and other government departments. In addition to official services there is the great and important volume of work carried out by many voluntary agencies for the promotion of health, notably in the provision of hospitals and convalescent homes and home nursing and health education. Some of these voluntary agencies receive subsidies from central or local health authorities.

Perhaps the most distinctive of all Scottish health services is that which caters for the sparsely populated districts of the Highlands and Islands. There had long been great difficulty in attracting good doctors to these outlying districts, and over a hundred years ago Dr. Coll Macdonald called attention to the lamentable condition of people in western Inverness and Ross from the want of medicines and medical attention. The people suffered acute or chronic disease without any attempt at relief. " What is required would be a dispensary in certain places, where medicines and instruments would be kept, and a few perambulating, intelligent, well-behaved medical men to attend and prescribe for the people." Little was done to improve conditions until 1920, when the Highlands and Islands Medical Service was instituted. It is provided for the counties of

Argyll, Inverness (except the burgh of Inverness), Ross and Cromarty, Sutherland, Caithness, Orkney, Shetland, and the Highland District of Perthshire. Grants are paid to doctors in these areas in return for the provision of medical care at uniform modified fees within the means of the patient, irrespective of the distance to be travelled by the doctor in looking after the case. The scheme is designed for the benefit of crofters and others of similar economic status, and over one hundred and fifty practices are subsidized in this way. Part of the doctors' remuneration is received from government subsidy, part from capitation fees under National Health Insurance, part from private practice, modified fee and otherwise, and part from local authority payments for services rendered. The local authority share often includes the provision of a house, and under the scheme many new doctors' houses have been built. A home nursing service is provided by subsidizing the County Nursing Associations. Similarly, hospital and specialist services have been subsidized in towns serving outlying areas which could not hope to provide such facilities unaided. An air ambulance service has been made available for the removal to city hospitals of cases in which highly specialized care is necessary. The Highlands and Islands Medical Service is in many respects a pioneer venture, and it has proved highly successful ; one of the interesting features about it is that doctors and patients alike seem to be well satisfied with the service and conditions provided, and more than once representations have been made urging that its administrative structure should remain undisturbed.

Another Scottish essay in the provision of health services that has commanded a good deal of attention had its roots in the early years of the war in the Clyde Basin Experiment. Concern was felt about the strain being placed by war conditions on the health of young workers, and it was decided to see what could be done to safeguard their well-being by the provision of facilities for detailed medical overhaul and convalescent care. It was decided to provide in addition to convalescent facilities beds in two base hospitals for the examination of patients requiring hospital examination, and to set up a panel of specialists to whom patients could be referred. For the first few months the scheme was nominally restricted in respect of age, geographical distribution, and occupation—in age to young adults, geographically to the counties of Renfrew, Lanark, and Dumbarton, and occupationally to essential war workers. The initial reference of a patient was from his own doctor ; travelling fares and subsistence allowances were paid. In the first instance an out-patient examination was made, and where necessary it was supplemented by hospital treatment and convalescent care. Where change of occupation was considered necessary the Ministry of Labour and National Service was asked to take the necessary action. Nearly 50 per cent. of cases referred were admitted to hospital for overhaul, and it was found that in some 6 per cent. of cases investigated change of work was necessary if the young person was to have a reasonable chance of leading a healthy working life. A large proportion of cases dealt with under the scheme were of general debility and vague ill-health : a number of cases of tuberculosis were brought to light. The scheme was a success, and after a year's preliminary work on its narrower original basis its scope was extended to cover workers throughout the Scottish industrial belt without limitation as to age : the new service came to be known as the Supplementary Medical Service.

Scottish medicine has not lost its flair for research. Of recent years much work has been done by Scottish doctors on the development of new chemo-therapeutic remedies, and some of it has already had far-reaching practical application ; the virus diseases, too, have been intensively studied, and there have been pioneer efforts in the study of rehabilitation, of peptic ulcer, and of rheumatism. Scotland took a leading place in the adoption of immunization against diphtheria in Britain, and much early basic research on problems of nutrition was done in this country. During the war Scottish surgeons have taken a prominent part in the treatment of brain injuries and of war wounds involving damage to the blood vessels and peripheral nerves. There has been a development of interest in the social aspects of medicine, an interest that seems to follow naturally on the brilliant work of Sir Robert Philip (1857–1939) on the care of the tuberculous. Sir Robert founded the first dispensary for consumptives in Edinburgh, with the object of detecting at as early a stage as possible evidences of tuberculosis and of preventing the spread of the disease within the family. From that beginning has evolved our national schemes for combating tuberculosis, in one aspect of which Scotland still leads the way : it has a high proportion of dairy herds free from tuberculosis. For several years before the war the sickness experience of the insured population in Scotland was studied in considerable detail and a mass of information collected on various aspects of incapacitating sickness that was in many ways unique. During the war work on social medicine has forged ahead : the problems of men invalided from the forces as no longer fit for further service have been investigated and efforts made to meet some of their difficulties. Early in 1946, under the auspices of the Tenants' Association at Hillington Trading Estate, a sheltered workshop was opened to afford employment for some disabled men, and the value of the enterprise was abundantly clear, alike as a contribution to the economic welfare of the men and in shaping their whole philosophy of life. The problems of the aged have been studied, and plans are afoot for a survey of the social and medical difficulties of youth. It has long been recognized that many of Scotland's gravest problems centre round the bad housing of her people, and the Scottish cities afford much research material for studies in social medicine.

LITERATURE

No account of the literature of Scotland, whatever its scope, can begin without making certain apparently damaging admissions. It is, by European standards, a literature that started late, suffered many long, catastrophic interruptions, and was limited, even in its productive seasons, by political, dogmatic, and social prejudice, by national poverty, lack of patronage, and linguistic disunity. It is to be considered as the literature of a small country, and one of these unhappy countries on whose pages Clio, in her most unamiable vein, has writ large, to the partial exclusion of several of her sister muses.

Few European literatures have provided as little for the stage as Scots. Between 1604 and 1616, the period of *Lear, Volpone, The Atheist's Tragedie,* and *The Duchess of Malfy,* Sir William Alexander published his stiff, undramatic, Senecan *Monarchicke Tragedies.* While Congreve, Etherege, Sedley and Vanbrugh were writing for the ungodly society of the restored court, tragedy was being enacted in Scotland, but not in the playhouses. On the Lowland and Galloway hills and moors, the Covenanters, the men of the Cameronian "societies," were being hunted like deer. Allan Ramsay, whose *Gentle Shepherd* (1725) is our only pastoral drama, braved the bigotry of his age and established a theatre in Edinburgh, but it was ruthlessly closed by the magistrates. And so more and more Scottish aspirants to dramatic fame trudged the long road to London, with tragedies in their pockets, none of them very good. And yet the tradition that produced the *Interlud of the Droichis Part of the Play* (c. 1500), Lyndsay's *Satyre of the Thrie Estaitis* (c. 1540), the *Fables* (published 1570) of Henryson and the tragic encounter of Troilus and Cressida towards the end of the *Testament of Cresseid* (first printed 1532), was not barren of great dramatic potentialities. In our own day, two of the most original manipulators of theatrical possibility have been Scotsmen—Barrie, whose easy and unfailing sense of what the public wanted was almost too great for his artistic integrity ; and Bridie, one of the most thoughtful and ingenious of contemporary dramatists.

And there are other admissions that have to be made. In many of the qualities that are central in the poetry of England, Spain, and Italy, Scots literature is singularly poor. There is little sensuous love of beauty, little mysticism, little philosophy, and little high imaginative creation in our poetry. There has been no Scots Blake, no Keats or Shelley, no Traherne or Crashaw, no Wordsworth or Coleridge. The Scots poets have cultivated the lower slopes of Mount Parnassus.

These would seem to be, and are indeed, damaging admissions, but it is wise to make them at the outset. One must look for other qualities—qualities more characteristic of the Scot himself—in our Scots literature. If for the purposes of this summary study Scots literature is to be regarded as literature written by Scotsmen, whether in English, in the Lowland vernacular, or in the synthetically enriched vernaculars (by which the early Scots poets and their latter-day disciples aimed at higher effects and a wider public), one should begin by considering what are the characteristics of the Scot to be looked for in his literature.

The Scot is credited with a strong sense of reality, an observant and accurate eye for detail, a practical, hard-headed shrewdness, a distrust of extremes and innovations, and a rigid moral sense, narrow, but consistent and strong. He is reputed to be sceptical, inquisitive, and unsentimental ; rough in his manners, quarrelsome and contentious by nature, sardonic in his humour, and apt (in the intervals of his theological pre-occupations) to be convivial to extremes. He is credited with an inordinate interest in his own history (family, parochial, and national) and with a natural antiquarian bent. How far are these qualities reflected in his literature ?

From quite early times the Scot himself has been aware of the differences, real or imaginary, between his southern neighbour and himself. The author of *The Complaynt of Scotland*, a mid-sixteenth century adaptation of Alain Chartier's *Quadrilogue Invectif*, writes :

There is nochit tua nations undir the firmament that ar main contrar and different fra uthirs nor is Inglis men and Scottis men, quhoubeit that thai be vitht in ane [*within one*] ile, and nychtbours, and of ane langage. For Inglis men ar subtil, and Scottis men ar facile [*candid*]. Inglis men ar humil quhen thai ar subjeckit be forse and violence, and Scottis men ar furious quhen thai ar violently subjeckit. Inglis men ar cruel quhene thai get victorie, and Scottis men ar merciful quhen thai get victorie. And to conclude, it is onpossibil that Scottis men and Inglis men can remane in concord undir ane monarche or ane prince, because there naturis and conditions ar as indefferent as is the nature of scheip and volvis [*wolves*].

The passage illustrates some at least of the qualities with which rumour has endowed the Scot, the dogmatic assurance, the rancorous patriotism, and the absence of humour as it is understood in the southern kingdom.

Thou lytill quair be eWir obedient
Humble subiect and symple of entent
Before the fare of eWiry connyng Wicht
I knaW quhat thou of rethorike may spent
Off all hir lusty rosis redolent.
Is noū in to thy gerland sett on hicht
Eschame thar of and draW the out of licht
Rude is thy Wede disteynit bare and rent
Wele aucht thou be aferit of the licht

Androv myllar

Plate 63   The title-page from a book printed in Edinburgh in 1508, showing the device used by Androw Myllar, Scotland's earliest known printer

Plate 64   Robert Burns, after the portrait by Alexander Nasmyth in
the National Gallery of Scotland

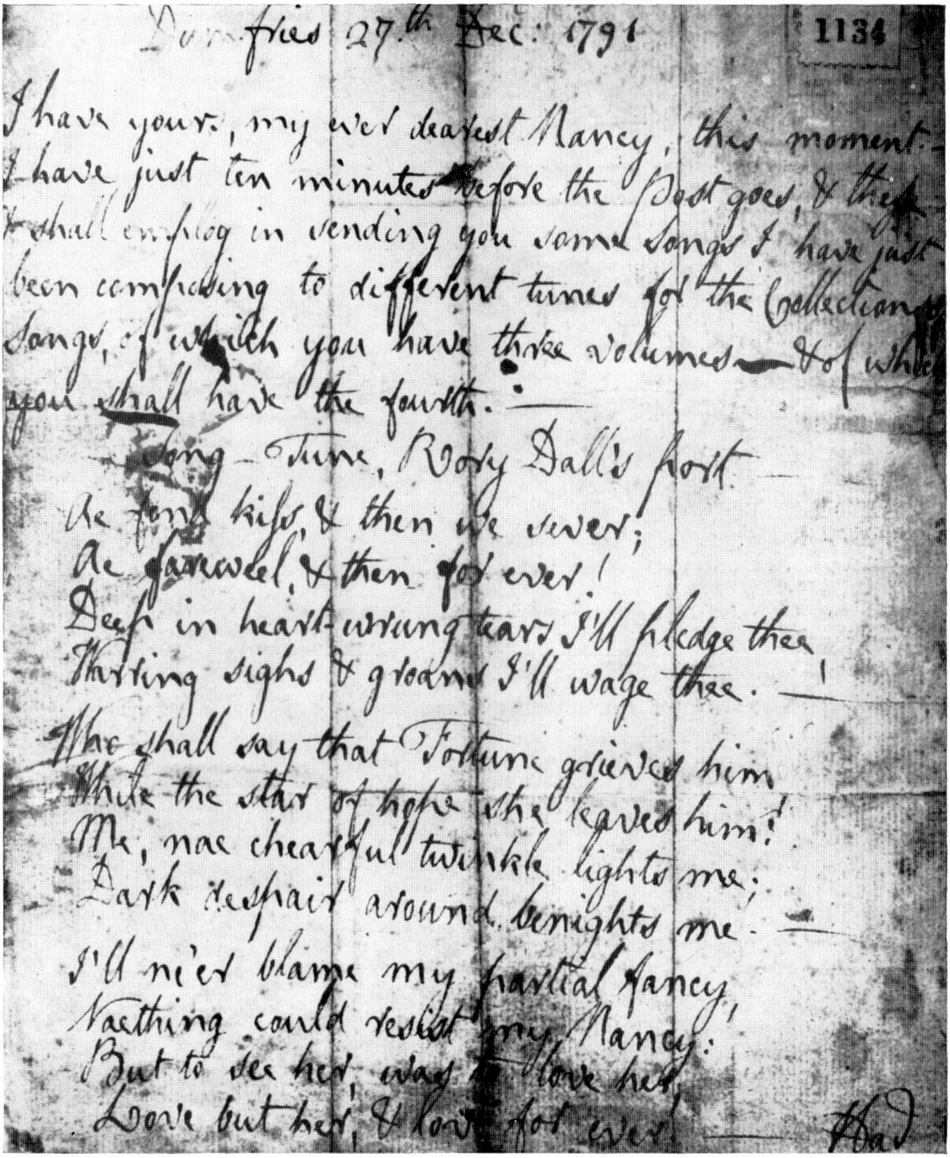

Dumfries 27th Dec: 1791   1134

I have yours, my ever dearest Nancy, this moment.
I have just ten minutes before the Post goes, & these
I shall employ in sending you some songs I have just
been composing to different tunes for the Collection of
songs, of which you have three volumes—& of which
you shall have the fourth.———

     ——Song——Tune, Rory Dall's port.——

Ae fond kiss, & then we sever;
Ae farewel, & then for ever!
Deep in heart-wrung tears I'll pledge thee,
Warring sighs & groans I'll wage thee.———

Wha shall say that Fortune grieves him
While the star of hope she leaves him?
Me, nae chearful twinkle lights me;
Dark despair around benights me.———

I'll ne'er blame my partial fancy,
Naething could resist my Nancy:
But to see her was to love her,
Love but her, & love for ever———

Plate 65   A page of Burns' poem, ' Ae Fond Kiss,' from the manuscript in the
National Library of Scotland

Plate 66   Abbotsford, the residence of Sir Walter Scott, on the
River Tweed

(*Photo : Valentine*)

No student of our earlier literature has failed to remark on the accuracy with which Nature, especially in her less genial aspects, is observed and recorded by the Scots poets. Gavin Douglas (c. 1475–1522), in the Prologue to the Seventh Book of his translation of the *Aeneid*, describes how :

> Puire laboraris and byssy husband men
> Went wayt and wery draglyt in the fen ; *wet and weary*
> The sely scheip and thair lytill hyrd gromis *poor sheep*
> Lurkis undir le of bankis, wodys, and bromys ;
> And wthir dantit gretar bestiall, *larger cattle*
> Within thair stabillis sesyt in to stall, *tethered in their stalls*
> Sic as mulis, horsis, oxin, and ky,
> Fed tuskit baris, and fat swyne in sty, *boars*
> Sustenit war by mannis governance
> On hervest and on symmeris purviance. *provision*
> Widequhair with fors so Eolus schouttis schyll *Everywhere/shouts shrilly*
> In this congelyt sessioune scharp and chyll,
> The callour air, penetrative and puire, *fresh air/pure*
> Dasyng the bluide in every creature,
> Made seik warm stovis, and beyne fyris hoyt, *comfortable hot fires*
> In double garmont cled and wyly coyt, *undergarment*
> Wyth mychty drink, and meytis confortive,
> Agayne the storme wyntire for to strive.

And Henryson, in the first stanzas of the "Testament of Cresseid," looks out from his chamber window on an equally austere scene, and withdraws to similar comforts :

> Throw out the glas hir bemis brast sa fair *Right through/burst*
> That I micht se on everie syde me by *I could see all around*
> The northin wind had purifyit the air
> And sched the mistie cloudis fra the sky,
> The froist freisit, the blastis bitterly
> Fra Pole Artick come quhisling loud and schill, *whistling/shrill*
> And causit me remufe aganis my will. *withdraw*
>
> . . . I mend the fyre and beikit me about, *warmed*
> Than tuik ane drink my spreitis to comfort,
> And armit me weill fra the cauld thairout. . . .

And the same painter-like fidelity is to be observed in the later landscapists—Ramsay, James Thomson, Stevenson (whose "Late in the Nicht" and "Ille Terrarum" are admirable examples) and in some at least of the vernacular poets of to-day.

As the Scots landscape poet seems to be naturally attracted to the " doolie sessoun " [*melancholy season*] when

> In the mirk nicht, the winter rain   *dark night*
> Dribbles an' blads,   *pelts*

so the Scots divines and theological controversialists seem inevitably drawn to the more forbidding and austere aspects of their study. In spite of the extent to which religion overshadowed and limited the lives of our forefathers, there is little real religious literature in Scots.

This is not to question the piety or devotion of those admirable, though formidable, men who stood equally resolved against Establishment, Indulgences, and the arts of life. When it is remembered that in the golden age of European letters Scotland was almost entirely given over to ecclesiastical pre-occupations, it is distressing to have to admit that no real religious literature emerges from the period. Knox's *History of the Reformation in Scotland* (c. 1566–67) is a magnificent achievement, to which there is no parallel in English letters. But (as one might expect) it is not sufficiently objective for history, and it is certainly not religious writing. There are few greater passages of descriptive prose in Scots, or English, literature than Knox's account of the St. Giles Day Riot or the grim story of the murder of Cardinal Beaton. After telling how the mutilated body of the cardinal was thrown into a corner of the sea-tower, to pickle in salt until his fellow-bishops should have prepared his exequies, Knox concludes : " All this we wreat mearelie [merrily]." This is reminiscent of no merriment in English literature, except possibly what Johnson called " the controversial merriment of Milton. . . . Such is his malignity, that hell grows darker at his frown." Nor is this untypical of the partisan literature of the age, an age which covers a century and a half. If the literary harvest of the Reformation was bitter, the crop of the Covenant was no more sweet. It was a seventeenth-century Scots divine, the " godly " Alexander Peden, who wrote :

And then, John, you and I, and all that will be found leaning on Christ's righteousness, will get day about with them [the " Malignants "] and give our hearty assent to their eternal sentence of damnation.

This traditional legacy of religious discord bred in the Scots certain qualities of mind and character. The assumption of familiarity with the divine purpose is common among the " elect " of the seventeenth century, and survived into the next two centuries to afford Burns and Stevenson their greatest satiric opportunities. Burns's " Holy Willie's Prayer " and the " Address to the Unco Guid," and Stevenson's " Scotman's Return from Abroad " are aimed at the pious professors of their day, the lineal descendants of Peden and Rutherford.

But the same history of discord developed that intellectual toughness, scepticism, and spirit of philosophical inquiry which has long been the most valuable inheritance of the Scot. In all classes of society he has been taught from his earliest years to read and think, that he might as soon as possible be able to interpret, to criticize, to make his own settlement with God and the world. Dissent, secession, a taste for litigation, and a natural disposition towards philosophic doubt are drawn from the same wellsprings in the Scots character. Even in pre-Reformation times, it is interesting to note that it is a Scots poet, Robert Henryson, who brings the frail and fickle Cressida to justice, and introduces the hanging Judge into the Court of Love.

One of the strongest recurring strains in Scots poetry is the poetry of revelry or of festive occasions—betrothals, bridals, fairs, and holidays, races, and games. This is a natural theme in the literature of a small country, with a scattered and mainly rural population, where the community meets but seldom for such memorable occasions as these. The earliest surviving examples of this literature, the fifteenth century " Peblis to the Play " and " Christis Kirk on the Green," though they commemorate popular celebrations, are, if early tradition is to be believed, of royal authorship ; but this is in no way exceptional or remarkable. It will be found that most of this popular Scots literature is of aristocratic origin—a pleasing testimony to the integrated character of Scots society before the Industrial Revolution. When what was in the main an agrarian population came to be centred in industrial areas, the significance of these local festivities disappeared, and the literature in which they were celebrated came to an end ; but well into the nineteenth century the theme survived. " The Blythsome Bridal " in Watson's *Choice Collection* (1706) revived the tradition, after the long and arid interval of the religious troubles, and thereafter in Fergusson's " Hallow Fair " and " Leith Races," Burns's " Holy Fair," and Tennant's "Anster Fair " (1811) it was continued and developed.

Apart from the love-songs, the themes in which Burns was

consistently greatest were revelry and satire, and in the "Holy Fair" we have these themes characteristically and inextricably intertwined. He was nearer in temperament to the English satiric age that preceded him than to the romantic age that followed, and in the pious professors and sanctimonious censors of his age (the degenerate and often unsavoury heirs of the Covenant) he found congenial subjects. There is a world of difference between the genial and cool satire of Fergusson's "Braid Claith" and the searing malice and irreverent exposure of such poems as "Holy Willie's Prayer" and the "Address to the Unco Guid."

Early criticism of Burns, as of Shakespeare, was distorted and invalidated by the assumption that they were poets of rustic origin, who owed little to learning. Carlyle writes of Burns that he was "one of those men who reach down to the perennial deeps, who take rank with the heroic among men ; and he was born in a poor Ayrshire hut. The largest soul of all the British lands came among us in the shape of a hard-handed Scottish peasant." So Gray writes of Shakespeare :

> To Him the mighty Mother did unveil
> Her aweful face : the dauntless Child
> Stretch'd forth his little arms, and smiled.

And David Hume, in his history of England, declares explicitly : "Shakespeare was born in a rude age and educated in the lowest manner, without any instruction from the world or from books." Such misconceptions as these are more easily planted in the popular imagination than eradicated from it, and Burns criticism still suffers from this legend. It was a more intelligent critic who wrote : "We see no propriety in regarding the poetry of Burns chiefly as the wonderful work of a peasant, and thus admiring it much in the same way as if it had been written with his toes." One should consider Burns alongside the other rustic bards, Bloomfield, John Clare, "honest Duck" and Burns's fellow-countryman and disciple, James Hogg, to realize the difference between them. Burns's father, true to the tradition of his age and country, procured the best tuition possible for his children, and the young tutor, John Murdoch, gave Robert a solid, if unorthodox, grounding in grammar, rhetoric and literature. Burns was far from being unaware of the literary fashions and influences of the south ; he studied Gray and Shenstone, and admired the didactic and elegaic, the picturesque and pathetic literature of sentiment, and often, to his cost, imitated it. He learned to read French and studied the classics in translation, as many another great man of letters has done with profit.

But his real literary connections were with the obscure, neglected but illustrious poets of older Scotland—with Dunbar, Henryson, Blind Harry, Barbour, Lyndsay, and Gavin Douglas, and with the poets by whom that great tradition had been revived after the publication of Watson's *Choice Collection* (1706)—Allan Ramsay (1686–1758), and Robert Fergusson (1750–74). Hamilton of Gilbertfield's version of "The Wallace" poured, he said, "a Scottish prejudice in my veins which will boil along there till the floodgates of life shut in eternal rest." Practically every poem that Burns wrote was dependent, either for theme or form, and often for both, on the work of the older Scots poets. He himself was not unconscious of his indebtedness to the native tradition, and again and again he acknowledges what he owes to "the genius of a Ramsay and the glorious dawnings of the poor unfortunate Fergusson." For the songs, though Allan Ramsay had to some extent shown the way, Burns turned rather to the song collections, and improvised on these traditional airs and on the refrains associated with them.

It is perhaps because Burns was so receptive to these various influences that it has been said, apparently unjustly, that he contributed nothing to Scots poetry but himself. But it is true. The forms were there, worked out and revived by his predecessors, but not even Fergusson had been able to make them more than locally significant. Burns infused into them his own ardent, turbulent and generous humanity, and used them for the expression of sentiments to which "every bosom returns an echo." Burns was no romantic, and at times one is grateful for it. One contrasts the sturdy, unashamed honesty of his "Lines to his Love-Begotten Daughter" with Wordsworth's beautiful but pontifical and irresponsible lines on a similar subject, and is grateful for their candour and decency.

The Scots tradition of convivial literature found in Burns a ready and congenial exponent. The natural reaction against the harsh and ignorant bigotry of Presbytery rule was an affectation of wine and women, and this was encouraged in Burns by his study of Ramsay and Fergusson, and coincided with an ardent, genial, and gregarious temper. It was this defiant impulse of reaction that impelled Burns, while pillorying the parish Pharisees, to erect for worship "muse-inspiring aquavitie" and sing the praises of "browster-wives and whisky-stills." But however foolish the affectations that motivated them, we cannot regret or reject " Scotch Drink," " Tam O'Shanter," and " The Jolly Beggars," any more than we can wholly regret the drug-inspired dream to which we owe " Kubla Khan." In later life Burns realized more clearly than anyone the folly of these excesses. " God have mercy on me," he wrote, " a poor, damned, incautious, duped, unfortunate fool ! the sport, the miserable victim of rebellious pride, hypochondriac imaginations, agonizing sensibility, and bedlam passions." Though there is perhaps a suspicion of Byronic affectation in this portrait of the damned poet, crowned with a cloud of gloom, it is probably honestly intended, but it should not blind us to the fact that it is to the other projection of the poet, to Ranting Robin, that we owe " Tam O'Shanter," " The Jolly Beggars," and the " Address to the Deil."

In the works of Ramsay and Hamilton of Gilbertfield, Burns found examples of the revived Verse-Epistle, and some of the most perfect things in Burns are cast in this form. The Epistles to William Simpson and James Smith, and the " Epistle to Davie " present the poet in his most equable mood and contain more of his philosophy of life than is to be found elsewhere. The form re-appears in the Scots poems of Stevenson, who uses it in the same discursive fashion.

The antiquarian predilection that made Burns a student of the early Scots poets and their verse-forms, and inflamed his imagination with jacobin and patriotic convictions, was equally strong in Walter Scott (1777–1832), and reveals itself both in his life and in his work as poet, novelist, editor, ballad-collector and historian. Though he was born and educated in Edinburgh, and though he was proud of his Edinburgh citizenship, he never forgot his Border ancestry and the past glories of his family, which he set himself to restore. The heroes of his boyhood, whose acquaintance he first made in the vivid reminiscences of his grandmother, were Wat of Harden, Wight Willie of Aikwood, and Jamie Telfer of the Fair Dodhead. This passionate pre-occupation with his own ancestral past was encouraged by the fact of his lame and lonely childhood, which developed his studious and imaginative tendencies and put a restraint on his strong love of outdoor activities, which remained strong until the last years of his life.

During his schooldays at the Royal High School of Edinburgh, and later during his apprenticeship in his father's law office he became, in his own phrase, " a tolerable reader," and revelled in romantic literature—in Ariosto, Boiardo, Spenser, in " The Castle of Otranto," and above all in collections of old songs and ballads—especially the balladry of the Scottish Border.

The importance of the ballads in Scott's literary life cannot be over-estimated. He read them, collected them, preserved them, annotated them, composed them and enlarged upon them. In them he found congenial literary material in which his regional patriotism, family pride, romantic ardour and love of the primitive and supernatural were all knit up. They provided the material for his first publication, a translation of Bürger's "Leonore"; and his second venture, a limited edition of his own ballad compositions, *Apology for Tales of Terror* (1799) marks the beginning of his business relationship with his old schoolmate, James Ballantine—an association which was to shape the whole course of both their lives. His appointment in 1799 as Sheriff of Selkirkshire confirmed his connection with the Border country, made possible his periodical " raids into Liddesdale " to forage for ballad material, and (like Fielding's appointment as a London magistrate) deepened his knowledge of men and affairs. No more severe verdict has been passed on Scott's great ballad collection, *The Minstrelsy of the Scottish Border* (1802, 1803) than that passed by Mrs. Hogg, mother of the Ettrick Shepherd, from whose sung versions Scott transcribed many of the best of them . . . " there was never ane o' my sangs prentit till ye prentit them yoursell, an' ye hae spoilt them a'thegither. They war made for singing, and no' for reading : and they're nouther right spelled nor setten down." In spite of this, and in spite of what has been said and written against the composite texts and modern forgeries contained in the collection, it was an anthology of the utmost importance to Scott himself and to romantic literature in general.

When, in 1805, Scott passed from ballad minstrelsy to verse romance, he chose, in the " Lay of the Last Minstrel," a theme which had " the simplicity and wildness of an ancient ballad," and his recital of the story to the Duchess of Buccleuch and her ladies at Newark, underlined the proprietary and family interest which counted for so much in all of Scott's literary adventures. The freedom of the ballad stanza gave place to a more fluid, plastic, metrical pattern, towards which Coleridge had already shown the way in the prosody of "Christobel." Thereafter a succession of these romances followed, and their popularity with the reading public was phenomenal. It is not to be denied that some of them, especially the latter publications, were of unequal and indifferent quality, and it is very doubtful if Scott could have competed indefinitely against the rising star of his countryman, Lord Byron. With his usual generosity, Scott himself declared : " He beat me out of the field in description of the stronger passions, and in deep-seated knowledge of the human heart." Such an avowal was typically modest and generous—perhaps excessively so—but it was a wise decision of Scott's to leave the field of poetic romance to Byron, and turn to prose romance, in which his supremacy was unchallengeable.

But even in the later and poorer verse-romances, Scott interwove a profusion of superb lyrics, which have deservedly outworn their settings. Songs like " Brignall Banks," " A Weary Lot is Thine," " County Guy," " Rosabelle," and " Proud Maisie," and martial lyrics and rollicking ballads like " Donald Dhu," " Bonnie Dundee," and " MacGregor's Gathering " have rarely been poured out with equal ease and profusion.

In the novel Scott found full scope for all his great and varied gifts and interests. During his long apprenticeship before, at the age of forty-three, he turned to the novel, he had experimented with lyric, ballad, and verse-romance ; written biography, history, and memoirs ; published standard editions of the English poets and prose writers, and collections of Scottish and Border antiquities. Now he turned to a medium on which he could spend his whole intellectual, imaginative, and personal resources. No writer before Scott's time had approached the novel with anything like equal equipment.

Within the great historical sweep encompassed by the novels, stretching from medieval France and England to the lawless Scotland of the generation just before his own—the Scotland of *Waverley*, *Guy Mannering*, and *Redgauntlet*, Scott assembled a Homeric profusion of characters, the most copious, authentic, and varied gallery between Shakespeare and Balzac. His heroes have been stigmatized as colourless, and Waverley himself described as " a sneaking piece of imbecility " ; and his heroines dismissed (with better justification in some cases) as insipid and unattractive. His understanding of the Celt was limited by superficial knowledge and imperfect sympathy, and his Highlander is apt to be rather a caricature. His historical accuracy has often been impeached, and his strong political sympathies were responsible for some unjust and indefensible representations.

But the vast majority of the portraits in Scott's immense gallery are completely authentic, and are painted with an ease and assurance that derive from his genial intercourse with all classes of society. Gentlefolk, professional men, rustics, law-breakers, and tradesmen—

Plate 67 Thomas Carlyle, after the portrait by Whistler in Glasgow Corporation
Art Gallery

Plate 68   Swanston Cottage, on the slopes of the Pentland Hill, an early
home of Robert Louis Stevenson
(*Photo : Valentine*)

no such world of credible and fascinating individuals had been created in English literature since the death of Shakespeare. His familiarity with the Lothians and his practice as a Border sheriff gave him a thorough knowledge of the Lowland Scot, and many of these creations—David Deans, Cuddie Headrigg and his mother, Mause, Peter Peebles, the eternal litigant, Dominie Sampson and Bailie Nicol Jarvie—might serve to illustrate the inventory of Lowland Scots characteristics quoted earlier. The indulgent humanity of Scott, which led him to assess too generously the work of his contemporaries and rivals, made him a great comic artist. His perception of moral issues, and of the conflict between good and evil in every human breast, though sometimes slightly facile, was always sincere. For this reason his comic and eccentric characters, though painted to the life, are never mere figures of folly, and many of his scoundrels, like Nanty Ewart, captain of the Jumping Jenny, are pathetically convincing. By his sanity and geniality, his learning and observation, and the spendthrift exertion of all the splendid mental and physical strength with which he was endowed, Scott gave the English novel a new content and significance, and set the course which romantic and historical literature in Europe and America was to follow for many generations to come.

Since curiosity, a sense of detail, and a strong interest in family and local history have been enumerated as Scots characteristics, it is perhaps not surprising that the two greatest biographies in English should be by Scotsmen. James Boswell was born at Auchinleck, Ayrshire, in 1740, the son of Lord Auchinleck, a Scottish judge. He was educated at the High School of Edinburgh and Edinburgh University, studied law at Glasgow University under Adam Smith, and later at Utrecht, travelled in Germany, Switzerland, Italy, and Corsica, meeting Voltaire, Rousseau, Wilkes, and Paoli. On his return to Britain, he was admitted to the Faculty of Advocates, Edinburgh, and published his *Account of Corsica* (1768) and *Essays in Favour of the Brave Corsicans* (1769). He had already made the acquaintance of Johnson in 1763, and in the twelve years between 1772 and 1784 this friendship was the main interest of his life. In 1791 the great *Life of Samuel Johnson, LL.D.*, the most remarkable work in eighteenth-century English literature, was published. Admittedly, Boswell had a great subject, but one has only to compare his work with the other records of Johnson that were left by his contemporaries—by Hawkins, by Mrs. Piozzi—to reject instantly and indignantly the thesis of Macaulay, that Boswell's weaknesses of mind and character made him the ideal recorder of the acts and sayings of this great man. Macaulay writes, " That he could not reason, that he had no wit, no humour, no eloquence, is apparent from his writings. . . . Nature had made him a slave and an idolater." Any single page of the biography is sufficient to reveal the absurdity of these judgments. Boswell's power of selection, his skilful juxtapositions, the balance maintained in this rich, voluminous work, the discreet self-effacement and the concentration of interest show Boswell as a deliberate and original craftsman, perhaps the most consummate artist of his age.

John Gibson Lockhart (1794–1854) was Sir Walter Scott's son-in-law, and was attracted to the writing of his *Life of Scott* by a motive similar to Boswell's own—an overpowering admiration for the great man who was his subject. If there is less variety and sparkle in Lockhart's biography than there is in Boswell's, there is greater unity and coherence. Motives of piety and respect, and occasional prejudice and vanity, are responsible for such omissions, misrepresentations and inventions as more recent research has exposed, but these do not seriously detract from the *Life* as literature. It is regrettable that the popularity of the *Life of Scott* has been responsible for the almost complete neglect of Lockhart's other writings. He published an admirable *Life of Burns* (1828) and an amusing study of Edinburgh society and manners, *Peter's Letters to his Kinsfolk* in 1819. His *Spanish Ballads* (1823) are unlikely to be revived now, but some of his light verse was among the best of a very good period. And one at least of his novels, *Adam Blair* (1823) might well interest the generation that to-day finds the *Waverley Novels* too priggish and prolix.

No account of Scots literature, however short, can well omit mention of the Ossianic fragments, in view of the immense contemporary popularity of these writings, the interest of the international controversy which raged around them, and their influence from a literary and historical point of view. With the possible exception of David Hume, James Macpherson (1736–96) was the first Scotsman, and certainly the first Highlander, to become a figure in world literature. To Mme. de Staël, Ossian was the modern Homer ; to Hazlitt, Homer, the Bible, Dante, and Ossian were " four of the principal works of poetry in the world." Goethe's *Werther* said : " Ossian hat in meinem Herz den Homer verdrängt ; " and Voss declared defiantly, " Ossian of Scotland is greater than Homer of Ionia ! " In France, Lamartine claimed the harp of

Morven as the emblem of his soul, Napoleon wept over Ossian and slept with the publication under his pillow; in Sweden, Napoleon's general, Bernadotte, introduced the fashion, and Ossianic Christian names have been common in Sweden from that day to this. In English literature, more interest centres on the violent controversy over the authenticity of the fragments than has ever been accorded to the writings themselves. A quarrel that embroiled Johnson, Gray, Blair, Horace Walpole and others gave inevitably a wide publicity to the suspect documents, but has not resulted in their being widely or seriously read. Johnson wrote to poor Macpherson one of the most superb abusive letters in English, and dismissed the fragments with : " Sir, a man might write such stuff for ever, if he would abandon his mind to it." But in Macpherson's defence it should be said that, like Columbus, only he had a mind to do the particular thing he did.

To Lowland Scotland and England, the publication of *Ossian* followed hard on an earlier shock. In 1745 the south was staggered by the spectacle of the Young Pretender, Prince Charles Edward, issuing from the Highlands at the head of a small but terrifying army of barbarous half-naked savages, outlandish in their customs, incomprehensible in their speech, and thrusting deep into the heart of England before hunger, dissension and weariness compelled their return. To certain elements of mid-eighteenth century society this was a monstrous and wildly alarming outbreak, but to others of a more romantic and imaginative character it was a revelation of the dignity and sublimity of uncivilized life. All over western Europe the time was ripe for a revolt against order, complacency and ennui. The melancholy, sentimental cadences of Ossianic prose, with its epic and Biblical reminiscences, and the evocation of a savage, untrammelled world of ancient nobility and austerity, were admirably calculated for the mood of the age. Fortunately, the romantic movement in English literature flowed from other and less suspect sources, but the influence of *Ossian* in Europe continued great for many years to come.

If the Ossianic fragments focused German attention on Scots literature in the eighteenth century, and excited Goethe, Herder, and Voss to extravagant admiration, Thomas Carlyle (1795–1881) by his discipleship to Germanic thought in the nineteenth, repaid the tribute in full. Himself the product of a Scots parochial and Calvinistic environment, Carlyle had to the full the national characteristics of spiritual and theological interest, dogmatic assurance, and critical and analytical temper. It was natural that he should think of the Church as a career, and it was equally inevitable that he should reject it. During his short schoolmastering period, he educated himself as well as his pupils, learned to read German, and subjected his belief, in the light of his new reading, to close and remorseless examination. His translation of *Wilhelm Meister* and *Life of Schiller* immediately preceded his marriage to Jane Welsh in 1826, by far the most important single event in his life. The publication of *Sartor Resartus* in *Fraser's Magazine* (1833–34), and in book form in 1838, and of the *French Revolution* in 1837, made him famous and established him as an apocalyptic, prophetic figure—something of a mystic, very much of a satirist, and the master of an English style, at once vivid, turbulent, evocative and startling. The personal qualities of Carlyle are nowhere to be observed better than in *Sartor Resartus*. No work was ever more derivative, and yet no work was ever more original than this treatise of " Clothes-philosophy," in which satire and symbolism, prophecy and preaching are themselves clothed in the language of faith—sometimes tender and lyrical, sometimes vehement and savage, but always appropriate and original. In the age of applied science and *laissez-faire*, in the teeth of the technicians, economists, and evolutionaries, he preached the evangel of ordered society on the medieval Christian plan, of authority, work, and silence. His doctrine of the Hero and his place in society, though it may have been discredited by history and may smell of Fascism to-day, found a ready and wide response. At least the mid-nineteenth conception of the Great Man was preferable to the mid-twentieth. Carlyle outlived his own influence, though not his fame, and died, a sad and lonely man, in 1881.

Scots patriotism, as has been already said, had always the suspicion of parochialism about it : and in the nineteenth century after the death of Scott and John Galt, whose *Entail* (1823) is as universal in its application as the best of Balzac, the scope of much of our literature became more and more local. Henley comments on the " local and particular " quality of much of the work of Burns, which, despite its technical brilliance, must for ever limit its appeal. Of the " Holy Fair " and even of " Tam O'Shanter " he writes : " the circumstances, the manners, the characters, the experience—all are local." If this is true of Burns, it was immeasurably more true of the vernacular writers who followed. Burns complained that

> . . . Irwin, Lugar, Ayr, an' Doon,
> Naebody sings,

but, largely due to his influence, the streams, the bonnie briar bushes and the kailyards of Scotland were sung with nauseating insistence in the second half of the nineteenth century. The authors of these parish idylls, in which rustic sentiment, artificial pathos, and crude humour are the main ingredients, came to be known as the Kailyard (or Cabbage-patch) school, and, but for the fact that the young Barrie was one of their number, would hardly merit notice in so short a study. Barrie's *Window in Thrums* (1889) and *Auld Licht Idylls* (1888) are possibly better than most of the Kailyard pieces, but nothing in the genre is as remarkable as the powerful *House with the Green Shutters* (1901), by George Douglas Brown. Cunningham-Grahame had written, "If it pleases the Kailyarders to represent half the population of their native land as imbeciles, the fault is theirs." George Douglas Brown's masterpiece might never have been written but for the pastoral puerilities of Pickletillie and Thrums, and would certainly have taken a very different shape. Walter Raleigh declared with gusto : "I love the book for just this—it sticks the Kailyarders like pigs." Like Barrie and Ian Maclaren, George Douglas Brown set out to depict the manners of a small rural community, but his theme is the malignant Scot, not the pawky sentimentalist, and if, like Hardy, he was guilty of manipulating character and circumstance to a too obviously contrived tragic conclusion, he nevertheless restored Scots fiction to a gravity it had not known since Galt's *Entail*. The influence of *The House with the Green Shutters* has been enormous. A. J. Cronin's *Hatter's Castle* is only one of the modern Scots novels to treat of the same theme in much the same terms, but none of its successors has anything of the Sophoclean gravity and simplicity of the original. Stevenson's *Weir of Hermiston*, had it been completed, would have been a greater novel, with a similar central theme, but with less complexity, and a tragic climax deriving more inevitably from the conflict of two very credible characters.

But for the ill-health that darkened and shortened his life, it is doubtful if Stevenson would ever have been a literary man at all. He came of a family of engineers and lighthouse builders, and in his moments of greatest candour he spoke of the artistic life with contempt. "A deification of pleasure," he called it—"a grovelling ideal." To one of his friends he wrote : "I could have wished to be otherwise busy in this world. I ought to have been able to build lighthouses and write David Balfour too." And he dismissed his verse with as little respect. "I do not set up to be a poet," he wrote to Symonds, "only an all-round literary man, who talks, not sings."

And yet, like many other artists who struggled with disease and weakness, his work is characterized by an excessive and fastidious pre-occupation with style and detail. Whether in prose or poetry, he

> did not think a day too long to make
> One line or letter bright.

George Moore and others have criticized Stevenson for his inordinate interest in stylistic perfection, and to some extent the criticism is justified. In many of the essays, the English poems, and some of the novel fragments, it is distressingly obvious that the writer is more concerned with the manner of his expression than with what he has to say. But when Stevenson had a theme worthy of his equal interest, as in *Thrawn Janet* or *Weir of Hermiston*, or when he was writing Scots verse in the native forms, his craftsmanship is no longer obtrusive. It is unfortunate that Stevenson, who was abnormally susceptible to literary influences, should have exposed himself to so many alien styles, unsuited to the themes in which he was most at home. His verse-epistles, mock-elegies, poems of sentiment and compliment, and philosophical fragments in the Scots vernacular are vigorous and natural as his English poems and his verses composed on French models seldom are.

Better novels were written in the last years of the nineteenth century than Stevenson's, but few were better written. Compared with his the prose of Trollope, Hardy, and Gissing is clumsy, and that of Meredith intricate and affected.

As a critic of his own work, Stevenson was untiring and relentless; as a critic of others he was, like Scott, often over-generous. In 1892 on the publication of the *Window in Thrums*, he wrote to Barrie: "There are two of us now that the Shirra might have patted on the head." For most of the Scots poems, *Kidnapped*, *Weir of Hermiston* and several of the short stories, Scott would certainly have acknowledged Stevenson.

On a more confidential occasion, Stevenson wrote of Barrie: "Barrie is a beauty. Stuff in that young man, but he must see and not be too funny." To Henry James he wrote, "There's genius in him, but there's a journalist at his elbow." In the early prose studies of Thrums and Kensington, the journalist prevailed, and he is never entirely absent from even the most successful of Barrie's dramatic works. Original and creative as Barrie undoubtedly was, one is always uneasily conscious that he is writing less well than he could;

that he has gauged the middle level of public taste and is resolved not to write above it. *Peter Pan*, though Peter and Wendy may have passed into European mythology, is, as a piece of dramatic construction, unworthy of the abilities of the man who wrote it, and there is less to be said for *Mary Rose*.

On the rare occasions when Barrie turns his back on facile sentiment and easy effect, as in *The Admirable Crichton, The Twelve Pound Look*, and *Shall We Join the Ladies ?* one is aware, not only of his exceptional sense of the theatre, but of the thoughtful, satiric and imaginative qualities which Stevenson and others hailed in his first publications.

Of recent Scots letters it is difficult to say much in a few closing words. John Buchan (Lord Tweedsmuir) was undoubtedly the greatest literary figure of our time, who in the intervals of a busy and distinguished public career, wrote historical novels, thrillers, memoirs, biographies, essays, and poems with equal ease and success. His novels were in the Stevenson tradition of high adventure and easy impeccable prose, and his biographies steered a careful middle course between the bleakness of factual memoir-writing and the temptations of the period novel. Neil Gunn is one of the most interesting of contemporary Scots novelists, and his studies of childhood and adolescence in the Highlands and Islands are sensitive, well-documented, and exquisitely written. The trilogy of Lewis Grassic Gibbon is in the anti-romantic tradition of *The House with the Green Shutters*, but has the added interest of a rhythmic, cadenced prose, the suitability of which for the purposes of fiction is doubtful. The picaresque novels of Eric Linklater, though their subjects are rarely of Scottish interest, have a goliardic quality which is in the oldest of Scots traditions, and recalls Dunbar, Burns, and Byron. Few contemporary novelists can carry a narrative or write English with Linklater's ease.

Stevenson, in his introductory note to his Scots poems, anticipates the dispute which to-day divides our Scots vernacular poets— whether the poetry of " our own dying language " should be written in the dialect of Lauderdale or Angus, Galloway, or the Mearns, or in a composite Scots, compounded of all these local elements, and enriched (where Scots fails) by coinages and importations. Much excellent verse is to-day being written in these regional dialects of Scots, but inevitably the purity of the speech is restrictive both to vocabulary and content, and most fatally restrictive to the size of its reading public. Stevenson admits : " . . . when Scots was lacking, or the rhyme jibbed, I was glad (like my betters) to fall back on English." The acknowledged leader of the younger Scots poets who practise the enriched vernacular is Hugh M'Diarmid, a lyrist of real genius, and the author of a number of long "satirico-polemical" poems of unequal quality. His work, and to some extent that of his disciples, not only enriches the vernacular by foreign and often startling importations and inventions, but aims at elevating the content of Scots poetry by drawing heavily on the literary, meta-physical, and political writings of other countries and continents. It is regrettable that the public capable of reading M'Diarmid is small, and must inevitably be smaller, for he is a real poet, and is a most potent influence on the young Scots writers of to-day.

THE PRESS AND PERIODICALS

IT is not surprising that Scotland, whose printers have a world-wide reputation, should have a strong journalistic tradition. Journalism, indeed, could be counted among the country's major exports. After acquiring a good, solid grounding in their profession on Scottish newspapers a great band of young Scotsmen have gone to Fleet Street, London, the centre of British journalism, and to all the corners of the Commonwealth to make their reputation as newspapermen.

Some of these young journalists, of whom the late Sir James Barrie is a notable example, have become famous as creative writers, but the great majority of them have confined their careers to the news-room. There is a logical, matter-of-fact, analytical element in the Scottish character which makes for success when it comes to the appraisal and presentation of news.

Despite this continual exodus of talent Scotland has by no means succumbed to the magnetism of Fleet Street. Her daily press enjoys a vigorous independence not attained, at any rate over a comparable area, in any other part of the British Isles. A striking proof of this is that Scotland, with one eighth of the population of England, supports two flourishing " quality " newspapers. In England the so-called popular press has left only two twopenny morning newspapers in the field—*The Times* and the *Manchester Guardian*. (During the war the price of *The Times* was raised to threepence.)

The reason why Scotland, a much smaller and poorer country than England, should be able to support two quality newspapers is probably psychological. The Scot, who has tended to idolize education, is by temperament canny, critical, and shrewd. He likes to get his news unpredigested and unadorned, and to assess its implications independently.

The two leading newspapers in Scotland are *The Scotsman* (surely one of the most happily named of all newspapers) and the *Glasgow Herald*. Roughly similar in format these two newspapers are national in the proper sense of that word and conform to the highest traditions of British journalism. Both of them, one in Edinburgh, the other in Glasgow, are published by Scottish firms.

171

The Scotsman is published by " The Scotsman Publications Ltd.,'' and was founded in 1817. Its sympathies, broadly speaking, are conservative, but its editorial emphasis is not dictated by party politics, and it frequently takes an independent line, especially where Scottish affairs are concerned, and in its news coverage is scrupulously fair to its political opponents. The photographic reproductions of *The Scotsman* are recognized to be of the highest quality in Britain, its mechanical equipment is unsurpassed in Europe, and its annual pictorial calendar is world famous. The associate publications are the *Evening Dispatch* and the *Weekly Scotsman* which is read all over the world by Scots abroad.

The *Glasgow Herald*, published by the Outram group, is even older than *The Scotsman*, and caters for the same critical and educated type of reader. Its editorial policy is similar to that of *The Scotsman* and, being published in the industrial west, it circulates more widely among the commercial class of the community. The Outram group also publish the *Bulletin*, a lively pictorial morning newspaper, and the *Evening Times*, which has the largest evening circulation in Scotland.

Outside Edinburgh and Glasgow the most active Scottish newspaper concern is the Thomson press in Dundee—a city which has trained hundreds of journalists. Its daily newspapers are the *Dundee Courier* and the *Evening Telegraph*. The Thomson press also publish, in addition to a large number of " juvenile " weeklies, two weekly papers which concentrate on local news and domestic affairs, the *People's Journal* and the *People's Friend*.

The metropolitan press is strongly established in Scotland. In Aberdeen both the morning and the evening newspapers, the *Press and Journal* and the *Evening Express*, are published by the Scottish branch of the vast Kemsley organization in London, which also publishes the *Daily Record*, the *Evening News*, and the *Sunday Mail*, in Glasgow. Glasgow is the centre of the *Express* newspaper group in Scotland and the *Scottish Daily Express* commands the biggest circulation of any newspaper in the country. The *Daily Herald* and the *News Chronicle* publish editions with a Scottish service of news, and there is a *Scottish Daily Mail*. In Edinburgh the *Evening News* is published by a firm with ramifications in England.

In addition to the daily newspapers there are well over a hundred local newspapers produced in Scotland, some of them of a high standard, but none of them with a nation-wide prestige.

So far as the periodical press in Scotland is concerned the days of resounding reviews are under eclipse. Scotland publishes no weekly review of standing. The famous monthly journals published by the well-known houses of Blackwood and Chambers, *Blackwood's Magazine*, founded in 1817, and *Chambers's Journal* in 1832, still serve a faithful public. The *Scots Magazine*, published in Dundee, the *S.M.T. Magazine* and the *Scottish Field* deal with historical, literary, and social affairs in Scotland. Recently a number of periodicals have appeared, of a progressive outlook, such as the monthly *Scots Review* and *To-day and To-morrow*, and various publications putting forward the point of view of the younger Scottish writers, issued by the Glasgow firm of MacLellan.

ARCHITECTURE

BEFORE any attempt is made to outline the story of architecture in Scotland there are certain basic factors which need to be clarified. They concern the environment, in the broadest sense, of the people who have inhabited this land over many centuries. It is worth remembering, then, that Scotland is on the north-west fringe of Europe and was the meeting-place of Celtic and Nordic influences ; and that in later years she had close affinities rather with the countries of North-west Europe, with the Low Countries and France, than with her southern neighbour. In earlier times her economic position was often precarious, and generally speaking her people were not able to afford the degree of sophistication in the arts possible for the inhabitants of more prosperous lands ; her architecture therefore tended to keep to essentials—and in considering those essentials the character of the climate must be remembered. Lastly, the building material until very recently was stone, a material which, while imposing a discipline on designers and builders, at the same time proved to be a medium for daring experiment in the hands of those who mastered its qualities—and at the lowest assured a naïve and solid type of building soundly based on functional needs.

Early Building

The earliest structure recognizable by the average layman as a building is the broch, an open, tapering, circular tower of dry-stone masonry enclosing a space of about 40 feet in diameter, with walls sometimes 19 feet thick and never less than 9, standing anything up to 60 feet in height. No windows pierce these walls, only a small easily defended door, but within their thickness are galleries, stairs, and cells. Round the circular enclosed space ran a wooden gallery, while in the centre was a hearth and a well. Brochs exist mostly in the north and west, the finest remaining being at Mousa in Shetland (Plate 19). Other more accessible examples are at Brora and Glenelg. They date mostly from the first to the fifth centuries A.D. and were used either as a defence against sea raiders or as the castles of a conquering aristocracy.

The arrival of Columba at Iona from Ireland in the sixth century and his missionary successes on the Scottish mainland among the

Picts, were two of the chief means of establishing cultural relations between Ireland and Scotland. From Adamnan's *Life of Columba* W. D. Simpson describes an early Celtic monastery with "its group of wooden or wattled huts—its barn, stable, and byre ; its mill, its bakery, its kiln for corn drying ; its refectory for the common meal, its guest house and its little heather thatched church of logs with a sacristy opening on one side where the monastic bell was kept—the whole establishment surrounded by a cashel, or fencible dry-built wall." Later these buildings came to be replaced in stone with beehive huts and underground cells ; and the remains on Eileach-an-Naoimh in the Garvelloch or Summer Isles and in Skye, convey a clear picture of the appearance of these Celtic monasteries. In addition there are scattered examples of tiny primitive chapels whose square-ends and converging side walls reveal Irish influence. A much altered version of this type of building exists on Inchcolm in the Firth of Forth, said to have been the cell occupied by the hermit who succoured King Alexander I when he was stormbound there in 1123. In addition to the square-ended chapel other signs of Celtic influence are the round towers, to be seen at Abernethy and Brechin, used as refuges for the clergy in times of hostile invasion, and the inclined jambs of doors and windows of which these towers contain examples (Plate 20).

The Romanesque Phase

Just as the Celtic missionaries brought fresh influences to bear on Scottish life and architecture, so Queen (later Saint) Margaret, the wife of King Malcolm Canmore, proved to be another means of linking Scotland with the culture of other countries. Queen Margaret was the grand-daughter of an English king but had been brought up in Hungary. Through her encouragement, and that of her son King David I, the organization of the Church of Rome with its elaborate monastic system finally absorbed the Scottish church, and the appearance of Romanesque or Norman architecture was a natural result. Characteristics of fully developed Romanesque architecture are the round arch, generally massive proportions, long narrow churches, and flat wooden ceilings.

The oldest of the churches designed for the Roman rite is the primitive and much altered cell-chapel of St. Margaret built on the highest point of the castle rock in Edinburgh. As Queen Margaret heard her last Mass here, the building must have existed prior to 1093. But the most striking of the early Romanesque churches is that dedicated to St. Regulus in St. Andrews, originally serving as the Cathedral and dating from the second quarter of the twelfth century. Only the earliest parts remain, that is the choir—narrow, high, and without aisles—and a lofty square tower ; in masonry and architectural detail it has affinities with the north of England and with France respectively.

Two Romanesque churches exhibit the influence of the north of England or Durham school—St. Magnus Cathedral, Kirkwall (begun in 1137), and the Benedictine Abbey Church of Dunfermline (Plate 25). Though small compared with continental cathedrals, Kirkwall is a noble and virile building developed from an orthodox plan, with a central tower, transepts with eastern chapels, a nave of seven bays, a choir of three, and a single eastern apse. The interior is, characteristically, very high for its width. Of the original aisled and cruciform Abbey Church of Dunfermline only the nave has come down to us intact, a structure of solemn dignity with massive piers, some of which are decorated with incised chevron and spiral ornament strongly reminiscent of Durham. Other large Romanesque Abbey Churches are at Jedburgh and Kelso.

Several small churches of this period are worth mentioning, notably St. Orans, Iona, with a square-ended Celtic plan (Plate 21), Dalmeny, near South Queensferry, described by Mr. G. P. H. Watson, a recognized authority, as " the most complete Norman church in Scotland," and Leuchars in Fife. The last two have walls enriched with arcading and end in apisdal sanctuaries.

Transition to Gothic

At the end of the twelfth century began the transition from Romanesque to Gothic. Although the pointed arch is always referred to as the chief characteristic of this next phase, in fact it had more fundamental implications. "Gothic" embodies a system of structure more scientific than Romanesque, enabling larger areas to be roofed and bigger windows to be inserted for the better lighting of the interior. As Gothic design developed, the structure gradually evolved itself into a framework of columns, buttresses, and ribbed vaulting, the walls tending to become stone screens pierced by increasingly large, traceried windows.

The most remarkable, and incidentally the most accessible, transitional building is the nave of Holyrood Abbey in Edinburgh, begun at the turn of the twelfth century. It was the first church to be vaulted throughout ; and the façade of the west front with its noble doorway, six-light window above, and rich arcading, is particularly fine.

Both Elgin and Glasgow cathedrals were reconstructed in the mid-thirteenth century. Although Elgin is partly in ruins it is even now possible to appreciate why it was regarded as the finest early Gothic building in Scotland at the Reformation. It has a uniformity almost as impressive as Salisbury, with which it is contemporary ; the east end with its two tiers of lancet windows surmounted by a rose window must have lit the interior magnificently ; while the high vaulted octagonal chapter house and the elaborately shafted west doorway are equally impressive features. One of the great glories of Glasgow Cathedral is its crypt, roofed by a complex system of vaulting which provides a rich setting for the Shrine of St. Mungo, the focus of many pilgrimages in medieval times—a factor obviously influencing the plan of the whole cathedral, which was designed to facilitate the orderly circulation of large numbers of pilgrims. Other great early Gothic remains are Arbroath Abbey and Dryburgh Abbey, near Melrose.

Decorated Gothic

From its early purity Gothic design developed into the middle, or decorated, phase with an increase in the ornamentation of vaulting and window tracery. English influence persisted despite Bannock-burn and King Robert Bruce's successful government. Sweet-heart Abbey, about eleven miles from Dumfries, is generally English in appearance. On the other hand, Dunblane Cathedral (lately restored by Sir Rowand Anderson and Sir Robert Lorimer) has the typically Scottish proportion of a long and narrow nave. The nave arcading at Dunblane is richly decorated and the clear vista from west to east is probably unique in Scotland.

Melrose Abbey, one of the most famous ruins in Scotland, comes within this period—on the plan associated with the Cistercian Order (Plate 24). It has no clear national characteristics, but is rather a blend of several. Mr. G. P. H. Watson states that no fewer than five master-masons worked at Melrose, and draws attention to the sharp contrast between the eastern arm (the Presbytery) " lofty and sheer, richly arcaded, and amply lit by great windows filled with curvilinear and perpendicular tracery," clearly the work of a Yorkshire master-mason, and the south transept, which shows unmistakable French influence. Again, the shafted pillars and moulded arches provide another example of Scottish arcading not unlike that at Dunblane.

There is a fine group of Fife parish churches of this period (T-shaped in plan with a broad tower topped by a blunt spire) of which St. Monans is the finest, with its good external proportions and decorated window tracery displaying both French and English influences.

The Growth of National Character

Late Gothic in Scotland seems to reflect not only the continued alliance with France but the development of national consciousness at home. England's " perpendicular " finds no echo in Scotland ; instead, certain French details become fused with a national idiom in both secular and religious buildings—the corbelling out of turrets in secular buildings and the revival of apses, along with the use of flamboyant window tracery in churches. Of the Scottish features which developed are the naïve curvilinear tracery, seen in Iona Abbey, stone slabbed roofing as at Corstorphine (Edinburgh), and Seton (near Tranent in East Lothian), the elaborate " Sacrament Houses " for the Elements, of which there are examples at Kintore (Aberdeen-shire) and Crichton (Midlothian) ; and lastly, the well-known open spires or crowns at St. Giles', Edinburgh, King's College, Aberdeen, and formerly St. Mary's, Haddington. This consciously national trend was largely due to the fact that church building, formerly sponsored by high-ranking ecclesiastics with an inter-national background, was now undertaken rather by burgesses spurred on by civic pride, by small landowners, or by friars. Accord-ingly the fifteenth century saw the building or reconstruction of several large medieval parish churches—Edinburgh, Linlithgow, Haddington, Stirling, Perth, and St. Andrews. St. Michael's, Linlithgow, is the finest of the four new buildings, with its five-sided apse and typically Scottish separate gabled roofs of transept and porch ; and it bears a striking resemblance to the Church of the Holy Rude at Stirling. The parish churches of Perth and Hadding-ton also have much in common with each other—the former, inci-dentally, having been most sensitively restored in recent years as the city war memorial by Sir Robert Lorimer.

Both Aberdeen and St. Andrews universities have fine, carefully restored chapels of this period, the original wooden stalls and screens in the former now being unique in Scotland and eloquent of the vanished glories of contemporary Scottish craftsmanship.

PLATE 69

Crown Steeple, St. Giles' Cathedral (Late Gothic)
(*Photo : Robert M. Adam*)

PLATE 70

Leuchars Parish Church (Romanesque)
(*Photo : Robert M. Adam*)

St. Regulus, St. Andrews (Romanesque)
(*Photo : Valentine*)

Elgin Cathedral, east end (Early Gothic)
(*Photo : Robert M. Adam*)

PLATE 71

Dalmeny Church (Romanesque ; tower modern)
(*Photo : Valentine*)

Corstorphine Old Parish Church (Late Gothic)
(*Photo : Valentine*)

PLATE 72

Dunblane Cathedral : nave looking east (Decorated Gothic)
(*Photo : Valentine*)

PLATE 73

St. Giles' Cathedral : south aisle (Late Gothic)
(*Photo : Valentine*)

Glasgow Cathedral : crypt (Decorated Gothic)
(*Photo : Valentine*)

PLATE 74

Roslin Chapel, Midlothian (Late Gothic)
(Photo : Valentine)

Amisfield Tower, Dumfriesshire (1600)
(Photo : Patrick Forman, Moffat)

St. Magnus Cathedral, Kirkwall, Orkney
(Romanesque and later styles)
(Photo : Thomas Kent)

Canongate Tolbooth, Edinburgh
(Late seventeenth century)
(Photo : Valentine)

PLATE 75

St. Machar's Cathedral, Aberdeen : west front (Late Gothic)
(*Photo : A. J. B. Strachan*)

PLATE 76

Holyrood Abbey : west front (Transitional)
(*Photo : F. C. Inglis*)

Lamb's House, Leith (sixteenth century merchant's house)
(*Photo : A. Reiach*)

PLATE 77

Midmar Castle, Aberdeenshire (early seventeenth century)

PLATE 78

Kildrummy Castle, Aberdeenshire (thirteenth century)
(*Photo : Robert M. Adam*)

The Palace, Culross, Fife (late sixteenth and early seventeenth century)
(*Photo : Crown Copyright*)

PLATE 79

Dunderave Castle, Argyllshire (restored by Sir Robert Lorimer)
(*Photo : ' Country Life '*)

Claypotts Castle, Broughty Ferry (late sixteenth century)
(*Photo : Valentine*)

PLATE 80

Traquair, Peeblesshire
(*Photo : Valentine*)

Kinross House and formal garden (late seventeenth century ; architect,
Sir William Bruce)
(*Photo : Valentine*)

PLATE 81

Farmhouse, near Tomintoul, Banffshire (eighteenth century)
(*Photo : Robert Hurd*)

Thatched and pantiled houses, Auchtermuchty, Fife
(*Photo : Robert Hurd*)

Entrance Hall, The Drum, near Edinburgh, showing low-relief plaster decoration (mid-eighteenth century ; architect, William Adam)
(*Photo : ' Country Life '*)

Round Drawing-room, Culzean Castle, Ayrshire (late eighteenth century ; architect, Robert Adam)
(*Photo : ' Country Life '*)

PLATE 82

PLATE 83   Aerial view of Culzean Castle, Ayrshire (late eighteenth century ;
architect, Robert Adam).   Presented to the National Trust for Scotland
by the Marquess of Ailsa

Bon-Accord Crescent, Aberdeen (early nineteenth century)
(*Photo : A. Reiach*)

North side of Charlotte Square, Edinburgh (late eighteenth century ;
architect, Robert Adam)
(*Photo : Paul Shillabeer*)

PLATE 84

Perhaps the most striking large church building of the fifteenth century, however, is the cathedral of St. Machar, Aberdeen, the west front of which has an heroic, almost saga-like, quality in the general design of its range of tall narrow windows and its twin spires, and in its simple treatment of that intractable material, granite; while inside is a remarkable flat oak ceiling which heraldically displays the ideal structure of Catholic Christendom.

From a number of characteristically Scottish all-stone churches such as Seton, Crichton, and Corstorphine, Roslin, about seven miles south of Edinburgh, stands out as an elaborate exotic, sponsored by the Earl of Orkney, probably an enthusiastic amateur, and built by foreign workers. The plan is a combination of borrowed features, but the surface is encrusted with a riot of carved symbolic and naturalistic embellishment which has to be seen to be believed.

Castles and Towers—the Larger Fortresses

Parallel with the establishment of a new order in the Church through the influence of Queen Margaret and her son King David I, came the settlement of a number of Norman families, from the eleventh century onwards, forming a governing class under royal authority. Their castles were not only military in character but served as local government centres. At the outset they consisted only of earthworks and timber buildings, the earthworks comprising a mount or mote protected by a ditch, and the buildings a dominating wooden house or tower enclosed in a wooden stockade, with an outer stockade or bailey enclosing subordinate buildings. By the early thirteenth century massive stone versions of the wooden prototype began to appear, as at Castle Duffus in Morayshire, Dirleton in East Lothian, Bothwell overlooking the Clyde, and Kildrummy in Aberdeenshire. In passing it should be noted that it was the upper parts of these buildings and surrounding walls which were of military importance, with their crenellations, machicolations, and corbelling, now loosely referred to by the omnibus term "embattlements." In writing of the confused and complex form of these earlier castles as they have now survived, Dr. Mackay Mackenzie rightly reminds us that they have been subjected not only to destruction by war, but to adaptations, reconstructions, and additions necessitated by the changing ways of life and warfare. It is not always easy therefore to define the stages of development.

Tantallon, an imposing fortress occupying a rocky promontory on the East Lothian coast, near North Berwick, illustrates a departure from the earlier type just described. Instead of being a dominating feature enclosed in the bailey, the main tower has now become part of a heavily fortified entrance, at once feudally impressive as well as efficient from a military viewpoint.

The " Palace "

Later still, the desire for a freer and pleasanter domestic environment became apparent in the tendency for the hall, a long two-storeyed domestic building, to be the chief building in a castle, often distinguished from the tower by the name " palace," a term which did not then have the particular social implication that it generally has to-day. Where former towers existed, they were sometimes linked by new ranges of lower buildings, as at Dunnottar, near Stonehaven in Kincardineshire, and at Linlithgow, where the whole group became known as the " palace " (Plate 27). A number of variations of this " palace " theme exist, according to the status and wealth of the owner and the character of the existing earlier buildings constituting the original castle, at, for instance, St. Andrews, Doune (South Perthshire), Craigmillar (in the south-east of Edinburgh), and particularly Castle Campbell at the foot of the Ochils, near Dollar, where the stages of castle development are clearly apparent. The design of palace buildings reflects, incidentally, the strong cultural influence of the Franco-Scottish Alliance, particularly in the architectural character of Linlithgow, Falkland (Fife), Stirling, and Caerlaverock (seven miles from Dumfries), the façade details in all of which exhibit many early Renaissance features of a charm and lightness hitherto rare in Scottish architecture. They provide a poignant reminder of the civilizing effect of Stuart sympathies, in the earlier days of that strangely brilliant but unfortunate dynasty.

Towers

In addition to these more important castles with their elaborate plan and complex development, there are the numerous towers such as Smailholm (six miles from Kelso), and Neidpath, near Peebles, and many others to be found in every part of the country, built and occupied by local lairds. At first these towers were of a simple shape, purely functional in character. They were built with thick walls which not only acted as a support for the stone vaulting at the basement and possibly other levels, but sometimes

Houstoun, West Lothian

contained the spiral stair giving access to upper floors as well as other
minor closets. The spiral stair also sometimes occupied an internal
projection or an external turret. These towers were often surrounded by a modest wall enclosing various outbuildings and pierced
by a dignified entrance archway—a good though later example
is Houstoun in West Lothian. At the beginning these towers contained only the minimum domestic accommodation, that is, the hall,
the room used by the laird's wife, their sleeping chamber, and the
kitchen with its store in the basement. Increased amenities were
later provided by the addition of a wing (or rarely, two wings),
to the original tower—a development in line with the "palace"
phase of larger castles; indeed in some cases the original tower
became a mere adjunct to a later house. Several "Z" and "L"
shaped plans gradually evolved, expressed in architectural forms
of great interest. Earlier in this chapter reference was made to the

181

military importance of the upper parts of castle walls. By the mid-sixteenth century this military need had diminished, and the fact that the upper storeys of these towers were domestically the most pleasant, led to an astonishing outburst of architectural invention in the effort to expand living accommodation at this level. In effect a house was superimposed on the tower below, supported by more or less elaborate corbelling where it projected beyond the tower walls. Claypotts, near Broughty Ferry, is at once the most accessible and explicit example of this phase, while Amisfield in Dumfries-shire exhibits the same tendency in a form which, as an architectural composition, is more mature and daring.

The larger towers, their owners no longer so absorbed by the need for self-defence, blossomed forth with an exuberant architectural virtuosity of corbels, balustrades, turrets, and roofing which is unique, and which, although generally reminiscent of French châteaux, can properly be considered as a native development. In particular, Craigievar, Midmar, and Castle Fraser, all in Aberdeen-shire, and dating from about 1600, stand out as striking achievements. It is worth noting that, despite their exuberance and naïve vanity these castles exhibit a firm grasp of aesthetic "rightness"; the relationship of turrets to the main mass of the tower roof, the corbelled emphasis that lends importance to the upper storeys, and the contrasting light-catching textures of harling, ashlar, and slating are all a delight to the eye, exhibiting none of those *gaucheries* of Victorian "castle" architecture to which the ironical soubriquet "Scots Baronial" has, perhaps a little unfairly, been attached.

The Burgh

Meantime from the sixteenth century onwards the Scottish burgh (though originating at a much earlier date) was taking a form still to some extent recognizable to-day, with its Parish Kirk, Tolbooth, Mercat Cross, and merchant burgesses' houses opening off its Market, "gates" (streets), "ports" (gates), wynds, and closes. It represented a traditional centre for trading and civil control, dating back in its essentials to the times of King David I, who initiated a system of burghs over the whole country. Culross in Fife, St. Andrews, Haddington and Stirling convey an impression of the architectural character of a typical burgh with its harled buildings, small windows, crowstepped gables, massive "lums" (chimneys), and general air of homely self-respect.

Of the larger parish kirks something has already been said.

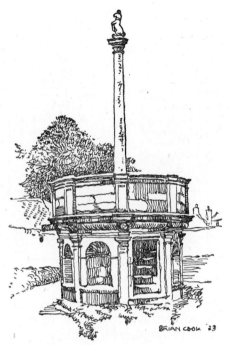

Mercat Cross, Prestonpans

Typical examples of smaller kirks can be seen in a number of Fife burghs such as Markinch. The earlier tolbooths with their strong towers reflect characteristics of castle architecture and, as one might expect from their trading associations, they also show affinities with the Low Countries, as examples at Musselburgh, Canongate (Edinburgh), and Tain indicate. Later tolbooths at Dunbar, Crail, Culross, Old Aberdeen, Dingwall, and Auchtermuchty—to quote only a few examples—show the development of a specialized type of building with the tower more as a formal mark of civic status than as a place of strength, thus reflecting a more settled way of life.

Domestic Architecture

But houses constituted the architectural bulk of a town. Of the fifteenth- and sixteenth-century stone dwellings few remain, the most remarkable being Provand's Lordship, Glasgow, now restored and beautifully furnished ; Loudoun Hall, Ayr, once the home of the Hereditary Sheriff and containing several contemporary features of domestic interest ; Lamb's House, a merchant's dwelling and

183

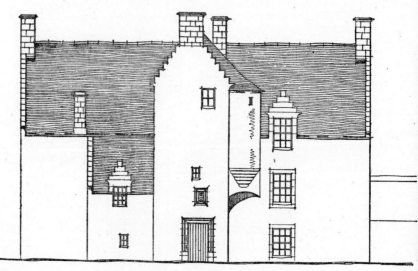

Pilmuir House, north elevation

warehouse near the old harbour of Leith, with a street frontage of vigorous character slightly reminiscent of castle architecture; and Huntly House, Edinburgh, which exhibits three distinct stages of growth, and has been restored for use as a City Museum. Later houses, dating from the seventeenth century, to mention only a few of architectural importance, are Argyll's Lodging, Stirling, Hamilton Dower House, Prestonpans, and Acheson House, Edinburgh, all courtyard houses; the Palace, Culross, and Gladstone's Land, Edinburgh, both with rare internal painted decoration, the former with a curiously Italianate terraced garden and the latter with open arcading on the ground floor, also found in Elgin; and Stenhouse Mills, Edinburgh. In the country, harled houses of similar character, such as Traquair—a rambling yet shapely masterpiece—Pilmuir in East Lothian and Ford House in Midlothian, still survive here and there. The simpler elements of Renaissance detail, first seen in the " palaces " within castles, also decorate these dwellings, with simple pediments above their dormer windows and crudely interpreted classical mouldings at string-course, door, and window. Further, the owners did not hesitate to proclaim their heraldic achievements, their initials and their national emblems in stone—a reasonable and pleasing expression of personal pride and self-respect. At no time before or since, indeed, had Scottish domestic architecture such individuality or so clearly expressed a native way of life ; and although this tradition was virtually extinguished among the wealthier classes by the architectural classicism that arose in the late seventeenth and early eighteenth centuries, it persisted throughout the eighteenth century in cottage and farm building as an indigenous style of simplicity and lasting charm.

Outside the main trends occur two buildings of some importance, Heriot's Hospital, Edinburgh (Plate 57), and Winton House, East Lothian. With their elaborate chimney stacks and other features they are both somewhat English in character, being designed by the same man, Wallace. The arcaded courtyard of Heriot's is in particular reminiscent of one of the Cambridge colleges, but each building contains many notable seventeenth-century details both externally and internally.

The Emergence of the Architect

Mention of Wallace, the first designer to be named, introduces the era of the great professional architect and the large country mansion. In the latter half of the seventeenth century Sir William Bruce of Kinross, a contemporary of Sir Christopher Wren's, embarked on a practice in which he achieved not only, it is said, the design of the traditional Merchants' Steeple in Glasgow, but later the superb neo-classical composition of Kinross House. This noble building is set in a formal garden which opens on to Loch Leven, through a gate surmounted by a fabulous cornucopia of fish, on the axis of Loch Leven Castle, the whole being a subtle blend of French and Scottish elements. The same could be said of his famous courtyard at Holyrood House, of the 1691 front of Caroline Park at Granton, near Edinburgh—not unlike a French manor house—and of the earliest part of Hopetoun House (South Queensferry), the completion of which was carried out in the grand manner by his pupil William Adam, the father of sons whose professional fame has eclipsed his own. William Adam, who practised during the first half of the eighteenth century, may be said to have bridged the gulf that had existed between Scottish and English architecture for two centuries, through his introduction of the Palladian style of neo-classic design. As an architect he was able, if a little stolid and uncertain in his handling of spatial values. He designed Yester House, near Gifford, in East Lothian ; the Drum, on the outskirts of Edinburgh, and Dumfries House, Cumnock, which is of particular interest owing to its superb condition and

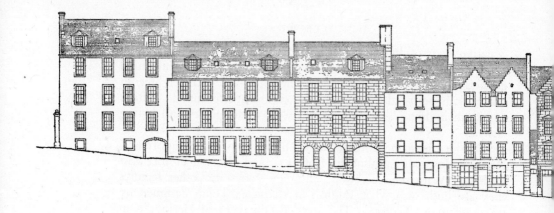

Broad Street, Stirling (mostly 17th century, now partly demolished), characteristic of burgh architec

Montgomery Square, Eaglesham, Renfrewshire (late 18th century)

Montgomery Street, Eaglesham, Renfrewshire (late 18th century)

the time

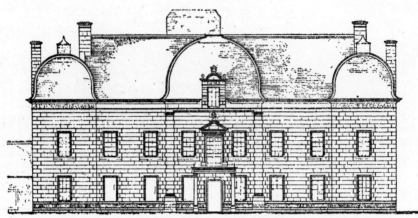

Caroline Park, south front (1691)

remarkably complete contemporary furnishings. He broke new ground by introducing into interior design the decoration of walls with elaborate low-relief plaster-work panels probably executed by Italian workmen. Hitherto such decoration had usually been confined to ceilings as in Sir William Bruce's Holyrood House, the walls being panelled in wood. One of his most unusual works, still extant, was the shooting lodge of Chatelherault, built in 1730 in the form of a grand entrance gate with flanking lodges, serving as the climax of a vista seen from the now demolished Hamilton Palace. He also designed the recently destroyed Dundee Town House. His most celebrated son, Robert, developed and enriched the neo-classic theme to a degree of almost excessive refinement, having been much influenced by the antiquities he studied on the shores of the Adriatic and Mediterranean. Most of his work was carried out in England, but some important buildings of his were built in Scotland. He designed, to take several instances, the Register House at the east end of Princes Street, Edinburgh, a sensitive composition with a flat central dome and light flanking towers ; the firm yet delicate façades of Charlotte Square ; and the earlier stages of Edinburgh University, subsequently completed by a later architect, Playfair. Experimenting in the castellated manner for his exterior, not too happily perhaps as regards detail, he also designed Culzean Castle, some four miles from Maybole in Ayrshire, the interiors of which must, however, be counted among his most successful and daring achievements, still to be seen with the original furniture and fittings *in situ*. Indeed he set the fashion for interior

Caroline Park, balcony railing over porch

design for a decade, with his delicate yet intricate ceiling designs and his development of the mantelpiece ; but although he is still widely and rightly admired for his interior decoration, his architecture deserves recognition as a major contribution to the civilized arts. In passing, it is interesting to compare his work with that of another contemporary Scotsman, Charles Cameron, who, though working entirely in Russia as the architect to Catherine the Great, had much in common with Adam.

Town Planning

The building of the first part of Edinburgh's New Town to Craig's design in the late eighteenth century is perhaps the best monument to an age when, as Voltaire said, Scotland led Europe in intellectual activity (Plate 31). Craig's plan was not perfect, and its original architectural integrity, albeit a little severe, has been savagely outraged by the commercial enterprise of later generations ; but even now the view along George Street from St. Andrew Square is impressive, and the spaciousness of his design has survived despite the many changes in the heights of the buildings bordering the main streets. Other interesting examples of town design at this time are Inveraray, and parts of Aberdeen and Perth, and there are as well several villages, such as Tomintoul, Eaglesham, and Ullapool, the layout of which have a quiet and spacious dignity.

The Greek Revival

Playfair, a leading architect of the Greek revival in the early nineteenth century, executed distinguished work in designing the eastern extension of Edinburgh's New Town, the façade of Royal Terrace being particularly impressive. He also designed the fine Academy buildings at Dollar, the vestibule of which is worth seeing, and his National Gallery in Edinburgh seems to underline the Athenian aspect of the capital with a nicely calculated emphasis. The Greek revival was strongly expressed by " Greek " Thomson in the west of Scotland, where his design for the St. Vincent Street Church, exploiting a difficult sloping site, and his monumental Great Western Terrace, seem to have exercised a wide influence on the street architecture of Glasgow. Hamilton was another important architect of the time, and his Edinburgh Royal High School, a building of grace and dignity on the slopes of the Calton Hill, is as successful in striking the right Athenian note as Playfair's National Gallery.

The Romantic Movement

Robert Adam had already given a foretaste of the romantic revival in architecture at Culzean. Stimulated greatly by the literary movement, architectural romanticism became widely fashionable. In particular, a version of Scots Baronial, abounding in restless lines, hard textures, and uneasy proportions, eventually became fashionable, its most constant interpreter being the undoubtedly able architect Bryce. This period was prolific in formidable castellated mansions—formidable, that is, in a social sense, since they were designed almost as much to impress as to accommodate. Balmoral, which was designed largely by the Prince Consort, is the best known, though by no means the most fantastic of this phase; and possibly, out of many, Kinettles near Forfar is the most extravagant in conception. The other aspect of revivalism was ecclesiastical. Only for about a century did the post-Reformation church in Scotland depart from Gothic, producing in that time, nevertheless, some excellent small churches in the native idiom, such as Burntisland in Fife, and Reay (Plate 53) and Dunnet in Caithness, these last two having a serene, almost Nordic quality, much enhanced by their glistening white-harled exteriors. The old church at Cromarty is particularly notable for its original interior furnishings. There were many late eighteenth-century neo-classical churches, some, as at Killin, near the head of Loch Tay, and Mearnskirk, seven miles from Glasgow, made more homely through contact with the traditional idiom; but in the main a revived, nostalgic gothic was *de rigueur* from the nineteenth century onwards, and little attempt was made to evolve a type of church suited specially for Presbyterian worship.

Mearnskirk

Sir Robert Lorimer

At the turn of the century Sir Rowand Anderson gave a whole-some lead in directing attention to the study of the real Scottish tradition, by now submerged and forgotten beneath decades of fierce industrialization, although most of his own work consisted of elaborate academic compositions of which the McEwan Hall, the Medical School, the National Portrait Gallery in Edinburgh, and Mount Stuart in Bute are typical. A more thorough return to the proper Scottish tradition was the keynote of Sir Robert Lorimer's genius. Although his best known work, the Scottish National War Memorial at Edinburgh Castle, is by no means his happiest, some of his restorations show a brilliant grasp of the native idiom—Dunderave is one of the finest—while his Thistle Chapel in the church of St. Giles, Edinburgh, exhibits an astounding virtuosity in handling the most elaborate Gothic detail, along with a real understanding of good craftsmanship—a sympathy which stood him in good stead in many of his commissions, particularly his restorations of churches and castles. Purely from the point of view of aesthetic values, the interior of his church St. Peter's, Falcon Avenue, Edinburgh, is worth study as a successful attempt to give a sense of

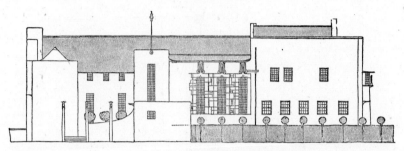

Design by Charles Rennie Mackintosh for a house for a patron of the arts

serene spaciousness within a comparatively small building. Sir Robert Lorimer, however, had his limitations, and his essays in modern design, as, for instance, in the West Mains Road science buildings of the University in Edinburgh, are curiously immature. It is perhaps best to recollect the wider interest he aroused by practical example in the architectural traditions of his own country.

Charles Rennie Mackintosh and the Modern Idiom

It is fitting to end with a brief appreciation of the genius of Charles Rennie Mackintosh, as an architect whose name means something furth of Scotland. Firmly rooted in the functionalism and homely charm of Scottish architecture at its most individual phase, in the seventeenth century, he was at the same time a restless experimenter with new forms of planning, new methods of structure and, with his wife Margaret MacDonald, with strange innovations in interior furnishing and decoration. His design for the Glasgow School of Art, which mightily disturbed the comfortable world of 1894, his designs for Hill House in Helensburgh, and Windyhill in Kilmacolm, and his interiors for Miss Cranston's restaurants in Glasgow, though strikingly original, could nevertheless have occurred in no other country but Scotland. This is a point which most of the recognized architectural critics of to-day persistently ignore when they write about Mackintosh. Laughed at by the Scottish people, he was, however, lionized by his European colleagues and exerted a wide influence on the growth of a modern idiom on the continent, particularly in Holland and Austria. He laid a new emphasis on the value of massing, texture, and spacing, and approached planning problems with a new directness, his judgment having obviously been matured against a Scottish background; while his conception of room design with delicately bizarre decoration, characterized by "square" *motifs* and attenuated forms for his numerous built-in fitments, also owed something to a study of past methods, albeit his creations took forms very different from those to which his clients were accustomed. His main value, however, is that, though breaking through the old conservatism, he made his loving interpretation of the Scottish tradition the bridge to a modern idiom and a freer approach to the architectural problems of to-day. The general standard of taste in architecture in Scotland—if one may judge from the average housing that has been built in recent years —is still suffering from the overwhelming and debasing effects of the industrial revolution, and it is too soon to assess the influence which Mackintosh's genius may yet have on the architecture of his own country. It can be said, however, that some of the present generation of Scottish architects, on whose shoulders rests a great responsibility, undoubtedly have a sound appreciation both of their own national background and of the technical problems in front of them. In that at least there is hope of a sounder foundation for the Scottish Architecture of the future.

THE ARTS

Painting

THE arts which belong properly to the field of archæology pass imperceptibly into art which is normally included under the general term "works of art." There is, indeed, a broad overlap, and in Scotland it occurred at a comparatively late date. Examples of art from pre-historic times will be found in the National Museum of Antiquities in Edinburgh, enough to show that Scotland did not in any way lag behind the cultural developments of corresponding ages elsewhere in either stone or bronze. In the Roman period Scotland lived its own life beyond the Wall, but Roman culture left its mark to the limits of its penetration and in regions surrounding occupied centres. The Celtic period is represented by a fine collection of sculptured stones and, to a lesser extent, by examples of metal work. The period of overlap when the graphic arts make their first appearance, and when arts of a similar kind were applied to many decorative purposes, is illustrated in examples of craft in a wide range of materials. No doubt our heritage would have been richer had Scotland escaped the many invasions and wars that swept over the southern and more prosperous counties. The peaceful arts had little opportunity of developing under such conditions, and the preservation of anything precious in itself was rendered almost impossible. There are records of artists being employed in the service of the early Stuart kings from 1397 when Robert II commissioned one "Andro the painter" to decorate the tomb of his parents, and there are innumerable references in the royal accounts to other artists, painters, and sculptors, both natives and visiting foreigners, during the following centuries.

The earliest paintings, which contain portraits that can be identified, and which can be attributed with some certainty to a known artist, are the Trinity College altarpiece panels. These pictures are the property of H.M. the King, but are on loan to the Scottish National Gallery. They doubtless formed the wings of the altarpiece of Trinity College Chapel, Edinburgh, a building founded in 1462, which stood on the slopes of Calton Hill. The panels contain portraits of James III and his Queen, Margaret of Denmark,

Copyright, Medici Society Ltd., London

ALLAN RAMSAY : Anne, second wife of the
22nd Chief of Macleod

(Collection, Mrs. Macleod of Macleod)

SIR HENRY RAEBURN : Mrs. Scott Moncrieff
(*Scottish National Portrait Gallery*)

Copyright, Medici Society Ltd., London

HORATIO MCCULLOCH : Glencoe
(Corporation Art Gallery, Glasgow)

G. PAUL CHALMERS : The Legend

(*National Gallery of Scotland*)

ROBERT ALEXANDER : The Happy Mother
(National Gallery of Scotland)

Copyright, Medici Society Ltd., London

WILLIAM McTAGGART : The White Surf
(*Collection, J. W. Blyth, Esq.*)

S. J. PEPLOE : Mixed Flowers

(*Collection, Ion Harrison*)

W. G.
GILLIES :
Flower Piece
(*Corporation
Art Gallery,
Glasgow*)

painted about 1470 or 1480. The attribution of these pictures to Hugo van der Goes is generally accepted. During the next hundred years there is a slow trickle of portraits which can be identified, but few that can be attributed to particular artists. There is, for instance, no portrait of Mary Queen of Scots that can be claimed as having been painted in Scotland during her reign. By the time of her son, King James VI, the first native Scottish painters emerge.

George Jamesone has long been regarded as the earliest of Scottish artists. The date of his birth is not known. The first date of which we can be certain is 1612, when he was apprenticed to his uncle, John Anderson, described as a "pictor" in Edinburgh; later he is supposed to have studied in Antwerp and to have been a pupil of Rubens. The earliest portrait by him is that of Sir Paul Menzies, Provost of Aberdeen, painted on his return to his native city in 1620 and now in Marischal College, Aberdeen. He continued an active career until his death in Edinburgh in 1644. However, another artist, John Scougall, for long a shadowy figure, has now become more clearly defined. He was probably senior to Jamesone. It is known that he painted a portrait of Henry, Prince of Wales, who died in 1612, which so pleased James VI. that he presented the artist with a ring. A self-portrait of Scougall, holding the ring in his hand, now hangs in the Scottish National Gallery. Scougall must have been active between the years 1610 and 1630, but so far no general outline of his work is possible. The name Scougall continues for another hundred years. David Scougall, active in the middle of the century, was possibly a son. Another John, a good painter, known as "Old Scougall" (which has helped to confuse the record), is fixed definitely between 1645 when he was born and 1730 when he died. His son George, an inferior artist, flourished in the first half of the eighteenth century. Jamesone had pupils of whom the best was Michael Wright. Wright made his way to Italy and returned to London where he was active in competition with Lely. He painted Charles II, and a series of portraits of the judges for the Guildhall, London, and a Highland Chief in full costume, now in the Scottish National Portrait Gallery, which is one of the earliest pictures showing the kilt.

Towards the end of the seventeenth century art in Scotland had sunk to a low level. The royal court was in London, and the national pulse had a very slow beat. In 1688 John de Medina, an artist of Flemish-Spanish extraction, was persuaded to settle in Scotland, and in his earlier years he produced many good, if rather heavy-handed,

portraits which had a considerable influence on later Scottish painting. Towards the end of his life he adopted a more summary
technique which degenerated still further in the work of his son and
grandson, both called John Medina, whose pictures are often confused with, or attributed to, the more distinguished man. John
de Medina received a knighthood—the last to be granted in Scotland
before the Union of the Parliaments in 1707.

The country suffered from political difficulties and disturbances
until the middle of the century, but after the Jacobite risings of the
'15 and the '45 there was a rapid development in Scottish art, due
in some measure to the gradually improving financial position of the
country.

William Aikman (1682–1731), a pupil of Sir John de Medina,
was a sensitive painter and enjoyed considerable success. After
training in Rome he returned to Scotland, but later moved to London
where his friends were the painters, poets, writers, and playwrights
of the day. He preserved his Scottish connection, and many portraits in the first quarter of the eighteenth century will be found
from his brush in Scottish collections. Next in succession was
Allan Ramsay, son of the poet, born in 1713. After a brief year or
two in London he set out for Rome and returned in 1738. He was
supported by the Scottish nobility centred on the Hanoverian court,
and was appointed Painter in Ordinary to the King in 1760. That
was perhaps his tragedy. George III was so pleased with the coronation portraits of himself and Queen Charlotte that he commissioned innumerable replicas. Ramsay had to employ assistants
and had a regular factory for the production of royal portraits.
His reputation has suffered at the hands of his assistants, but in his
own work he was a charming painter, particularly in portraits of
women. He was in Horace Walpole's phrase, "formed to paint
them." His work has great elegance and refinement with pleasing
and unforced colour. He remains one of the greatest artists of the
Scottish school, reflecting as has so often happened since, a peculiar
sympathy with the art of France.

One of Ramsay's pupils, David Martin, was the link with
Raeburn, although he did no more than give the boy some pictures
to copy. Raeburn was born in 1756, apprenticed to a goldsmith
at the age of sixteen, and is reported to have started his self-training
by copying miniatures which came to his master to be framed.
He quickly passed to portraits in oil, and soon married a lady of some
little fortune in the village of Stockbridge, now part of Edinburgh,

where he had been born. He developed rapidly in proficiency and reputation. He decided to visit Rome and set out for Italy. He returned in 1787 and little beyond increased confidence marks that experience. Later he paid a visit to London for a few weeks, but otherwise he was never south of the Tweed. Within a few years his position as the outstanding painter of the day was unassailed. He built a new studio in York Place, Edinburgh, in 1795, and there for the next twenty-eight years he produced the remarkable series of portraits which have preserved for us the most vivid presentation of the greatest generation Scotland has known. There are few outstanding figures of that time who were not painted by Raeburn. He was an artist of great competence with command of a technical accomplishment which ensured that his work seldom fell below a very high standard ; but he was responsive to exceptional conditions, and when placed on his mettle or challenged by a noteworthy opportunity he seldom failed to produce a masterpiece. His portrait of Sir Walter Scott, painted in 1823, and now in the Scottish National Portrait Gallery, was probably his last work.

Throughout the eighteenth century portrait painting had many exponents. Aikman, Ramsay, and Raeburn are the outstanding figures, but many artists, of whom we know all too little, added their quota to the work produced. Few of these have a reputation beyond Scotland. Native art was carried forward by a body of painters of respectable merit, building the foundations for their more brilliant brethren.

Landscape painting started in the early years of the century in the work of the house-painter James Norie, who encouraged a taste for painted panels in the rooms he was called upon to decorate. It is true that he had an ambition to be " classical," and his paintings are scattered with Roman ruins ; but there are hints of local scenes to show that he walked abroad with his eyes open. The Norie workshops were the training ground for a whole generation of artists—indeed for nearly a hundred years house-painting under the Nories was a main avenue leading to the practice of the fine arts.

In 1753 the first art school, the Foulis Academy, was opened in Glasgow, followed by the Trustees' Academy in Edinburgh in 1760. Both were modelled on the academies which had been established on the Continent and both aspired to the standards of Rome. A surprising number of young artists succeeded in visiting Italy and many spent long periods there. Alexander Runciman, who had been a Norie apprentice, went to Rome and returned to become

Master of the Trustees' Academy. He was succeeded in the Mastership by David Allan, who had been a pupil at the Foulis Academy. Allan, like other painters returning from Rome, had an ambition to paint large historical compositions, but there was no demand for such work and he interested himself in making drawings of the quaint characters who were part of the street life of Edinburgh. He also did a series of illustrations for the poet Ramsay's *Gentle Shepherd*, and many drawings of events in the town or incidents with rural settings. These may be said to have blazed the trail that Wilkie was to follow a generation later. The poems of Burns and pictures or engravings by the Dutchmen directed attention to aspects of Scottish life corresponding to the subjects made famous by the " Little Masters " of Holland, but Wilkie did more than merely translate these into a Scottish idiom. He was an artist of rare gifts, and drew upon recollections of a childhood and youth spent in a Scottish village with the manse as his background and the life of the village as his constant study. Several painters followed Wilkie, with less accomplishment, but sometimes even more direct contact with the Scottish scene. The traditon started by Raeburn of a robust portraiture was continued in the work of several able painters. He had many followers of whom Sir John Watson Gordon was the most distinguished. Andrew Geddes, who spent the greater part of his life in London, was in many ways a more sensitive artist. Both were portrait painters of real merit.

The Royal Scottish Academy was founded in 1827 and, after some initial difficulties, became the main exhibition centre and principal art society. The most noteworthy feature of the next fifty years was the gradual development of landscape painting. Alexander Nasmyth was an original member of the academy. His earlier work continued in oil the style of the topographical draughtsmen, but he acquired a more pictorial approach in his later work, and he has been called the Founder of Scottish landscape. The Rev. John Thomson of Duddingston, under the influence of Sir Walter Scott, struck a more romantic note. The works of Sam Bough, Horatio M'Culloch, Milne Donald, and Alexander Fraser show a gradual approach to a more intimate rendering of nature.

In 1852 Robert Scott Lauder was appointed to the Mastership of the Trustees' Academy, and under his inspired teaching an outstanding group of artists arose. Lauder did not impress his own personality upon his pupils, but developed the individuality of each of his students. This group included Orchardson, Pettie, Tom and

Peter Graham, MacWhirter, the Farquharsons, the Faeds, the Burrs, all of whom moved to London; and McTaggart, Hugh Cameron, and George Paul Chalmers, who stayed at home. The training these men received directed their attention to certain standards of performance and qualities of paint, which, in the new approach to Nature, developed in the landscape painter, William McTaggart, the greatest interpreter of light, air, and atmosphere, in a very personal form of impressionism, that the school has produced.

Impressionism, however, brought its own reaction and the Scott Lauder group was followed by the " Glasgow School." Many cross currents were evident in the work of the new group. The Japanese print, Whistler, Bastien-Lepage and the *plein air* movement all had an influence in shaping the course they pursued. Decoration became of importance : " values " was their key-word. The leader was W. Y. MacGregor, a painter of rare ability but sadly hampered by indifferent health, so that the leadership devolved on Sir James Guthrie, who was elected President of the Royal Scottish Academy in 1902 at the early age of forty-three. Prominent in the group were Walton, Roche, Lavery, Hornel, Henry, Paterson, and the sculptor Pittendrigh Macgillivray. Round this nucleus there revolved a larger circle including many fine painters. Their fame spread far beyond Scotland and they received wide recognition. They were bold craftsmen and used their material with freedom and vigour. The qualities which were most notable were the rich full colour and sense of pattern. These are the qualities which are perhaps most characteristic of Scottish painting as a whole, and in the work of the painters of the Glasgow School they found a new and more complete expression. The aims of these painters threw into prominence the peculiar virtues which have marked other aspects of native art in several of its applications. The Lowland tweeds with their rich textures and quality of both colour and substance are matched by the pattern and stronger colour of Highland tartans ; a certain robustness in architectural form and skill in structural engineering are other manifestations of characteristics which found a new alignment in the work of the Glasgow painters.

These artists came into prominence in the late 1880's or early '90's, and they may be said to have dominated the scene up till the war of 1914–18. Other painters outside the group carried on a more traditional art. Sir George Reid, Guthrie's predecessor in the Presidency of the Academy, was a portrait painter with great powers of characterization. He painted portraits which were excellent likenesses, and when stirred beyond his normal professional efficiency he produced a few pictures of penetrating insight. Wingate, Guthrie's successor, was a landscapist with something of McTaggart's gifts of observation but a less virile form of expression. He was the ideal sketcher from Nature, and in canvas after canvas of small size he performed miracles of delicate notation of the subtleties of atmospheric effect. Landscape painting, as a whole, proceeded along the path of a modified impressionism. Figure painters found that life in Scotland was strangely like life in France or in Holland, according to the individual inclinations of the artists to see in terms of Paris or of The Hague. A group of admirable animal painters arose, of whom Robert and Edwin Alexander, father and son, were the most notable.

The first Post-Impressionist Exhibition in London in 1911 raised the curtain on a new scene. The leader in this was S. J. Peploe. He was an artist who had already made a reputation for his paintings of still life in a very fluid medium which he had used with great distinction and a most sensitive appreciation of tone. In 1910 he went to Paris. Perhaps he already felt that he had carried his method of painting as far as was possible within the limits of the technique he had adopted. He found himself in the midst of the controversy raging in Paris and he was convinced that development, for him, lay in the region of colour. He started to acquire a new language in art, to seek for the combination of form and colour in the new relationship that Cézanne had shown to be possible. His earlier work in this manner was clearly inspired by Cézanne, but he developed in a quite personal way. In his later pictures of still life, flowers and landscape, particularly a great series painted in Iona, he found a new expression of the qualities which have already been claimed as characteristic of Scottish art—fine colour, pattern, and craftsmanship, all informed by a rare respect for the use of his medium. Other painters of this group were F. C. B. Cadell and Leslie Hunter ; both were fine colourists, more spontaneous than Peploe, but lacking the depth of his more considered appreciation.

The work of these men may be regarded as leading directly to the present position in Scotland. The release of art from the more academic standards of representation has led to a great number of experiments in methods of self-expression, and to a far wider recognition of the artist's freedom or right to express in his own way his response to the impulse which prompts him to paint. These responses are too varied and diverse to lend themselves to easy classification, but they do not differ widely from the aims of artists elsewhere in Europe who have gained the same freedom.

SCULPTURE

Sculpture has never held an important place in Scottish art. From whatever cause, the urge to give shape to thought in terms of volume and planes has offered less attraction than the possibility of using colour and pattern. It is indeed in " pattern " that sculpture has had some distinction. During the Celtic period the crosses with carved interlacing ornament, and with bosses and other methods of enriching the surface, were high developments of a very decorative art. The use of more naturalistic form begins in the animal or human figures represented on later carvings, but these are often so flat in character that they have little sculpturesque shape. Carvings in ivory or bone " in the round " are often excellent in their economic use of form.

From Gothic or Medieval times there are a few surviving fragments. The work of one or two outstanding carvers can perhaps be traced from centre to centre or abbey to abbey, as there are carvings which seem to hold individual character, but this is a speculative field. The roundels from the King's Room at Stirling Castle, dated about 1530, are fine examples of wood carving. Several pieces of good panelling have survived to find a home in the National Museums.

Sculpture, in the generally accepted sense, made a late appearance. Even the more active architectural periods of the seventeenth and eighteenth centuries produced little in ornament or enrichment. Ambitious but untutored carvers sometimes attempted more than their accustomed tombstone, but no great monument marks their sense of adventure. A few good examples of lettering and one or two family vaults with pillar or pediment or a coat-of-arms are all that can be mentioned. The nineteenth century might be described briefly as the era of the public statue and portrait bust. Enough has already been written about the humours of public monuments. The late Lord Rosebery described Edinburgh's loyal tribute to a respected monarch as " George IV going for a brisk walk with his Sceptre," and nothing could be more apt. Regarded as merely historical, the monuments have their interest. The first statues were imported : Charles II in lead sits on his horse in Roman armour in Parliament Square, Edinburgh; George III, in gladiatorial costume stands in bronze in the Old Council Chamber; Lord Forbes in marble, a fine example of Roubiliac's work, sits in Parliament Hall.

Sir John Steell, sculptor to Queen Victoria, produced a great many statues. The figure of Sir Walter Scott, in the Edinburgh monument, is from his chisel. He modelled the Duke of Wellington and his horse outside the Register House, Edinburgh, and innumerable busts in marble and bronze. He was a straightforward representational sculptor, competent, but not deeply inspired. John Henning and Handyside Ritchie are other early names and later, Burnett, who did the fountain in Princes Street Gardens, Edinburgh. Brodie, who excelled in portraits, John Rhind, Hutchison, Lawson, Calder Marshall, Birnie Rhind, and the Stevensons were all working in Victorian times. With the rise of the Glasgow School, Pittendrigh MacGillivray emerged, an artist whose interests might have turned to either painting or sculpture, but he chose the heavier medium. MacGillivray is the most distinguished figure who has appeared. His work is marked by an instinctive classicism which sets him apart from his fellows. The sum total of his work is comparatively small. He was a deliberate worker, not easily satisfied, and never employed as fully as he should have been.

At the present day there are a number of carvers and a greater number of modellers. Sculpture, in the sense of architectural decoration, has virtually ceased to be used; it now flourishes mainly in the detached figure or group, often on a small scale, with an occasional portrait bust, invariably in bronze rather than in marble. In Scotland sculpture has a lingering regard for realism, sometimes with a hint of stylism or convention within the character of the medium, but, so far, the more rarefied abstractions have not found a foothold.

THE CRAFTS

Examples of the earlier crafts, and their continuation down till about the end of the seventeenth century, will be found in the Museum of Antiquities. Examples of later or contemporary crafts must be sought elsewhere; unfortunately there is no public gallery or collection dealing with this aspect of art.

The Scottish crafts have found expression in all the arts based on wool, in weaving and embroidery; in carving and woodwork; in pottery from local clays; in wrought iron and smith's work, and to a lesser extent in the precious metals. To deal first with the metal crafts. Wrought iron was used in relation to architecture. There are examples of early screens or railings in styles which we recognize as Scottish. A few domestic staircases have survived with decorative rails of an ornate and foliated type. Wrought iron was used extensively in articles for the kitchen, and many of these have interesting or characteristic forms. When cast iron came into more general use, fire-backs with armorial bearings took distinctive forms, and later, in the eighteenth century, the brothers Adam created many designs for architectural purposes from fireplaces to decorative vases in the light and delicate style which is associated with their name. Locksmiths produced many examples of fine craftsmanship. A more characteristic phase lay in the art of armourers and gun-smiths who in the seventeenth and eighteenth centuries produced swords, pistols, dirks, and other small arms of excellent workmanship with fine decoration. In heavier armaments the " Carronade," that played such an important part in naval warfare, took its name from the Carron iron works.

The pewterers produced many distinctive vessels, including the " Tappit Hen," articles for domestic use, and communion cups or other ecclesiastical vessels of good shape and simple ornament. The silversmiths were working on similar lines, and some of the finest examples of their work are still the treasured possessions of several churches. Domestic silver was, on the whole, simple in style and depended more on good proportion and elegance of form than on ornament or elaboration of shape. It attained a very high standard. To-day only a very few firms have their own craftsmen and these are engaged mostly in reproducing traditional designs with little that reflects contemporary standards or ideals. Goldsmithing has played a much more restricted part and has not even found a place in jewellery of a marked character. Modern jewellery in silver is limited very largely to reproductions of " Celtic " designs, and the setting of precious or semi-precious stones in a more modern style by artist craftsmen and craftswomen, who exhibit in the craft sections of a few art societies.

Pottery had very considerable developments in the eighteenth and early nineteenth centuries. A large number of firms, many of them small or " family " businesses, were established on the Clyde and on the north and south shores of the Forth. Most of these were active in the production of domestic articles, but a few produced decorative items such as figures or ornamental groups. " Portobello ware " has a well-deserved reputation. The single figures or groups were doubtless inspired by examples from Staffordshire, but the Portobello craftsmen produced figures of local interest such as Newhaven fishwives, Highlanders, and other Scottish types. The work was crude, but the colours were gay and effective, and these figures are now highly prized by collectors. The demand for such work gradually disappeared, the Scottish potteries declined in numbers, and only one or two firms survive in the mass production field. The individual craftsman in pottery is now represented by a few art school trained potters, doing good work, often in local clays, and exhibiting in the craft sections of the art societies.

Glass also had its craftsmen. Edinburgh became a centre for cut crystal, and one firm still continues to produce work of traditional style. A few artists have been engaged in glass engraving, and more recent developments suggest that glass design may take a much more important place than it has done hitherto. About a hundred years ago there was a revival of interest in stained glass. A few artists produced windows of some merit, but unfortunately limited by the taste of the period and influenced by the painted glass of Germany. More recently, largely under the inspiration of the architect, the late Sir Robert Lorimer, and the work of Dr. Douglas Strachan, stained glass developed a new importance. Several artists settled in Edinburgh or received their training at the Edinburgh College of Art, and Edinburgh became a recognized centre where work was carried out which found its setting all over this country and abroad. Dr. Strachan designed the windows which were Britain's contribution to the Palace of International Justice at The Hague. Sir Robert Lorimer was deeply interested in all the crafts and gathered round him a group of artists who carried out excellent work, as may be seen in the Thistle Chapel at St. Giles' Cathedral and the National War Memorial at Edinburgh Castle. The tradition lingers, but few opportunities arise for these craftsmen and they are already scattered.

Woodwork is now represented by the large furniture industry centred mainly in north Ayrshire. Craftsmen are mostly absorbed into industry and only a very few retain an independent position. A few smaller firms of high standing produce furniture of excellent quality, but modern methods of mechanical production leave little opportunity for the long apprenticeship necessary for the training of fine craftsmen in wood.

Printing is another industry in which the work of the individual craftsman tends to disappear in the ever-increasing mechanization of the craft. Scottish printing, both in the sense of setting and layout, and in the actual production of the impression, has maintained high standards with a conservative regard for tradition. Design for the industry, either for illustration and decoration or in the broader field of commercial art, has been less highly developed than it might have been.

Wool has played a very important part in Scottish life. In all forms of weaving and knitting it is the medium for not only handcrafts but also for major industries developed from these crafts. Scottish tweed derives its special quality from the method of preparing the yarn or thread. The wool is " carded " or " teased " into a ruffled mixture within the thickness of the thread, whereas in the English " worsted " the wool is combed so that its strands lie along the length of the thread. This carding of the wool gives to tweed its characteristic texture. Added to this there are traditional weaves and patterns which are the product of a long-established technique. The wool is frequently used in its natural colours— white, brown, and black, or in mixtures of these and, until recent years, with a limited range of dyes from natural rather than synthetic sources. The industrial production of tweed is centred largely in the Borders, but weaving is being revived in other districts where it had all but disappeared. In the Hebrides and Western Highlands hand-weaving is carried on, and the excellent products of this home craft can be seen at the headquarters of the Highland Home Industries in Edinburgh and at other centres.

Knitting, as a craft, is the basis of the great Scottish Woollen Industry with products, covering a very wide range, based on a knitting as distinct from a weaving technique. Among the handcrafts the beautiful lace-like Shetland knitting, which is dependent on the peculiarly fine texture of Shetland wool, and the polychromatic patterns of Fair Isle knitting may be mentioned. On a more utilitarian plane, the knitting of socks and other garments, soberly domestic or gay and frivolous, is perhaps the most actively pursued of surviving crafts.

In the early eighteenth century linen manufacture was one of Scotland's most important industries. A few crafts based on linen weaving and various forms of lacemaking, embroidery, drawnthread work, and crafts based on the fine linen and cotton thread that was produced at the same time were carried on. The linen industry is now relatively of less importance and crafts based on it have almost completely disappeared, such as the beautiful Ayrshire embroidery. The manufacture of thread continues, but the crafts of crochet, tatting, netting, and other forms of " fancy work " using that thread passed out of fashion with the last generation. On the industrial plane the manufacture of lace curtains and various kinds of net is a reminder of earlier crafts. Of other forms of special weaving, the making of tartan calls for high skill in the craftsman. Another art that has disappeared, the weaving of Paisley shawls, recalls memories of a century ago.

Scotland has never had a highly developed peasant art. The use of local materials to meet simple needs by the exercise of handicrafts has seldom found the added grace that would constitute an art. The outlook of the average Scot is severely practical, but in his own practical way he has found beauty in practical things. If he makes a shepherd's crook from a ram's horn it can be a serviceable crook and at the same time a thing of elegant shape. He applies the same art to an Atlantic liner or a concrete dam ; and when he looks at his work on that scale he may, with some justification, set his bonnet at a more jaunty angle.

CONTEMPORARY ART

CONTEMPORARY painters in Scotland, as in most countries, range from those who elect to follow in the tradition of their immediate predecessors to those who seek after new forms or press forward into regions of fresh experience.

There are artists who work in Scotland and are little known beyond the borders ; others who have ventured afar and have made reputations in a wider field. In etching, Sir D. Y. Cameron (died 1945), Sir Muirhead Bone, and James M'Bey are known internationally. Russell Flint, as a popular member of the Royal Academy, is widely recognized especially for his brilliant water colours. David Alison and H. J. Gunn, both portrait painters, are centred on London. Colquhoun and MacBryde are among the " moderns," and Duncan Grant, an artist of Highland descent, is one of the leaders of contemporary English painting.

These artists have perhaps adopted or accepted more cosmopolitan standards, but many painters working in Scotland to-day within the tradition, or influenced, consciously or unconsciously, by the qualities which have been claimed as characteristic of the school, are less well known than they should be. Scottish painting escapes in large measure the ephemeral excitements of vogue or fashion and proceeds calmly on a high plane and with considerable accomplishment.

The two main exhibitions, the Royal Scottish Academy, in Edinburgh during the summer months, and the Royal Institute of Fine Arts, in Glasgow in the late autumn, lead to an arbitrary subdivision of the artists into East Coast and West Coast ; but the work of most of the outstanding painters is to be found in both exhibitions irrespective of their immediate domicile or professed loyalties to one or the other centre. In Edinburgh in the autumn, the Society of Scottish Artists is the popular venue for the younger and more adventurous spirits. The Royal Scottish Society of Painters in Water Colours exhibits in both Edinburgh and Glasgow, the Scottish Society of Women Artists in Edinburgh ; and annual exhibitions are arranged by the Art Societies of Aberdeen, Dundee, and other centres.

Who then are the artists who call for special mention ? Limitations of space would demand a mere catalogue of names; selection must necessarily leave many blanks.

Of painters who find their main inspiration in landscape, and who express with individuality and affection their appreciation of the beauties of Scotland in a straightforward, technically efficient record, George Houston and Charles Oppenheimer, both members of the Royal Scottish Academy, James Wright, Robert Eadie, Douglas Macleod, and Harold Storey may be taken as representative of the West. In the East, A. R. Sturrock, Spence Smith, Mervyn Glass, J. M. Aitken, D. M. Sutherland, and Stanley Cursiter (also a portrait painter), all members of the Academy, have each their characteristic approach, based broadly on "impressionism," but each accentuating some personal preference for pattern, rhythm, or colour. W. O. Hutchison (recently Principal of the Glasgow School of Art), David Ewart, Henry Lintott, and David Foggie concentrate their interests chiefly on portraiture, as does E. S. Lumsden, who is well known also as an etcher.

Some years ago there was more than a promise that another group of young men were about to repeat the "rebellion" which, in the nineties of last century, started the "Glasgow School"—Sivell, M'Glashan, Cowie, and Crawford were the nucleus. Circumstances compelled them to devote themselves to teaching, perhaps to the restriction of more creative work, but they have exercised a very considerable influence—Sivell in Aberdeen, Cowie in Arbroath, Crawford in Glasgow. M'Glashan alone has preserved his freedom and is known especially for his portraits of children.

To-day if one seeks for the centre of artistic energy, enthusiasm, and originality in Scotland one must turn towards Edinburgh. The Society of Scottish Artists, as the forum of the younger men, has fostered a group of painters who can be mentioned here only by name—Gillies, MacTaggart, Moodie, Bruce Thomson, Maxwell, Westwater, and Wilson. All of these have responded in various ways to influences mostly French, and they have fused them—not mixed them—with a true Scottish tradition which comes through the earlier McTaggart and the notable Scottish colourists, Peploe, Cadell, and Leslie Hunter. Maclauchlan Milne, from a retreat in Arran, produces landscapes which make their bow in the direction of Cézanne. Telfer Bear in figure subjects and flower pieces remains faithful to his pictorial ideals of decorative shape and colour. Another isolated figure, rapidly emerging as a considerable personality, is William Crosbie. His versatility is remarkable, and he certainly promises to be one of the most distinguished graduates of the Glasgow School of Art.

Three women artists have been elected to the Academy : Miss Phyllis Bone—a sculptor with a flair for rendering animals—to full membership, Mrs. Josephine Miller and Mrs. Mary Armour, both painters, to Associate rank. Miss Anne Redpath, President of the Society of Women Artists, with a personal and decorative approach to still-life, Katherine Cameron, Penelope Beaton, Margaret Hislop, and Anna Dixon, are all painters more than able to maintain prominent places in the annual exhibitions. Two earlier painters associated with Glasgow, Annie French and Jessie M. King, are now all too seldom seen.

J. D. Fergusson has returned to Glasgow and has become the inspiration and mentor of a new group, advanced in thought and courageous in expression.

In the annual exhibitions sculpture takes a prominent place covering a wide range in bronze, stone, and wood. Notable among the sculptors are Proudfoot and Schotz in Glasgow, and Whalen, Jackson, Forrest, Lamb, and Lorimer in Edinburgh.

MUSIC

THERE are two distinct levels on which Scottish music may be approached. There is the folk-music level with its rich legacy of songs and fiddle and bagpipe tunes and dance music ; and there is the level on which we find Scottish composers trying in one way or another to win a place in the general body of European music in its more highly organized forms. On the first level Scotland is, by common consent, unsurpassed by any other European country. Her folk-song collections are vast and varied, deriving partly from the Highlands, where Gaelic speech and song contribute a character-istic Celtic atmosphere, and partly from the less spectacular but no less distinctive Lowlands of Scotland, where Scottish folk-lore and customs have produced a body of tunes and poetry perhaps more accessible to the visitor. At any rate, whenever an attempt has been made to bridge the gap between Scottish folk-music and music-making in Scotland in what may be called the " art " forms, it has generally been related to Scottish as distinct from Gaelic music. That is partly because the Gaelic language is quite unintelligible to the vast majority of Scotsmen, and partly because from an English point of view—and that, of course, means also the point of view of those who visit Scotland bringing with them some knowledge of the English language and traditions—there are, to put it simply, more points of contact with dialect and fiddle than there are with bagpipe and a foreign tongue.

This, however, has had its disadvantages as well as its advantages. Certain of the more obvious characteristics of Scottish music have been easily fastened on and imitated to the point of burlesque. In the latter part of the eighteenth century there was a craze in London for songs with a " Scotch snap," and they were easily manufactured by popular " pleasure-garden " composers like James Hook. Such songs as " Within a Mile o' Edinburgh Town " and " Robin Adair " may well have passed for genuine Scots melodies when they were written or adapted, but the discovery of ancient Scottish manuscript collections and the series of collected editions of Scots songs, begin-ning with Johnson's *The Scots Musical Museum* (1787–1803), with all the various editions and commentaries based on it, and coming up to our own day with the Kennedy-Fraser collection of Hebridean

Plate 85 Massed pipe bands of the 51st and 52nd Divisions, in Princes Street, Edinburgh

(Photo : Valentine)

Plate 86   Cinema 'still' from the film *Bonnie Prince Charlie*: the Gathering of the Clans at Glenfinnan

songs, sifted out the genuine from the false and gave composers, if they wanted it and knew how to use it, an abundant source of inspiration for creative work in more elaborate musical forms.

It may be readily admitted that few of our composers until quite recently have known how to use it. There has been endless " arranging " of the material for accompanied and unaccompanied solo and choral singing. But when it came to writing original work our composers were apt to seek their inspiration elsewhere. Even when they attempted to introduce a Scottish element into their music it seemed either so imperfectly assimilated that it stood out incongruously from the work as a whole, or was so conventionally understood that it lost any character which it might originally have had. We are perhaps rather apt to underrate nowadays the music of those who might be called " the three Macs "—Mackenzie (1847-1935), MacCunn (1868-1916), and McEwen (b. 1868)—but whatever may be the final estimate of their contribution to the store of European music, it cannot be said that they achieved any striking originality in the use of such Scottish material as they employed. They belong to a generation which accepted the German musical tradition as the basis of musical craftsmanship, and there is no indication in their work that a distinctively Scottish material might, for its appropriate higher artistic expression, require a different technique, an altogether different kind of musical thought. They had not the advantage of examples like Sibelius, Bartók, Moussorgsky, or even, in a different way, Debussy and Falla. Their northern composer was Grieg, their Russian Tchaikovsky, their Frenchman Saint-Saëns, and their Hungarian probably Joachim and the Brahms of the Hungarian Dances. What is more, they had no magnificent heritage of secular and church music such as Elizabethan England could provide—a heritage which, coupled with an unerring instinct for the proper use of folk-song material, was to result in the unrivalled work of Vaughan Williams.

There was, however, a comparatively simple and straightforward church music tradition of congregational singing, which, given the opportunity, might have led to something. And it is characteristic of Scottish music of a later day than the three Macs that this too has found, and is still finding, ways to influence healthily what we may, I think, make bold to call a national school of composition.

Among names that must be mentioned in this connection are David Stephen (1869-1946); his pupil Ian Whyte, born in 1903, who, in addition to his work as a composer, exerts a healthy influence as conductor of the B.B.C. Scottish Orchestra; Erik Chisholm (1904), who, however, recently left us to work in South Africa; Francis George Scott (1880), distinguished chiefly as a song-writer, and Cedric Thorpe Davie (1913), Lecturer in Music at St. Andrews.

But if Scotland can as yet claim no composers of world renown, she has contrived in one way or another to extend hospitality to composers of other countries. If we glance back at the musical life of Edinburgh in the eighteenth century, we find the amateurs of the Musical Society strongly predisposed in favour of Italian musicians to give what we would now call " professional stiffening " to their concerts. Tenducci, Urbani, the Corris, the Pasquales, the Passerinis, and others all contributed something to Edinburgh's musical life. But music in those days was apt to flourish only in very select circles, and the popular organization of music and the large public concert belong of course to a day much nearer our own.

As in England, the backbone of a great deal of musical activity here has been the choral society and the church choir. The works by which Handel is best known, his oratorios, were both the result of a natural predispositon to choral singing and an incentive to the formation of bigger and better choirs. Handel has been no less popular in Scotland than in England, and it is not without signi-ficance that the parent body of the Scottish Orchestra is the Glasgow Choral and Orchestral Union. The Orpheus Choir, the best known in Scotland, is also based on Glasgow.

The Scottish Orchestra provides the main orchestral fare in Edinburgh and Glasgow during a season which runs from October to March. Since its foundation in 1891 it has played under many distinguished conductors, but none of them have been Scotsmen. It has been suggested in one well-known work of reference that the fact that the conductorship " has been consistently in the hands of English or foreign musicians points, perhaps, to the lack of higher training in music in Scotland." But the Chair of Music at the University of Edinburgh is over a hundred years old, and although in its early days it seems to have been more decorative than educational, the years during which it was occupied by Sir Donald Tovey saw a great increase in the scope of the musical training provided by the University, and the Reid Symphony Orchestra (1915–46), mostly conducted by Professor Tovey, con-tributed much that was valuable to the community.

It can hardly escape notice, however, that neither Tovey nor his two immediate predecessors had any Scottish blood in their veins, and the Chair of Music at Glasgow University, which is coupled with the Principalship of the Royal Scottish Academy of Music, seems since its foundation to have followed this precedent. Not that Scottish musicians have any cause to complain of the administrations of their adopted leaders, but when so many of our " key " posts are occupied by distinguished and obviously bene-volent musicians from the South, there is no use pretending that as a nation the Scots are musically self-sufficient.

It would ill become us, however, to build up a protective wall against external musical influences ; and that has never been our policy. Indeed, at this stage of our artistic development, probably the highest hopes for our musical future lie in more frequent and more direct contact with international art. I am reminded in this connection of some words written by the distinguished Swiss conductor, Ernest Ansermet. Discussing the music of his own country, he said, " We may talk about Swiss composers, but we may not particularize about Swiss music. . . . We are, of course, affected by our origin, but our spiritual boundary is European, and it is perhaps more necessary for us than for others that it should be so."

The International Festival of music and drama, inaugurated in Edinburgh in 1947, will become, it is hoped, an annual feature of Scotland's musical activity, and should lead to a heightening of its standards, a further enrichment of its heritage, and a greater opportunity for the development of whatever native genius it possesses.

DRAMA

It may surprise visitors from other countries to find that Scotland has comparatively little to show in the field of drama—Scotland whose history is so intensely dramatic, full of episodes like the tragic story of Mary Stewart, Queen of Scots, of the Scottish Covenanters, of the Jacobite Rising under Prince Charles Edward in 1745. The Scottish Ballads, too, are starkly dramatic. Yet in play-writing and theatre-craft her flowering has come very late.

If you ask the reason you will be told that the Reformation killed the drama in Scotland, and even those who most admire the work of the religious reformers of the sixteenth century must admit it is true. In pre-Reformation days the Church encouraged and used drama "to point a moral and adorn a tale." Sir David Lyndesay, teacher and counsellor to King James V of Scotland, wrote, in the sixteenth century, his *Satire of the Thrie Estates*, which certainly pointed a moral in dramatic form, commenting with ribald humour on the evils of the day, especially of the evils within the Church itself. But after Lyndesay's *Satire* there is a long gap until late in the eighteenth century. John Knox and the Presbyterian Church courts frowned on dramatic enterprise. The theatre was regarded as a gateway to hell. When John Home, a Scottish clergyman, wrote his *Douglas Tragedy*, and had it presented in Edinburgh in 1756, the pious were much scandalized, although it was a solemn enough affair, by modern standards, in heavy blank verse. The prejudice continued strongly during Victorian days. People scarcely middle-aged to-day remember how in their youth even the Christmas pantomime was frowned upon, and to go to the " Circus " and see performing animals and acrobats was the only dissipation permitted. If a dramatic performance is given in a country place, the village folk even now are much more likely to refer to it as " the concert " or " entertainment," avoiding that doubtful term, " play."

But the dramatic instinct and the creative imagination were there. Sir James M. Barrie, Scotland's first prominent modern dramatist, set them free at last at the beginning of this century. He came to write for the theatre from writing stories and novels about one of the strictest and narrowest religious sects in Scotland, the " Auld Lichts," in whose doctrines he was brought up in his native village. His early tales of Scottish ministers and farmers and weavers seem far removed from the magic he made later for countless theatre-goers in *Dear Brutus, Mary Rose*, and above all, *Peter Pan*. But the flair for the theatre he possessed could not be ignored, the light in him could not be hidden, and perhaps he is typical of the Scot, naturally inclined to the dramatic but long suppressed.

But it was really after the first world war that drama in Scotland had its true renaissance. The Little Theatre movement had its pioneers in such a group as the Scottish National Players in Glasgow which began on an amateur basis. They produced Scottish plays by new Scottish playwrights—John Brandane, John Ferguson, Hal D. Stewart and others, and especially by a Glasgow doctor, O. H. Mavor, who took as his pseudonym James Bridie. Bridie has become Scotland's major dramatist. But in spite of the native pioneers, it was not until his work became known in London that his own country fully appreciated his quality. Bridie's charm, less sugary than Barrie's, and his entirely individual humour are abundantly evidenced in his earlier plays—*The Anatomist*, based on the story of the Burke and Hare murders in Edinburgh to procure corpses for experiment, *Tobias and the Angel* where, as in a later play, he has taken his plot from the Apocrypha, *The Sunlight Sonata, The Sleeping Clergyman*, and many more. Of his recent successes, *Mr. Bolfry* presents an attempt to raise the devil. *It All Depends What You Mean* makes riotous fun out of the Brains Trust form of popular education and entertainment, and *The Forrigan Reel* adopts an almost surrealist technique in a Scottish idiom.

But to go back to the early twenties of this century. It was then that an enterprising little travelling theatre run by the Arts League of Service, whose aim was to bring the arts into everyday life, literally blazed the trail of the drama all over Scotland. With a very simple fit-up stage and curtains and a company of about six or seven they presented one-act dramas, tragedies and comedies, mimed ballads and songs, and ballet items in small towns and lonely villages which had never seen anything of the kind before, and where the theatre had been regarded with even deeper suspicion than in the cities. The drama became the fashion with the Women's Rural Institute and with young people's church clubs as well as in industrial areas. People began to want to make their own plays and take part in the many activities of this community art—scene-painting, costume-making, and so on.

The Scottish Community Drama Association arose, working on the same lines as the British Drama League. It held local festivals in which companies competed in one-act plays marked and placed by an experienced adjudicator, with semi-finals and finals in the large towns. The movement boomed throughout the twenties and continued during the difficult years of the thirties when groups of unemployed people often found community dramatic effort a means of escape from despair and, more, a way of education and mental development.

The verse-play also became a feature of this amateur movement. John Masefield, the poet laureate, had given a lead to the experiment, holding festivals in his private theatre at Oxford. Gordon Bottomley, the poet, wrote several plays based on old Scottish stories in a verse which had a new freedom and flexibility, using verse-choirs in something of the style of the old Greek chorus to support and explain the action of the play. Realistic plays of the coalminer's life by Joe Corrie, and Andrew P. Wilson's comedies of Scottish life were among others favoured by the amateurs.

The professional repertory flourished in the twenties, notably in the hands of the Masque Theatre group, playing at the Lyceum Theatre, Edinburgh. These brilliant players gave Scottish audiences work of an international scope—Strindberg, Tchekov, Ibsen as well as Oscar Wilde and Barrie. They had the courage to experiment, and they set a standard which has never been excelled. Other repertory companies followed them, and to-day Wilson Barrett keeps up the tradition at the Lyceum with a very catholic selection of plays including from time to time the work of new Scottish writers. Meanwhile professional repertories sprang up in smaller towns. The Perth group, before the war, under David Steuart, were drawing audiences from all over the country as to a festival to see a new Bridie performance. They still flourish, and recently put on for the first time a striking new play by Moray McLaren, well-known Scottish man of letters, on the theme of Hamlet returning to the modern world to find himself as a human being, not merely a character in Shakespeare's brain. The Dundee Repertory Company, under A. R. Whatmore, has also built up a reputation for excellent work.

Glasgow, to-day as always, is keenly alive to the arts. There the Citizens' Theatre group has been formed, supported and encouraged by James Bridie, and aims at the highest achievement of repertory—the classics of all nations as well as new and genuinely experimental work. Glasgow also provides a theatre in miniature at the Park, Charing Cross, built by private enterprise in an ordinary dwelling-house of the spacious Victorian type, and seating only about a hundred and twenty, but presenting to audiences on a club-membership basis, plays of merit and unusual interest of a professional standard.

Here must be mentioned the valuable work, during the war years, of the Council for the Encouragement of Music and the Arts, known more briefly as CEMA, and now re-styled the Arts Council. It was thanks to CEMA that the Citizens' Theatre was enabled to make a start under war conditions, and other cultural efforts also have been sponsored in the same way.

Broadcasting too has played its part in shaping the dramatic movement in Scotland. It has produced new work by Scottish playwrights as well as giving Barrie, Bridie and the better-known native dramatists to the public. Memorable broadcasts during the war years included dramatic dialogues, featuring the Immortals from Abraham Lincoln to Rabelais in conversation among the Elysian Fields, by Eric Linklater, the distinguished Scottish novelist, author of *Juan in America*. Linklater's stage play, *Crisis in Heaven*, was in the same genre as the dialogues. The technique of the studio show may be rather different, with requirements of its own, but there has been, and is, a close link between Scottish broadcasting and the various local repertories and more experienced amateur groups.

In the field of lighter entertainment the Scottish comedians— " the comics "—have a large place. It was Harry Lauder, of course, who may be said to have founded the tradition of the Scottish comedian. Lauder came of mining folk but he had the gift of a fine voice and native humour. To-day his lilting songs, his kilt, and crooked walking-stick are famous, and he himself still lives—and sometimes sings—at a good old age, in the west of Scotland. Following him came the inimitable Tommy Lorne, who died comparatively young and who had a genius for comic mime. To-day Dave Willis inherits that gift of mime, purely ridiculous ; Harry Gordon brings a tang of north-eastern humour in character-studies from Aberdeen, and Will Fyffe has established his benign personality with film audiences as well as theatre-goers.

The visitor to Scotland may find these " comics " and other younger artists in their tradition giving " summer shows " in Glasgow or Edinburgh, or perhaps in pantomime if he happens to pay his visit during the winter. He will find, probably, excellent touring companies from the south in the commercial theatres of our cities. He may see the try-out of a new play by a leading London dramatist like Emlyn Williams, or a piece of international distinction like Thornton Wilder's *Skin of Our Teeth*. But he should not miss the work of the repertories at Perth, Dundee, and Glasgow. Incidentally, if he is a ballet fan, he will be lucky if his visit coincides with a performance of the Edinburgh Ballet Club, a group of young dancers of professional standard and great enterprise and originality.

The visitor may be surprised to find no repertory of the more daring and purely experimental kind in Edinburgh, Scotland's capital, which has always prided herself on her reputation as a centre of culture. If, however, he ventures to the Little Theatre, Pleasance, he may find one of the more advanced amateur groups putting on a less usual type of play with considerable merit. He may, if the weather is kind, enjoy a performance of Shakespeare at the town's open-air theatre at Braidburn.

He may be interested to note, too, the Gateway Theatre on the main thoroughfare to the port of Leith, a building reclaimed by the Church of Scotland, where not only films but plays, sometimes, but not always, religious in character, are produced largely with the hope of educating a young audience in what is best in drama.

The wheel, it would seem, has come full circle. At long last, the Presbyterian Church of Scotland has come to realize what the pre-Reformation Church accepted—that in drama, the poet and the artist speak to a community, not merely purging the soul by pity and terror, nor educating an audience by holding the mirror up to Nature, but also healing the strained nerves of these difficult times by beauty and by laughter.

THE CINEMA

" If films were steam-driven I am sure we should be making very good ones in Scotland by now," said a Scottish writer some years ago when discussing the prospects for a Scottish film industry. His point was that films seemed frippery things in comparison with great bridges and giant liners, and those other massive projects which by tradition have engaged the creative efforts of the Scots. Perhaps there is something in the argument that film-making is to be classed among those light industries which have so long been neglected in Scotland.

At any rate, it is significant that Scotland's greatest contribution to the cinema has been made, not in the featherweight spheres of fiction or fantasy, but in the development of a film style based solidly on facts. John Grierson's name is now inseparably linked in cinema history with the documentary film—what he has called " the creative treatment of actuality." It was this Scotsman who, in *Drifters*, his story of the herring fleets, first went to everyday life for a film theme, and by discarding studio trappings and insisting on reality, set a style and a standard which have come to be recognized as the distinguishing characteristics of the British film.

It was Grierson's influence as the leader of the documentary movement which both stimulated the interest of other young Scotsmen in the film medium, and also turned as many documentary occasions as possible to Scotland's advantage. *Night Mail*, on the northward journey of the travelling post office, and *North Sea*, on the drama behind the ship-to-shore radio service, were notable among the films located in Scotland. They were also milestones in the evolution of the documentary film, and, with *Drifters*, served to underline the movement's close link with Scotland.

This association was carried a stage further when, in the year of the Empire Exhibition (1938), the first deliberate attempt was made in Scotland to use the film as a medium of national projection. There was acute dissatisfaction with the screen picture of Scotland as drawn by alien hands ; and there was also a stirring of national feeling which it was thought should find expression in terms of film. The seven films which resulted, describing in graphic summary the country's character and traditions, its planning for industrial development, its agriculture, education, and sport, told the story of Scotland in vivid and authentic terms. " These films of Scotland, so imaginatively planned and so artistically made," wrote one observer, " set up a model for other nations to follow, in that they show Scotland as it really is."

Scotland as it really is . . . we have seen so much that is false on the screen that the real thing has a startling novelty. The studio film-makers have thought of Scotland in terms of Rob Roy and Mary Stewart and Annie Laurie ; of the Bonnie Banks of Loch Lomond, the Massacre of Glencoe, and Over the Sea to Skye. The Scot has appeared in the likeness of either an " Auld Licht " elder of the Kirk or a students' Charities Day Highlander. History, habits, and clothes have been repeatedly travestied in films which, made four hundred or six thousand miles away, showed little difference. Perhaps the blame does not lie entirely with the film-makers : the kilties and the comics of the music hall have something to answer for. But we have grown weary of the exploitation of Scotland as a comic strip.

John Grierson put the point well when he wrote : " The synthetic picture of kilties and comics hurts when a nation remembers that it has been in its time both Robinson Crusoe and Paul Jones, conquered large slabs of Russia for the Czars, been so eager to fight out the fate of Canada that it provided warriors for both armies at Quebec, emancipated a couple of South American countries, developed steam and steam-hammers and bridge-building and shipbuilding and Macadam road-building and modern surgery, founded logarithms and the Bank of England, and travelled first down the big rivers of Africa, and across Canada and Australia, and, as the map will testify, many other places as well."

To tell that story would mean a five-year plan for a major film industry, and Scotland does not have a major film industry as yet. It does have a group of half a dozen units which are steadily expanding and developing, and hold the promise of national film production on the modest model of Sweden or Switzerland ; and Scotland does have a constant flow of documentaries describing the country's achievement and dramatizing its problems. Early in the war the Scottish Office adopted a positive policy in the use of films. There were films of production in the fields and factories, of health plans for the Highlands, and new types of schools in the Lowlands, of experiments in preventive medicine, and of enlightened methods with young delinquents. Later there were films of the forward-looking projects—the hydro-electric scheme, the new mines with their modern techniques, research in agriculture and fishing.

Wherever the skill exists these films are being made by the Scottish units. But the English film-makers who will come to Scotland and keep the Scottish touch are also being encouraged. Notable among them is Michael Powell, whose film on Foula, *The Edge of the World*, combined the qualities of a studio story and a natural setting, and who returned to strike an authentic note in another Scottish film, *I Know Where I'm Going*. Neil Gunn collaborated in the production of a film version of his novel, *The Silver Darlings*—the story of the crofters who lost their land but conquered the sea. Sir Alexander Korda, who made that pleasant Scots fantasy, *The Ghost Goes West*, returned to film the story of Bonnie Prince Charlie. And there seems every promise that the version of Margaret Irwin's *The Gay Galliard* will eliminate the dark memory of Katherine Hepburn's *Mary of Scotland*.

Scotland's support for the documentary is only one evidence of the country's interest in the service the film may render in providing for moods of resolution as well as of relaxation. The oldest and largest of Britain's film societies are in Scotland. The earliest experiments in relating the cinema to the school curriculum were made by Scottish teachers. Early in the war mobile cinemas were organized to give shows for evacuated children—the genesis of the Ministry of Information's country-wide network. The latest example of this social use of film is the scheme for mobile cinemas in the Highlands and Islands which will add a welcome amenity to life in remote areas.

Scotland does not have vast studios and mammoth productions ; but its record in film achievement is not negligible, and may indeed outlive the transient triumphs of the commercial movie-makers.

LIBRARIES

THE larger libraries in Scotland are south and east of the Highland line, in Edinburgh, Glasgow, Dundee, St. Andrews, and Aberdeen. In the rural areas every county education committee, with one exception, administers a library system which covers also the lesser burghs without, and some with, libraries of their own. The county systems vary in size with the population. At one end of the scale is Lanark county with a stock of 170,000 volumes or more, in six full-time branch libraries, one part-time branch, and over 200 centres, from which a circulation of one and a quarter millions a year is recorded, while at the other end is Bute with fewer than 3,500 volumes and a circulation of 8,300 a year. In support of all popular libraries, whether in counties or burghs, is the Scottish Central Library for Students at Dunfermline. This clearing-house, which is financed by the Carnegie United Kingdom Trustees, works in liaison with the special and the bigger general libraries in Scotland and in England, including its counterpart, the National Central Library in London, and from them it borrows, for readers applying through their local libraries, any books not in its own stock of about 20,000 volumes. The Union Catalogue of books in Scottish libraries has been in compilation for some time. But the general reader in want of something to read has few opportunities, outside the cities and the larger burghs, of choosing books from standing stocks. Even so his state will be no worse, and perhaps rather better, than if he were sojourning in parts equally thinly populated in any other country.

In burghs with their own library services readers can inspect book-stocks of a quality normally varying with the size of the burgh. Only the city and university libraries have large stocks. Perth has a Public Library of 47,000 volumes, 15,000 of them being for reference. Aberdeen municipality, in a central and six branches, provides 174,000 volumes, 61,000 of which, as in all British town reference libraries, may be freely consulted. For books and other material about the North, and Aberdeenshire in particular, the best collections (outside the National Library in Edinburgh) will be found in the Aberdeen Public Library or the University Library of that city. Founded in 1494, the University Library now stores over a quarter of a million volumes, among them the indispensable books on Scotland, the Celts, the Jacobites, and psalmody.

At St. Andrews the University Library (1456) houses about 300,000 volumes, including valuable collections of or on : Bibles ; MSS., including Eastern ; early printed books ; George Buchanan ; St. Andrews ; mathematics—the McKay library ; Norway—the Beveridge library ; and the Sir James Donaldson, R. D. Mackenzie, Crombie and Baron von Hügel libraries. St. Andrews is also the home of the extensive and valuable Hay Fleming library of Scottish history.

Dundee City owns nearly 270,000 volumes in a central and several well-placed branch libraries ; 55,000 are in the central reference library, which contains much of value on Dundee and the neighbourhood, and on Scots music. University College Library has 40,000 volumes.

Glasgow is well supplied with general and special libraries belonging to the city, the university, or societies ; while it supports good bookshops and subscription libraries. The University, besides its great general library (1475), has a number of special collections, among them : the Euing—Bibles, and fifteenth-century books, black-letter ballads, and other specimens of early presses ; the Simson—older mathematical books ; the Hamilton and Veitch—mainly ancient and medieval philosophy ; the Arnott—botany ; the Ferguson—alchemy and chemistry ; and the Hunterian—early printed books and MSS., many very fine. There are also valuable libraries belonging to the Church of Scotland, the Physicians and Surgeons, the Faculty of Procurators, the Technical College, and the Royal Philosophical Society. The city's libraries offer a great service. More than a score of district lending libraries containing over half a million books are backed by two branch reference libraries—one at Govan and the other at Stirling's Library—by the Commercial Library, also at Stirling's, and above all, by the Mitchell, a 400,000-volume reference library known all over the world to Scottish readers and students. Special collections in it worth noting are : Celtic civilization ; genealogy ; Burnsiana ; music ; the Moir—rare and valuable ; the Jeffrey—natural history (especially ornithology), archæology, and art ; the Dyer—the Far East ; the Gourlay—architecture ; the Munro—archæology ; and the Andrew Bain—Glasgow books, Burnsiana, and other rarities. Naturally this library is rich in Scottish lore. Issuing over one and a quarter million books a year, it is the busiest reference library in these islands, apart from the British Museum.

Of Edinburgh as an educational centre it has been said that a young man may train himself there for any occupation anywhere in the world. Citizen for citizen, Edinburgh is hardly second to London in the services its bookshops offer. The wars have retarded progress at the greater libraries, for they still lack enough accommodation of a modern type. When the new National Library is completed, and the Central Public Library is extended as proposed, the main hindrances to development will have been removed. The libraries of the municipality comprise this Central building, sixteen branches, and a number of travelling collections at schools, social service centres, and business houses. Nearly 150,000 of the half a million books in stock are for reference. At the Central there are four special collections, unique in these islands because organized for home reading as well as for reference : that on art is the best outside London ; that on Edinburgh is incomparable ; that on music is surpassed only by the Henry Watson Music Library at Manchester ; and that on economics and commerce is good and extensive. The main reference department is general, but the divisions for Scottish affairs and for English literature will rarely be found wanting by serious students ; for manuscripts recourse must be had to the National. The lending libraries also are general (430,000 volumes), of a high standard in most classes of books, including fiction, which however is not their strong suit ; and they contain perhaps the largest number (24,000) of the best books on Scottish history, literature, topography, and affairs to be found anywhere for *home* use.

Space is lacking to name all the society and special libraries in Edinburgh. The chief are : the Signet (over 150,000 volumes)—law and (abundantly) general ; the Advocates'—law ; the S.S.C.—law and general ; the Royal Society (50,000)—science ; the New College (100,000)—theology ; and the Royal College of Physicians (100,000). Smaller but considerable collections of (for the most part) indispensable books belong to the Royal Medical Society, the Royal Scottish Geographical Society, the Royal Scottish Museum, and the Society of Antiquaries.

The University Library of Edinburgh (1580) contains about half a million printed books and 8,000 MSS. The special collections, apart from the Faculty libraries, include : the Clement Little—theology and law ; the Drummond of Hawthornden—Elizabethan, French, Italian, Spanish literature in early editions ; the Halliwell-Phillipps—Shakespeariana, including twenty-eight of the rare quarto plays ; the Laing—MSS. and charters, mainly of Scottish interest ;

and the Royal Observatory, under the charge of the Professor of Astronomy—rare early-printed books on astronomy, mathematics, and physics.

The National Library of Scotland stands at the head and at the back of all the other libraries glanced at above. As the Advocates' Library it was founded by Sir George Mackenzie of Rosehaugh in 1682, and formally inaugurated in 1689. Since 1709 it has enjoyed the right of receiving a copy of every book published in the British Isles. In 1925 it became National. With well over a million volumes it is the largest collection in Scotland, and one of the few libraries of Alexandrian volume in Great Britain. A new building for part of the library was being erected when war came in 1939. Among the special collections may be noted : the Marquis of Astorga's—early Spanish books ; the Thorkelin—Scandinavian history and antiquities ; the Dietrich—tracts, including Luther, Melanchthon, and other reformers in original editions ; the Lauriston Castle—Scottish, furniture and general ; the Rosebery—early Scottish ; the Hugh Sharp—rare and early editions and Americana ; the Blaikie—Jacobite pamphlets ; the MacCurdy—Leonardo da Vinci ; the Methven—" Ossian " ; the Allhusen—French literature and art ; the Warden—shorthand ; the Balfour—Handel early editions, one of the finest extant ; the Glen and the Inglis—Scottish music ; and some 400 fifteenth-century books. In so brief a chapter it would be quite impossible to do more than hint at this library's treasures. The MSS. of Scott, Burns, the Carlyles, and other Scottish authors would make any library famous. The Scott and Carlyle correspondence is unequalled anywhere. About 1,800 MSS. and 900 charters are catalogued in the first volume of the *Catalogue of Manuscripts acquired since* 1925 (published 1938), and the most cursory examination of this volume indicates clearly its literary wealth. Let it suffice to say that the National Library is the main source of knowledge for the student of anything about Scotland, and Scotsmen the world over, besides being a rich library for a multitude of other subjects.

MUSEUMS

THERE are some sixty museums in Scotland, varying greatly in size and content, from the large institutions in Edinburgh and Glasgow to the smaller ones in the county towns. The following brief survey of the more important ones indicates their main characteristics.

In Edinburgh are concentrated the national institutions : the Royal Scottish Museum (Chambers Street), the National Museum of Antiquities of Scotland (Queen Street), and the Scottish National Naval and Military Museum (the Castle). The Royal Scottish Museum consists of three major sections : (a) Natural Sciences—geology, including the collections of H.M. Geological Survey, and zoology. (b) Applied Science—physics and chemistry leading to mining, metallurgy, civil and mechanical engineering, and shipping ; and (c) Art, Archæology and Ethnology, dealing with the arts and crafts of mankind from the earliest to recent times, and illustrated with stone and metal implements, glass, pottery, and porcelain, ivories, bronzes, silver, pewter, textiles, and embroideries. As well as material of great scientific interest, the collections contain items of especial appeal to the general public, such as habitat groups of birds and beasts, working models of various types of engines, outstanding examples of craftsmanship, and pieces of historic importance. The National Museum of Antiquities of Scotland houses material illustrating life in the Stone Age, Bronze Age, Iron Age, and Roman times. Of particular interest are the gold ornaments of pre-Christian times, relics from the Stone Age dwelling at Skara Brae, Orkney, from broch excavations and Viking burials, and the Roman period treasure of silver discovered on Traprain Law, East Lothian. In the collections of the later period are the crosier and bell of St. Fillan, the Guthrie bell shrine and the Monymusk reliquary, carved sculptured monuments, and many objects of historical interest, such as the personal belongings of Mary Queen of Scots, Prince Charles Edward, Robert Burns, Walter Scott, and others. The only surviving ancient Scottish harps are to be seen in this institution. The Scottish National Naval and Military Museum in Edinburgh Castle contains arms and armour, flags, paintings and documents, and numerous personal relics of famous soldiers and sailors. The series of oaken statuettes showing the details of the uniforms worn by Scottish regiments provides a striking panorama of the development

Plate 87 Chessmen carved from walrus ivory, found in an underground
chamber in the island of Lewis ; now in the National Museum of
Antiquities, Edinburgh

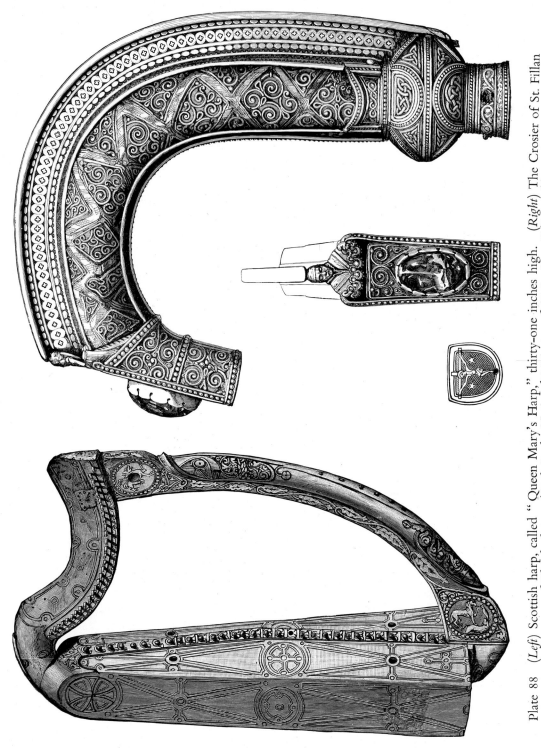

Plate 88 (*Left*) Scottish harp, called "Queen Mary's Harp," thirty-one inches high. (*Right*) The Crosier of St. Fillan

of military dress and accoutrements. The National Library, the University Library, and the Historical Department of H.M. Register House have each exhibitions of some of their treasures.

The Corporation of Edinburgh maintain three period museums, Huntly House in the Canongate, Lady Stair's House in the Lawnmarket, and Lauriston Castle to the north of the city. The collections include objects of local interest and such furnishings and fittings as might be considered appropriate to houses of that type. The birthplace of Robert Louis Stevenson, at 8 Howard Place, is administered as a museum by the Robert Louis Stevenson Club.

Glasgow presents a group of important museum, financed and organized by the Corporation of the city. They centre on the Art Galleries and Museum at Kelvingrove, and provide extensive exhibition series in geology and zoology, the latest additions comprising large habitat groups on a regional basis. In the ethnological galleries are typical examples of weapons, implements, pottery, basketry, and metal-work arranged in racial and geographical groups. Archæology is represented by reconstructed cists, stone implements, urns, etc., many of them from local sources. There is a particularly fine collection of arms and armour, together with the Burrell Collection of pottery, glass, and silverware. The Technological Section displays series of models illustrative of the development of heavy engineering, shipbuilding, and marine engines.

There are, in addition to the Kelvingrove Museum, several branches. The People's Palace, Glasgow Green, is devoted to the history of Glasgow, its development and personalities ; Camphill Museum, Queen's Park, contains objects of art and natural history specimens ; Aikenhead Museum, King's Park, is a period museum displaying furniture, dresses, and textiles ; Tollcross Museum is a children's museum, with natural history material and an aquarium. There is the Hunterian Museum of the University of Glasgow, containing collections of manuscripts, books, pictures, coins, and department of zoology ; and, finally, a period museum in Provand's Lordship, a sixteenth-century house.

The cultural centre at Perth, a composite museum and art gallery building, in part old and in part new, reflects the twofold character of the collections. The natural history material, originally accumulated for the Perthshire Natural History Society, gives a general view of the geology, botany, zoology, and archæology of the county ; the art objects represent a much wider field. The Dundee Corporation maintains two museums. One, together with the Free Library, is housed in the Albert Institute, and illustrates the part played by the town in the heyday of whaling. The natural history collections include a representative series of Arctic animals, and there are numerous relics of the whaling industry, now dead. In the Dudhope Museum, Dudhope Park, are archæological and technological exhibits.

In Aberdeen the museum facilities are provided partly by the university and partly by the corporation. The University Anthropological Museum at Marischal College contains prehistoric remains from north-east Scotland, classical, oriental, and Egyptian antiquities, and an extensive series of ethnological material from world-wide sources. The Art Gallery and Industrial Museum administered by the Town Council houses collections of porcelain, pottery, glass, enamels, and textiles, and, in addition, the nucleus of material to form a regional museum illustrating the wild life, natural resources, and history of the north-east.

Inverness possesses a municipal museum situated in the Castle Wynd. Its collections are essentially local and fall into two well-defined groups. In one room is a fine series of Highland and Jacobite relics, such as old hard tartans, weapons, and accoutrements of a varied character. A small room is equipped to represent a Highland cottage kitchen of about a hundred years ago. The third room contains mounted birds and animals of the Highlands.

Am Fasgadh (Gaelic = the Shelter), Kingussie, is a unique museum in that it represents the labours of its founder, Miss I. F. Grant, to preserve Scottish Highland material, and is the first Folk Museum in the British Isles, on the lines of the well-known open-air museums of Scandinavia. The outstanding feature of this museum is the erection, with appropriate material in the hands of experienced craftsmen, of distinctive types of old houses.

Highland exhibits and history are inevitably associated in the mind of the visitor to Scotland with Bonnie Prince Charlie, and the scenic attractions of his western wanderings can be enhanced by the interesting relics housed at the West Highland Museum, Fort William. Tartans, their vegetable dyes still bright, weapons, maps, and letters, snuff mulls and powder boxes provide a vivid picture of a not very distant past. The prehistoric remains from the crannog (fort) in Loch Treig rank high with archæologists but pale before the lure which the secret portrait of Prince Charlie exercises on most spectators.

The wild life of the Orkneys, the homely things of everyday use, and models of the local craft, so rapidly dying out, provide attractive exhibits in the museum at Stromness, Orkney, but the unique feature of the collections is the model of the wonderful prehistoric settlement at Skara Brae, supported by examples of the implements found there. There must be few visitors, with time available, who do not seek out the actual settlement without delay. Elgin, Forres, and Banff have each a local museum : the first named presents a collection of the famous sculptured Burghead bulls, and at Forres there is a good display of flint arrowheads and implements gathered from the Culbin Sands, which engulfed valuable agricultural land in historic times. The Abbot's House, Arbroath, houses exhibits from the locality, appropriate to a better understanding of the life of the period. Later times are represented by the collection in the museum at Peterhead, where models, relics, and implements deal with the home fishing industry on the one hand, and the distant whaling in the polar seas on the other. Both Stromness and Peterhead possess examples of Eskimo material brought home as trophies by the local sailors.

In the Midland Valley of Scotland there are several museums within easy reach of either Edinburgh or Glasgow. Kirkcaldy houses in a modern building its art collections and natural history material illustrative of the geology and natural history of the district. The Smith Institute at Stirling contains an extensive series of Scottish domestic and agricultural appliances, the well-known " Stirling Heads," carved oak medallions from the presence chamber in the palace of King James V at Stirling Castle, and a wide range of antiquarian exhibits. Paisley Museum, while displaying material illustrating the natural sciences and the history of the town, is naturally renowned for its collection of Paisley shawls, products of its local industry. It is to be regretted that the weaving for which the Southern Uplands belt is famous has not so far been selected as a theme for a museum. Hawick may yet add this to its exhibits of local history and natural history. At Melrose the Abbey Museum, administered by the Ministry of Works, displays in a picturesque old building the interesting objects found during excavations, and examples of architectural features such as stone carvings and floor-tile displays. There are local museums at Kirkcudbright, and Thornhill in Dumfriesshire. The Chambers Institution at Peebles is devoted to a large extent to archæology, ethnology, and natural science. The museum at Dumfries houses collections illustrative of local wild life and the history of the town. At Kilmarnock, the

Dick Institute possesses natural history and ethnological material. The museum, housed in part of the library building at Ayr, exhibits local birds and beasts, together with antiquities from the district. At Rothesay, on the island of Bute, the local natural history society has its museum devoted to natural and antiquarian objects from the island, and presents the holiday-maker with a good picture of its resources and history.

Among the historic houses, which to some extent combine the attractions of an authentic period setting with the sentimental associations of an historic figure, are the Hugh Miller cottage at Cromarty, the home of the stonemason who became a famous geologist, the Burns Cottage, Alloway, the Arched House at Ecclefechan, the birthplace of Thomas Carlyle, and the Andrew Carnegie Memorial at Dunfermline, which includes the cottage where the steel magnate and benefactor first saw the light. No list would be complete without reference to the Scottish National Memorial to David Livingstone at Blantyre, housed in a three-storied tenement, on the topmost floor of which the famous explorer and medical missionary was born. . Much of the original furniture and fittings remains, and in the adjoining room are relics of Blantyre of Livingstone's early days. The middle floor and annexe contain exhibits associated with his life and work, while the ground floor remains as the school he attended.

Several castles and mansions, open to the public, display collections of arms and armour, furniture and fittings. Of these, Dunimarle Castle, Culross (Fife) and Blair Castle, Blair Atholl (Perthshire) are typical examples. Culzean Castle (Ayrshire) has been made into a national guesthouse and showplace, the first guest being General Eisenhower. The museum portion will remain as it was when first tenanted towards the end of the eighteenth century, with period furniture designed by the famous Robert Adam, architect of the castle.

The annual report of the National Trust for Scotland for Places of Historic Interest or Natural Beauty (4 Great Stuart Street, Edinburgh) contains a list of its properties, including Culzean Castle, shown on a map of Scotland.

ART GALLERIES

THE public art collections in Scotland have a long and honourable history. They bear witness to the public-spiritedness of many distinguished citizens.

The Scottish National Gallery in Edinburgh is beautifully situated at the foot of the Mound, which stretches from Princes Street up towards the High Street and the Castle. The foundation stone of the building, designed by W. H. Playfair, was laid in 1850. The quiet dignity of the exterior is reflected in the general lay-out of the interior. In the light of modern methods of display, the double row of octagonal rooms may not appear to be eminently suitable for exhibiting notable works of art. Nevertheless, it has often been reported that a visit here is much less fatiguing and more rewarding than in the case of comparable experiences elsewhere. The National Gallery is maintained and administered by the State. Control is vested in a Board of Trustees which is also responsible for the Scottish National Portrait Gallery in Queen Street.

Of the collection itself, it is almost sufficient to say that it is comprehensive in nature, ranging from Italian and Flemish Primitives to the early nineteenth-century French, English, and Scottish schools. Outstanding works, many of them discussed and reproduced in standard works, should be noted, for example : Rembrandt's " Hendrickje Stoffels " ; Botticelli's " Portrait of a Youth " ; Vermeer's " Christ in the House of Martha and Mary " ; Tiepolo's " The Finding of Moses " ; Watteau's " Fête Champêtre " ; Boucher's " Madame de Pompadour " ; Goya's " El Medico " ; Gainsborough's " The Hon. Mrs. Graham " ; Constable's " The Vale of Dedham " ; Gauguin's " Jacob wrestling with the Angel " ; Degas's " Diego Martelli."

It is, of course, a special function of the gallery to exhibit Scottish Art, and therefore one can see the finest examples of Jamesone, Ramsay, Raeburn, Geddes, Wilkie, McTaggart, with an introduction to the " moderns " in Peploe and Hunter.

The National Portrait Gallery building (which houses also the National Museum of Antiquities) is devoted to the illustration of Scottish history—on the gallery side by the portraits of the men and women who have shaped it. Arranged chronologically, the collection features important figures and events associated with the life and times of Mary Queen of Scots, John Knox, the Jacobite adventures of the '15 and the '45, Hume, Burns, Scott, and other notable characters in the realms of law, politics, literature, and the church.

Throughout the rest of Scotland, art galleries are administered by the municipal authorities. In many of the smaller towns they are still associated with the city library or museum ; but when the collections begin to assume some degree of importance, the tendency is towards accommodating pictures, sculpture, and *objets d'art* in separate buildings with specialized direction. Glasgow is an exception, and it has been able, because of the size of the building, to devote considerable space to the very notable art collection. The Art Gallery and Museum in Kelvingrove Park was opened in 1901. It is a formidable piece of architecture in a lovely setting, with the University as a background. The city records show that the Corporation's first art purchase was made in 1618, but the present collection, generally acknowledged to be superior to all other municipal collections in the United Kingdom, actually dates from 1856, when the city acquired the M'Lellan pictures for £15,000. Subsequently through gifts, bequests, and purchases, many fine examples of all the European schools of painting have been accumulated. Among these may be mentioned, " St. Victor and Donor," attributed to the Maître de Moulins, Rembrandt's " Man in Armour" (one of seven examples by the great Dutch master), Giorgione's " The Adulteress brought before Christ," Millet's " Going to Work," Rubens' "A Wild Boar Hunt," and Whistler's "Thomas Carlyle." The Glasgow collection is especially known for the quality and variety of works by the " lesser " Dutch and Flemish masters, such as Cuyp, Teniers, Van Ostade, Bril, Van de Velde, Hobbema, and Ruisdael.

Glasgow has recently become culturally enriched to an outstanding degree by the gift of the Burrell Collection. This includes pictures, tapestries, stained glass, furniture, porcelain, sculpture, silver, etc., to an extent of approximately 5,000 items. The donors have also provided for the erection of a special building to house the collection in a suitable setting, along with adequate funds for the purchase of additional works. Special preference is to be given to the art of the Gothic period. Pending the completion of these plans selected items from the collection will be on view in the city.

The University of Glasgow has prepared plans for a new Art Gallery which will provide modern facilities to view the fine pictures at present hung in the Hunterian Museum and in other parts of the university buildings. Chief among the attractions are three excellent Chardins, some fine portraits, and a unique collection of Whistlers, in addition to the MacCallum collection of prints.

The Aberdeen Art Gallery, from modest beginnings in 1885, has become in many respects a model for civic enterprises of this nature. Placed in the heart of the city, the practice of holding temporary exhibitions at frequent intervals serves to maintain interest. The collection, built up by gifts and purchases, includes modern paintings in oil and water-colour, engravings, etchings, and lithographs, modern sculpture, and casts of Greek, Roman, and Renaissance sculpture. Contemporary Scottish and continental art is well represented. The policy, under the terms of the Macdonald bequest, of acquiring works produced within twenty-five years of the date of purchase, gives Aberdeen a unique place in municipal art galleries, in virtue of the support given to living artists.

The first museum in Perth was the outcome of a meeting held in 1784, when the Literary and Antiquarian Society was formed. The studies and discussions were to be of a general character embracing natural history and the encouragement of the fine arts. This latter object received its first impetus when the Earl of Breadalbane presented a series of valuable paintings, mostly Italian. In 1926, the Brough bequest led to the building of a new art gallery and museum, a popular centre with its permanent collection and frequent temporary exhibitions.

In Dundee, the Albert Institute combines the central library, the museum, and the art gallery. The Fine Art collection has grown beyond the capacity of the building, and the civic authorities await the appropriate opportunity for re-organization. Paintings on view show a preference for literary values and portraiture, but the corporation has shown catholicity in the selection of " visiting " exhibitions and in recent purchases.

The Kirkcaldy Art Gallery, opened in 1925, was presented to the town by John Nairn. It is admirably suited for its purpose and, thanks chiefly to the energy and generosity of private citizens, an excellent collection of pictures is being created. At present it is largely representative of Scottish Art from the latter part of last century. Orchardson, Graham, Fraser, McTaggart, Lorimer, Alexander, Wingate, Colin Hunter, are to be seen in typical works. The Glasgow School, with W. Y. M'Gregor, Melville, Paterson, Hornel, Walton, and D. Y. Cameron, and some isolated examples from the nineteenth-century Dutch, add variety to a well-arranged collection.

In Stirling, the Smith Institute Art Galleries and Museum very properly feature the work of Thomas Stuart Smith, who, in addition to his skill as a practising artist, founded the Institute and bequeathed the nucleus of the collection which has been developed along lines of special local interest.

Kilmarnock has the Dick Institute, a fine building which combines library, museum, art gallery, and lecture hall. Interest in the arts is fostered chiefly through occasional exhibitions, although a small permanent collection of paintings and prints by British and French artists is always on view.

The Museum and Art Galleries in Paisley are the outcome of the interest of the Philosophical Society (founded in 1808), but the financial needs for development in the early stages were met chiefly through the generosity of Mr. Peter Coats. Space is almost equally divided between art, history, and natural science.

In Greenock, the Art Gallery is the Lecture Hall of the M'Lean Museum, but recent bequests in pictures and funds have resulted in plans which only await favourable building conditions in order to become effective. Meanwhile the Caird Collection is on view, and additions, chiefly contemporary Scottish painting, are made from the income of a substantial trust fund.

Reviewing the art galleries in Scotland as a whole, it will be seen that the significant collections of works of art are in Edinburgh and Glasgow. In other cities and in the smaller towns, there is evidence of an increased awareness of the importance of art in the general life of the people, and this is gradually being reflected in both the quality and presentation of works on public view. In many places which have not been mentioned in this brief survey the collections are mostly related to the pictorial aspects of local history, and the visitor is not infrequently surprised and delighted by the productions of artists who may yet be acclaimed and honoured.

LIST OF CULTURAL INSTITUTIONS AND SOCIETIES

CULTURAL institutions and societies are a prominent feature of Scottish life. The following are the more important, arranged chronologically according to the date of their foundation :

THE SOCIETY OF ANTIQUARIES IN SCOTLAND was founded in 1780 for the promotion of archæology, especially as connected with the antiquities and history of Scotland. It publishes annual *Proceedings*. The Fellows (F.S.A.Scot.) number over 800. There are also Honorary Fellows, mainly foreign.

THE ROYAL SOCIETY OF EDINBURGH was founded in 1783 for the promotion of science and literature, but for many years has been wholly scientific. It publishes *Transactions* and *Proceedings*. The Fellows (F.R.S.E.) number approximately 800. There are some 70 Honorary Fellows, British and foreign.

THE ROYAL PHILOSOPHICAL SOCIETY OF GLASGOW was founded in 1802 for the advancement of the mathematical, physical, and natural sciences, and to promote the diffusion of scientific knowledge. It has a membership of 900, and publishes *Proceedings*.

THE ROYAL SCOTTISH ACADEMY of Painting, Sculpture, and Architecture was founded in 1826 to encourage the practice of the Fine Arts in Scotland. There are some 30 Academicians (R.S.A.), a similar number of Associates (A.R.S.A.), as well as Honorary Academicians (H.R.S.A.). Since 1827 it has held annual exhibitions in Edinburgh confined in principle to works of living artists. The exhibition is normally open from April to October. Others are arranged from time to time.

THE SCOTTISH TEXT SOCIETY since 1882 has issued over 100 volumes containing unpublished texts in Scots.

THE ROYAL SCOTTISH GEOGRAPHICAL SOCIETY was founded in 1884 to popularize and diffuse geographical knowledge in Scotland. It has some 100 Fellows (F.R.S.G.S.) and about 2,000 members. It has centres in Edinburgh, Glasgow, Dundee, and Aberdeen. It publishes *The Scottish Geographical Magazine*.

THE SCOTTISH HISTORY SOCIETY, founded in 1886, has issued over 120 volumes of unpublished documents illustrative of Scottish civil, religious, and social history.

AN COMUNN GAEDHEALACH (The Highland Association) was founded in 1891 to encourage the study and cultivation of Gaelic literature, history, music, art, etc. It has over 100 branches, mainly in the Highlands. It holds an annual National Mod or Gaelic Festival. *An Gaedheal* is its monthly magazine.

P.E.N. (Poets, Playwrights, Editors, Essayists, and Novelists). The Scottish Centre of the International P.E.N. Club was founded in 1927. It has 110 members and meets alternately in Edinburgh and Glasgow.

THE STAIR SOCIETY was founded in 1934 to encourage legal historical research and the study of the history of Scots Law. It issues volumes of unpublished material.

THE SALTIRE SOCIETY was founded in 1936 for the preservation, encouragement, and development of Scottish Art, Literature, and Music. It has some 2,000 members, with centres in Edinburgh, Glasgow, Aberdeen, Ayr, and Kelso. It publishes pamphlets.

In addition to these listed above, the following selection indicates their age and variety : The Royal Medical Society (1737) ; The Royal Physical Society (1771) ; The Highland and Agricultural Society (1784) ; The Royal Celtic Society (1820) ; The Royal Society of [Industrial] Arts (1821) ; The English, the Geographical and the Historical Associations ; The Edinburgh Bibliographical Society ; The Ecclesiological Society ; and the Franco-Scottish Society. The Zoological Society of Scotland maintains the Zoological Park, Edinburgh. Nearly all these societies issue publications. Some of them, the Franco-Scottish Society, for example, have centres in the chief towns. The various societies interested in French culture find a natural home in the French Institute, Edinburgh, established by the French government in 1946. Many of the towns have also local societies such as the Gaelic Society of Inverness. Most of them are listed under " Scotland " in the *Official Year Book of the Learned and Scientific Societies of Great Britain and Ireland* (last issue 1939). There is also a *Catalogue of the Publications of Scottish Historical and Kindred Clubs and Societies, 1780–1908,* by C. S. Terry, continued to 1927 by C. Matheson. A world list of Scottish Societies of all kinds is published in *The Scots Year Book.*

The Scots Ancestry Research Council (4 North St. David Street, Edinburgh 2) is a non-profit-making organization to aid Scots at home and overseas to trace their family history.

FOOD AND DRINK

FOOD

WHAT sort of food has Scotland to offer the stranger within her gates? In normal times he may be assured of some of the best food and drink to be found in any country. There are many admirable foodstuffs in Scotland, and there is also a sound culinary tradition; but, as in other countries, during the last hundred years industrialization and commercialization have played havoc with both. The high-water mark of Scottish housewifery was reached just before the dawn of the industrial era, when everything that is now supplied by the factories was made in the home, and besides cooking and baking, there were preserving and pickling, brewing, and the distilling of simple wines. But now much of the best Scottish produce goes to the London markets, and in the industrialized areas particularly, cheap imported foodstuffs have largely replaced the wholesome native fare. Traditional dishes tend to disappear, and too often the wayfarer sits down to frozen mutton followed by a " shape " and tinned fruit, or something equally unimaginative. On the other hand, in the better-run hotels and guest-houses, as well as in many Scottish homes, both high and humble, one may enjoy as appetizing a meal as anywhere in Europe. " France," writes Mr. H. V. Morton, " for the man who has to be led gently to his food, but Scotland for the man with a good healthy appetite ! "

Like all the arts, the cookery of a nation always has its roots in the soil : it draws its basic materials from the soil, and its basic methods from the people who have lived longest on the soil and who therefore know best how to use its products. What are these products, and how are they used?

What with the bounty of Nature and the skill of her farmers and stock-breeders, not only is Scotland virtually self-supporting in all essential foodstuffs, but she is able to send a considerable surplus over the Border. It is true that her soil is, on the whole, poorer than that of England, and that she enjoys less sunshine, so that neither her wheat crops nor the larger fruits ripen to the same perfection. On the other hand she grows very good barley and oats of superlative quality. Her moors and forests abound with game—the stags that roam habitually among the stony heights make incomparably the best venison, and the heather-fed red grouse, which is peculiar to Scotland and the North of England, is the most exquisitely flavoured of all feathered game. Scots mountain mutton is on a par with the Welsh, the English South Down, and the *pré-salé* of France, whilst the beef of the Aberdeen–Angus herds is unrivalled the world over. The rivers, lochs, and seas teem with salmon and trout ; the seas with white fish of unsurpassed firmness and flavour and herring that are the pick of all markets. Scotland excels, too, in tomatoes and all berry fruits, the flavour of which is greatly improved with slow ripening, whilst her heather honey is as delectable as it is abundant. Again, some of the finest varieties of potatoes in the world bear the names of Scottish cultivators ; and, finally, there is the dairy produce afforded by the famous Ayrshire, Galloway, and Dumfriesshire herds.

With such a lavishly equipped larder, how is it that Scotland does not possess a national cuisine to rival the highly sophisticated cuisines of, say, Hungary and France ? For one thing, the Scot does not take kindly to high sophistication in cookery or anything else ; and for another, his native foodstuffs do not require sophisticated treatment—rather they reject it, just as Highland homespuns reject anything but the severest tailoring. It takes a good tailor, however, to make a severely cut garment, and it takes a good cook to roast a joint or grill a steak to perfection ; but granted that one's cook is skilled in the basic culinary methods, what better can one offer a guest than a cut from a roast sirloin of prime Scots beef, with mealy potatoes, a simply cooked second vegetable, and its own delicious gravy ; or a slice of boiled salmon, again with potatoes, fresh green peas, and a little of the salmon bree for sauce ; or a roast grouse with potato chips, fried crumbs, watercress or French beans, mushrooms, and clear gravy ; or a slice from a round of salt beef or fresh gigot (leg of mutton) with dumplings and the appropriate vege-tables ?

Since his instinct dictates the simplest methods in dealing with materials of the first quality, it is not surprising that the Scots cook does not display much ingenuity in the cooking of meat. Still he (or, more generally she) produces a number of very satisfactory dishes —among them a singed sheep's head (a genuine *plat de gourmet*) ; Scots collops—a savoury dish popularly known as "mince" ; sausages as good as you will find in any country ; small mutton pies

—the most popular of Scottish snacks—which must be served piping hot ; and the immortal haggis. And no country has a greater variety of puddings and pies, creams, jellies, and trifles.

The excellence of Scottish soups has been attributed to the early and long connection between Scotland and France ; but whilst French influences may be detected in such soups as Feather Fowlie, Lorraine Soup, and possibly Friar's Chicken, it is certain that long before the days of the Auld Alliance many a savoury odour arose from the kail-pot on many a humble Scottish hearth. Among the best-known soups are Barley Broth (known to the world as Scotch Broth), which is to Scotland what the *pot-au-feu* is to France and the *minestrone* to Italy ; Powsowdie or Sheep's Head Broth ; Hotch Potch or Hairst Bree (Harvest Broth)—for it is made only when the kail-yard (kitchen garden) is in its prime—which is fragrant with the sweet juices of young growing things ; Bawd Bree (Hare Soup), nuttily flavoured with toasted oatmeal ; Cock-a-leekie (praised by Soyer) ; Cullen Skink (made with a smoked haddock), a fishwife's soup from the shores of the Moray Firth ; and Salmon Soup, which is said to be provided for good Scots in Heaven.

What is most characteristic in the Scots treatment of white fish is the use of the elements to give them *goût*. Thus (after being slightly salted) they are variously " rizzared," or sun-dried ; " blawn," or wind-dried ; rock-dried ; or, as with skate, earth-dried—that is, left on the grass for a day or two with a grassy sod reversed on them. Sometimes, again, they receive a touch of the forest, being smoked over silver birch or oak sawdust with a few juniper twigs or pine cones thrown over it. There are few more delectable breakfast dishes than a rizzared haddie (haddock), a blawn whiting, a home-cured Loch Fyne kipper, a buttercup-yellow finnan haddie (Findon Haddock—Findon being a fishing-village near Aberdeen), a pale " Moray Firth " (a lightly smoked haddock, excellent with bacon) or a copper-coloured Arbroath " smokie."

Plenty of ingenuity is shown, too, in the preparation of both oatmeal and milk. Porridge, properly made with home-milled meal and fresh spring water, and served with thin cream or rich milk, is food for the gods. There are several kinds of brose and crowdie, as well as that immemorial dish, sowans (Gaelic *sughan*), which is a sort of gruel made from the fermented " sids " or inner husks of the oats. A combination of oatmeal, suet, and onions is the basis of several nutritious and appetizing dishes, including

" skirlie " (skirl-in-the-pan), white or mealie puddings, stuffing for a boiled fowl, and, with the addition of a minced pluck, the haggis. Lastly, there is the national oatcake, which a French gastronome has described as " a masterpiece."

Some of the traditional " milkmeats " are unfortunately hardly more than names to-day. These include (apart from cheeses like Dunlop and Coll) Hattit Kit ; Corstorphine Cream and its rival, Ru'glen (Rutherglen) Ream ; Highland Crowdie (a sort of cream cheese) ; Cranachan or Cream-Crowdie ; Oon (Gaelic *Omhan*) or Frothed Whey—a Highland specialty ; and Blaand or Sparkling Whey, a popular Shetland beverage.

As a nation the Scots are definitely better bakers than cooks, the standard being very high among both amateurs and professionals. To beat the best Edinburgh bakers one must go, it is said, all the way to Vienna. There is an endless variety of bannocks, scones, and teabread, as well as of cakes and shortbreads ; and the biscuits of Scotland, like its jams and marmalades, travel to the ends of the earth.

The meals *par excellence* are breakfast and tea. (The modern tearoom originated in Glasgow.) " If an epicure could remove by a wish in search of sensual gratification," wrote Dr. Samuel Johnson, " wherever he had supped, he would breakfast in Scotland." A typical pre-War breakfast in a Scottish country house consisted of porridge and cream ; a choice of hot dishes—kippers, finnan haddies, or grilled trout ; bacon with eggs, kidneys, mushrooms and so forth ; toast, floury baps (the traditional breakfast roll), white or barley bannocks, and crisp oatcakes ; butter, honey, and marmalade ; fresh fruits in season ; and, of course, tea and coffee— a grand prelude to a long day on the hill !

DRINK

Until far into the eighteenth century French wines of excellent quality were cheap and plentiful in Scotland. The Englishman, however, preferred the wines of Portugal—a choice dictated less by his palate than by his country's foreign policy—and the United Parliament, by imposing prohibitive duties on French wines, deprived the Scot of modest means of his claret, whilst allowing the English-man to go on enjoying his port. One recalls the lines of John Home, the friend of David Hume, which Sir Walter Scott never failed to repeat on appropriate occasions :

Haughty and fierce the Caledonian stood ;
Old was his mutton and his claret good.
"Let him drink port," an English statesman cried ;
He drank the poison, and his spirit died.

Since then the manufacture of beer and whisky has greatly developed.

Although the Scots are not a nation of beer-drinkers in the sense that the English are, some of the best beers in the world are brewed in the Lowlands of Scotland—the bulk of them in Edinburgh and Alloa. " That the great English beers are supreme of their kind is indisputable," writes Donald Carswell ; " but on the other hand there is an unconscionable amount of bad beer in England. . . . The great English brewers recognize the uniform quality of Scotch beer and take their Scotch trade seriously. Hence the bottled Bass or Allsop you drink, when you can get it, in Glasgow or Edinburgh is a more heartening drink than any contained in bottles bearing the same labels in London or Manchester. How else could they compete with our M'Ewans, our Ushers, and our Youngers ? "

Glasgow manufactures a special light lager of which even foreigners, says the same authority, " speak with a reverence verging upon awe." Then there is the so-called " sweet " or " Scotch " ale —a noble liquor, but requiring to be drunk in strict moderation.

But however good Scots beer and ale, it is universally conceded that, in the words of an eighteenth-century traveller, " the glory of the country is Usky (whisky)." The word whisky comes from the Gaelic *uisge-beatha*, meaning " water of life," and, like the bread of life, it is provided by the harvest of pale gold barley. By the process of distillation the substance is converted into vapour, which, in turn, is condensed into liquid form. " The distillation of the barley brew by the Celtic peoples," writes Neil Gunn in his authoritative and fascinating *Whisky and Scotland*, " seems to have preceded by untold centuries the distilling of fermented wine by Greek and Latin." (The distilling of wine, incidentally, produces brandy.)

Until about a hundred years ago Scotch whisky had always been distilled from a brew of malted barley by a pot-still ; but with the invention of the patent still, which managed to extract alcohol much more cheaply, in much greater quantity, and from all sorts of materials, there came greatly increased commercialization and a marked deterioration in quality. Patent-still whisky is legitimately used for blending, but the best blends are pure malt. " Patent-still spirit," writes Neil Gunn, " is no more a true whisky than, at the opposite extreme, is any of those cheap juices of the grape heavily fortified by raw spirit which we import from the ends of the earth a true wine. . . . I have never yet met any blend of all malts or of malt and patent that had the individuality and distinction of a perfect sample of single whisky. . . . Perfect knowledge and appreciation," he adds, " beget natural temperance."

Plate 89   Raeburn pictures in the National Gallery of Scotland, Edinburgh

(*Photo : Harold Hood*)

Plate 90   A yacht race on the Clyde during the Clyde Fortnight

(*Photo : G. L. A. Blair*)

SPORT

A LOVE of athletic achievement is inherent in the Scottish character, as is witnessed by the many tales handed down to generations of clansmen of the might and prowess of some forebear, not necessarily in battle. From early times Scotsmen have hunted their native hills and glens and fished their lochs and burns to provide food for their families, but it was in playing games and trying feats of agility and strength that sport and recreation were found, and not until much more recent times that shooting and stalking were developed for purely sporting purposes.

This love of sport was characteristic in Highlands and Lowlands alike, and seems to have caused King James II some anxiety, for in 1457 he gave orders that football and golf, both very popular Sunday pastimes in those pre-Reformation days, " be utterly cryit downe," to be replaced by the more serious and profitable practice of archery, in which he had good reason to wish that his Scottish soldiers should excel those of the King of England.

There is much evidence, however, that the kings and queens of Scotland themselves shared their people's enthusiasm for playing games. Mary Queen of Scots was accused by her enemies of playing golf and another game, " Pall Mall," at Seton shortly after her husband's murder. A much earlier sovereign of the house of Stewart, King James I, lost his life through an ill chance arising out of a game of ball he had been playing while staying at the Black Friars Abbey at Perth. Seeking refuge in a vault under the Queen's bedroom from a band of assassins who had broken their way into his apartments, he found that his only means of escape—a narrow opening leading on to the court where he had been playing—had been built up on his instructions three days earlier to prevent the balls rolling down it. Thus trapped he had no alternative but to await a death he might well have otherwise managed to escape.

Highland Games

As might be expected, both Highlands and Lowlands have exercised an individual influence on the growth of Scottish sport, although many characteristics are common to both. The Highlander in particular prided himself on speed of foot, and races to the top of a mountain crest were popular, as was the old Highland foot race, which always included a hurdle leap. His prowess covered a wide field, and the Highland games, which include tossing the caber, putting the weight, throwing the hammer, and piping and dancing, were the natural outcome of a characteristic athleticism, and are still flourishing throughout the Highlands to-day. These games are the traditional gathering of local folk around their chieftain. Taking place frequently at some historic castle for the special enjoyment of the people of one or two neighbouring estates or parishes, the under-lying spirit is a family one.

Of the greater " gatherings " the northern meeting at Inverness, the Braemar Gathering on Deeside, and the Oban Games are the outstanding examples. Here Highlanders, chiefs and clansmen, have gathered for centuries, and are now reinforced by large numbers of sightseers who come from all over the world to see not only the sports themselves, but to witness the spirit of the gathering under-lying the whole meeting. Although one cannot help regretting that modern conditions have to some extent deprived the Highland games of the homeliness and simplicity which characterized them in the days when the contests were almost entirely of a local and parochial nature, it is indeed good that so much of the original form of these ancient sports still survives.

The Lowlander, too, has shown all-round skill in games, but he particularly prides himself on his Rugby football ; and Seven-a-Side football, a variant of the game introduced in the Borders, is regularly played.

Golf

Of all the games played in Scotland in days gone by, three stand out as claiming Scottish origin and being particularly Scottish in character—golf, curling, and shinty, and of these golf has now achieved world-wide popularity. The frequent denunciations after the Reformation of golf-playing on Sunday, sometimes ending in the prosecution of the delinquents, bear witness to the centuries old popularity it has enjoyed. The " Royal and Ancient " game has indeed earned its title, for there are many examples in history of the enjoyment it afforded the Royal House. In 1503 the Royal Accounts show an item of £2, 2s. " for the King to play at golf with the Earl of Bothwell " ; only 9s. was paid for the club and balls, so perhaps a bet made up the balance. Exactly one hundred years later James VI appointed William Mayne to be Royal clubmaker, and gave a certain James Melville a monopoly of ball making. His son, Charles I, was playing on Leith Links when he received news of the Irish rebellion, and the match was never finished in consequence.

Although the presence of ladies on the links has not always been smiled on, the Musselburgh Club, founded in 1774, appears to have set a chivalrous example by offering the prize of "a creel and shawl" to the best golfer amongst the fishwives.

The best country for golf is a large expanse of uncultivated soil not too much broken up by hills ; and in Scotland the links, particularly along the east coast, where they are most extensive, form ideal ground. Of all Scottish golfing centres, St. Andrews, with the Royal and Ancient Club in the East Neuk of Fife, is the shrine of golfing tradition and the Mecca of golf enthusiasts. On the south side of the Firth of Forth, at North Berwick, the course is a sporting one which is extremely popular, being within easy reach of Edinburgh. Six miles nearer Edinburgh, Gullane boasts two good courses, and on the west coast, in Ayrshire, Prestwick and Troon are famous.

Curling

Curling, or the "Roaring Game," is played on a sheet of ice and is known by its devotees as "Scotland's ain game." There is certainly some reason for this, as curling in Scotland has four centuries of history behind it, and has long been recognized as a national sport. In Edinburgh the magistrates used to march in procession behind a band playing the Curlers' March to open the season on the Nor' Loch, a stretch of water formerly lying at the foot of the Castle rock. Like golf, curling can claim to be both Royal and Ancient. Tradition has it that the Stuart kings were curlers, and both Mary Queen of Scots and Darnley are reputed to have played. It was in the reign of Queen Victoria that the Prince Consort gave his patronage to the Grand Club, which thereafter became the Royal Caledonian Curling Club. Like golf, it too has won popularity outside Scotland, although to a lesser extent, and there are curling clubs in England, Canada, New Zealand, Newfoundland, U.S.A., Russia, and Switzerland. The game appears to have originated in a fairly simple form as quoiting on the ice with a large round stone. Now curling stones are cut from hard rock, rounded and polished, and fitted with a wooden handle.

Bowls

Curling is somewhat akin to the game of bowls, which, although probably English in origin, maintains a long-standing popularity in

245

Scotland where a distinctive Scottish variety of the game is played, the Scottish game differing widely from that normally played south of the border. There is a Scottish Bowling Association, founded in 1891, and the Scottish game has gained a fairly far-flung popularity. In a number of places in England, as well as in Ireland, Australia, and New Zealand, greens have been made, and the game is played as in Scotland. Great care has to be taken in laying the turf of a bowling green to ensure sufficient drainage, turf taken from the seashore being much the best. For many years the Ayrshire coast was the chief source of supply, but on that becoming exhausted, excursions were made as far afield as the islands of Colonsay and Islay for the purpose. In comparatively recent years a very large number of bowling clubs have sprung up in the industrial areas of Scotland, showing that the game is in no way losing its popularity.

Shinty

Amongst games less widely popular than of old, but still played with great enthusiasm, shinty is one of the most traditional. Played with a ball made of cork and leather and a wooden club, it used to be popular amongst all ages, particularly round about the season of Christmas, but now is usually indulged in only by the more youthful members of the community. In the old days it was the custom for local parishes to engage each other in this game, and the prize, according to one tradition a keg of " genuine mountain dew," was attractive, for Highland whisky was appreciated no less then than to-day.

Shinty is a fine free game, much less restricted by rules but otherwise not unlike hockey which is derived from it. In olden times a field of shinty must have borne some resemblance to a battleground ; its usual accompaniment being skirling pipes and waving banners. To-day the pipes still play a picturesque part, marching their teams on to the field of play and hailing their victories with piercing blasts of triumph.

Youth Hostels

The story of Scotland unwinds itself largely against a backcloth of wild and beautiful scenery, for although our Lowland landscapes are richer and more gentle, in a small country the size of Scotland the hills are never far distant. This is indeed a boon to a modern Scotland, suffering all the attendant ills of a rapid growth in industrialism, and now turning more and more to the treasure house of its countryside for sport and recreation. Mountaineering, rock climbing, and rambling are essentially sports which all can take part in regardless of their means.

For some time past an ever-growing pilgrimage of modern youth has set off with rucksacks and saddle bags, and the fact that this is so is largely due to the excellent work being done by the Scottish Youth Hostels Association, the facilities which they are providing being of great value to mountaineers and ramblers alike. The first enthusiasts to set forth in search of the countryside were few in numbers. Walking or cycling, they journeyed by day and sheltered by night where they could, perhaps in some lonely barn or hut or even beneath a hedge or rock. In the 1930's there took shape in many countries the Youth Hostel Movement, and amongst the foremost in the field was Scotland. The opening took place in May 1931 of the first hostel of the Association, a row of cottages in Broadmeadows in the valley of the Yarrow Water, amid country famed in the songs and verses of Sir Walter Scott and James Hogg, the Ettrick Shepherd. By the summer of 1946 more than seventy hostels extended over the face of Scotland, placed at convenient distances for walking or cycling along many ancient routes trodden by our countrymen in days gone by. From the Heart of Midlothian the rambler can set out to the rounded hills and historic castles and abbeys of the Border country or he may leave behind him the black chimneys of the lowland cities and townships to take the Road to the Isles. If his destination is the Cuillins of Skye he may shelter in the hostel at Glen Brittle, and thence journey to the shores of Torridon, Maree, Gairloch, Inver, and Eriboll; whilst to the east of him lie the rugged recesses of the Grampian range, accessible only to those who will face its storms by routes where a man's limbs alone can take him.

By providing simple hostel accommodation for wayfarers on their travels the Scottish Youth Hostels Association fulfils its aim, which is to help all, but more especially young people of limited means, to know and enjoy the Scottish countryside. At these hostels, for a nightly small charge, sleeping accommodation and simple washing and cooking facilities may be had. Members attend to their own needs and lend a hand in the general service. Visitors can join the Association, and those seeking particulars will find them in the Handbook, price 9d. (11d. by post), obtainable from the National Office, 13 Rutland Square, Edinburgh. As might be expected, life in a hostel is coloured by the same spirit of freedom and simplicity which has set this pilgrimage of youth upon the road.

The characteristic atmosphere is one of comradeship, ignoring barriers of nationality and creed. Thus the youth of many countries may be brought together in common quest for that true recreation which is as much spiritual as physical, and which contact with Nature and the elements alone can provide.

Mountaineering

Mountaineering has not been developed as much as it might have been in Scotland, for there is much sport and recreation to be found in the Scottish hills. Weather should hardly ever be an impediment to an experienced party getting to the top of any hill in Scotland at any time of the year, there nearly always being an alternative route by which summits can be reached safely. Safety does, however, lie in the ability of a party to use competently a map and compass. The summits of most mountains in Scotland can be reached by an easy way, although there are some, particularly in the Cuillins of Skye, whose summits could not be reached by a climber keeping his hands in his pockets. Simple mountaineering, consisting in way-finding and hill walking, is possible throughout the year, and from December to April climbing up gulleys in snow, particularly on peaks above 3,000 ft., is an interesting sport. On occasion the ski-ing conditions can be very good indeed, although they can never be relied on.

There are 543 summits in Scotland above 3,000 ft., twelve of these above 4,000. There is thus plenty of scope for mountain sport in many districts.

In summer rock climbing is possible in many places, the chief centres being as follows :

CENTRE	PEAK	ROCK
Fort William	Ben Nevis	Porphyry
Glen Coe	Bidean-nam-Bian group	,,
Kingshouse	Buachaille Etive Mor	,,
Aviemore and Braemar	The Cairngorm group	Granite
Arrochar	Cobbler, Narnain, etc.	Schistose : Porphyry
Dundonnell and Loch Maree	An Teallach and Ben Eighe group	Sandstone : Quartzite
Inchnadamph and Loch-inver	Ben More Assynt, Suilven group and Ben More Coigach group	,, ,,

CENTRE	PEAK	ROCK
Isle of Skye :		
Sligachan and Glen Brittle	The Black Cuillins	Gabbro
Isle of Arran :		
Brodick and Corrie	Goat Fell group	Granite

The above centres, with the exception of Arran and the Inchnadamph group, are also suitable for snow-climbing, and the following may be added as being more accessible :

CENTRE	PEAK
Crianlarich, Tyndrum, Inveroran, and Loch Awe	Ben Lui, Ben More, Cruach Ardran, Ben Doran group, Black Mount group, and Cruachan group
Dalwhinnie and Newton-more	Ben Alder, Drumochter Hills and Monadliaths (sometimes suitable for ski-running)
Spean Bridge	The Grey Corries and Aonachs
Killin and Lawers	Tarmachans and Lawers group
Cluanie Hotel	The hills to the N. and S. of Glen Shiel

All these are within easy access of Youth Hostels.

Rock-climbing

Rock-climbing, particularly in the Cuillins, compares favourably with any in the world, and snow-climbing provides excellent and rigorous training. The study of weather is essential and the time factor a vital consideration, for weather in Scotland is more treacherous than in Switzerland or most other parts of Europe. Fog and blizzard come down with very little warning, and the climber has to be extremely competent in " way-finding," and in winter especially accurate in his timing and judgment of distance. All the qualities required for climbing in the Alps are necessary in Scotland too, for a climb in Scotland is much more in the nature of an expedition. Most accidents have occurred through people losing their way and becoming exhausted, possibly through not being properly equipped, and it must be emphasized that full Alpine equipment should always be carried in winter.

Scottish mountaineering has distinctive features of its own, the scale being grander than in England or Wales, although less grand than in the Alps. Offering as it does not only training for Alpine conditions, but first-class sport of its own, mountaineering in Scotland could be developed as a distinctive national sport far more than it is at present. With its varied scope and opportunities it is to be hoped that the future will see a much wider enjoyment of this sport. The Scottish Mountaineering Club has published excellent volumes about the chief climbing centres—the Cairngorms, Ben Nevis, Central Highlands, etc.—with maps, diagrams, and illustrations.

Fishing

There are many hotels in Scotland in situations which provide an ideal centre for all who love to be among mountains and enjoy the many forms of recreation they offer. Most of these cater specially for the angler, many having private stretches of salmon and sea-trout river, and nearly all having several lochs where good trout fishing may be had. In most cases the hotel provides boat and boat-men at a nominal figure, and charges for the right to fish are included in the hotel bill. Whole books could be written about the lochs and rivers of Scotland and still leave much untold. There are the great salmon rivers : the Spey, the Dee, the Tay, and the Tweed, and a host of smaller rivers full of salmon, sea, or freshwater trout, to say nothing of the many small burns where trout of smaller size abound. The four big rivers mentioned are fished mainly from a boat, but on the Tay it is nearly all trolling, and the angler has less chance to make use of his skill than the ghillie, on whose artful manœuvring of the boat much depends. There are freshwater lochs where trout up to eight or nine pounds can be caught, and a variety of lochs on the west coast of the mainland and on the shores of the Western Isles where sea-trout give excellent sport. In North Uist on Loch Skealter, a large freshwater loch, one may have the unusual experience of fishing for salmon in most unlikely surround-ings, for in summer its backwaters are bright with large white water-lilies.

Most of the big rivers in Scotland are broken up into beats, some of which have changed hands for large sums, and others which are let monthly at high charges. Nevertheless, there is fine fishing for the humble pocket. Town councils and angling associations in many parts of Scotland own the fishing rights on local rivers, and anglers can fish for a few shillings per day. Loch and reservoir fishing for trout is also obtainable at a daily charge on application to the local town hall.

Plate 91   A Scottish Youth Hostel on the shore of Loch Eck
(*Photo : S.Y.H.A.*)

Plate 92 (*Above*) An international football match at Hampden Park, Glasgow. (*Below*) Curling on Duddingston pond, Edinburgh

(*Photos : ' The Scotsman '*)

Plate 93 (*Above*) Gliding (*Photo: The Duke of Hamilton*). (*Below*) The 'Twelfth':
Grouse shooting near Dunkeld (*Photo: Central Press Photos Ltd*)

Plate 94   Tossing the Caber

(*Photo : Topical Press*)

Sailing

The Firth of Clyde is the principal yachting ground on the west coast of Scotland, and offers to the racing man, in the open waters of the lower Firth, an opportunity to sail in ideal surroundings in almost tide-free water, and to the cruising man, remote anchorages in Loch Fyne, Loch Goil, and the Kyles of Bute, which have a beauty rivalled only by the loveliest parts of the Western Highlands. Between Castlebay in Barra, the westernmost of the Hebrides, Eriboll in the north, and Oban in the east is a triangle offering to the sailor every possible aspect of more adventurous sailing, whether in a sailing-boat or in a motor-yacht. There are also a few enthusiastic clubs on the east coast, but here less shelter is afforded.

There is no doubt that Scotland has something to offer the sailing-man which he can get nowhere else, for there is an atmosphere about these waterways and islands which even the most hardened traveller finds difficult to withstand.

Gliding

Gliding is a sport which first started in Scotland in 1929. Since then enthusiasts have carried on until the beginning of the war in 1939. A fresh impetus was given when the Air Ministry started gliding for the Air Training Corps, mainly as an interest value in obtaining recruits for the Royal Air Force during the war. A day spent as a member of a gliding school provides much healthy exhilaration, but the sport is at present practised only in its elementary stages, except in a few isolated cases. It is likely that in the next few years much expansion of gliding will take place and more gliding clubs will start in various centres. It seems probable that when advanced gliding or soaring becomes more popular, Scottish topography and weather conditions will prove to be particularly suitable to the development.

Within the limits of an article of this kind one can only attempt to give a rough outline of what is implied by Scottish sport, placing the emphasis on those sports which are, or may be, most widely enjoyed. For example, much has been written elsewhere about deer-stalking and grouse shooting, but although game is present or abounds in almost all country areas in Scotland, those who indulge in shooting as a sport must inevitably be limited in numbers.

Football

By contrast Association Football, although played by relatively small numbers, is supported by a widespread enthusiastic public, and in this way has become the most popular " sports feature " in the national life. Although it may be fair criticism that there are too many watchers as opposed to players, to judge by attendance at first-class football matches, it should be realized that a very large proportion of the spectators are, or have been, themselves players, for every locality has its football team. In fact every boy is born and bred on football ! Boxing is also popular, but it is the gladiatorial side both of football and of boxing which gains the limelight, attracting often vast multitudes of spectators. Both Rugby (Rugger) and Association (Soccer) football are, however, quite generally played by the young men of Scotland, and amateur boxing holds a worthy place. Indeed the " noble art " as practised in the gymnasium as opposed to the competitor's ring is widespread and has a very real if unpretentious value.

The effect of environment, and in particular of contact with the elemental forces of Nature, on the character of a race is well known, and has long been appreciated by a seafaring people. Now in this new air age realization of the air as a potent elementary and formative factor is dawning, and its true assessment is of vital importance. In all countries contact with the land has played a fundamental part in tempering the nature of its inhabitants, and in Scotland the hills have done much to form the character of our people and determine our way of life. In such sports as sailing, gliding, and the rediscovery of the hills and all they offer, release may be found from the conditions of the work-a-day world, counteracting the artificiality of a town existence, by sports which inevitably bring a close and vitalizing contact with Nature.

A SCOTTISH CALENDAR

THE whole life of nature is, as we know, dominated by periodic events, and primitive calendars were based upon this periodicity. The cycle of the seasons constitutes the year, and from time immemorial men have celebrated each season with a festival. In ancient Europe there were two methods of dividing the year. The non-Celtic peoples (including the Anglo-Saxons) divided it in accordance with the solstices and equinoxes, their two main festivals being Midsummer and Midwinter or Yule, and their minor ones falling on what are now Lady Day and Michaelmas. The Celtic peoples (including the Picts and Scots), on the other hand, divided it in accordance with the entry of the seasons, their two main festivals being Beltane (1st May) and Samhuinn or Hallowmas (1st November), and their minor ones, Bride's Day (1st February) and Lunasdail or Lammas (1st August). (It is noteworthy that to this day, allowing for a slight dislocation in the calendar, the English quarter days coincide with the ancient non-Celtic, and the Scottish with the Celtic divisions of the year.) But there is also a strong Scandinavian element in Scotland, and whilst Beltane and Hallowmas, or Hallowe'en—for the festivals always began with the rising of the moon on their eve—are of Druidic origin (Druidism being a form of sun-worship peculiar to the Celtic peoples), Midsummer and Yule were celebrated by the Viking immigrants and their descendants. In accordance with the policy of the Church to invest the pagan festivals with a Christian significance, Yule was identified with the Feast of the Nativity, and henceforward was celebrated throughout Scotland as a religious festival, *i.e.* as Christmas, up to the Reformation.

There are many survivals of our archaic seasonal festivals in the modern Scottish calendar. Beltane, now merged in the Midsummer festival, is celebrated chiefly in the Common Ridings of our ancient burghs, the pilgrimages to wishing-wells, and the May dew ceremonies ; Hallowe'en in the bonfires, the " guizards " (mummers), and the divination rites ; whilst the Yule season (formerly known as the Daft Days), which embraces Christmas and Hogmanay, is still celebrated with such traditional Scandinavian rites as the Burning of the Clavie at Burghead, the Fireball Festival at Stonehaven, Burning the Old Year Out at Biggar, and the Lerwick festival of Up-helly-a', which in its modern form must surely be the finest fire-festival in Europe.

The year in Scotland begins with " first-footing " in the " wee sma' hours " of New Year's morning ; but as this custom forms part of the general Yule celebrations it will be dealt with under that heading.

Bride's Day (*Candlemas Eve*). The original Bride was the Celtic goddess of Spring. The day was re-dedicated by the Church to St. Bride of Kildare, but the remarkable ceremonies associated with the festival, in which the decorated sheaf—the Spirit of the Corn— was predominant, prove the truth of Sir James Frazer's assertion that the saint is but the goddess "in a threadbare Christian cloak." These ceremonies are now only a memory. In due course Bride's Day was merged in Candlemas, which survived as a school-bairns' festival until within living memory ; but the prohibition by the School Board of the Candlemas offerings that were part of the dominie's perquisites ended the historic custom of electing the Candlemas King and Queen. The Ba' (handball) game, however, which invariably concluded the celebration, has been carried on continuously in some of the Border towns, and notably in Jedburgh, where the office of Candlemas King has recently been revived. Jedburgh has in fact two Ba' games—the Callants' (lads') Ba', which is played on Candlemas Day, and the Men's Ba', which is played on Fastern's E'en (Old Shrove Tuesday). The contending sides are the "Uppies" versus the "Doonies," those born above the site of the Mercat Cross playing towards the Castlehill, and the downward men to the Townfoot. At 2 o'clock, amid scenes of wild enthusiasm, the ball is thrown up in the Market Place by the Candlemas King. The game, though governed by no written rules, is fought with the utmost good nature and regard for fair play. The Fastern E'en Ba' is followed by a dinner given by the Jethart Callants' Club.

Another festival associated with Candlemas, though held at a later date, is celebrated by the students of St. Andrews University. With its ecclesiastical ruins, its fine old colleges, its spacious streets, and its grassy links, the city provides an ideal setting for the pageantry of Kate Kennedy Day, when the Lady Katherine Kennedy, who is represented by a beardless " bejant " (first-year student) in medieval dress, is the principal figure in a great pageant of historical figures who have been associated with the life of city or university.

The origin of the custom is obscure. Some derive it from the

Celtic festival of Spring and identify Kate with Bride. The students themselves, however, are not interested in tracing it further back than the fifteenth century, nor its principal figure to any other than Bishop Kennedy's charming niece, Lady Kate, who visited her uncle at St. Andrews in 1451 and became the toast of town and gown. It is by no means improbable, however, that the relatively modern festival was grafted on to an earlier one.

Beltane. The dates of the two chief Celtic festivals were of major importance to a community whether at the hunting or at the pastoral stage of development. At Beltane the flocks and herds went out to the summer pastures ; at Hallowmas they returned to the fold. By Beltane the seed had been committed to the ground ; by Hallowmas the crops were " inned." Thus Beltane may be regarded as a Day of Supplication, when a blessing was invoked on hunter and herdsman, on cattle and crops, and Hallowmas as a Day of Thanksgiving for the safe return of the wanderers and the renewal of the food supply.

To the Druids, the sun was the seat and centre of the divinity, and fire, because of its affinity to the sun, was their mystic medium of worship. At Beltane great bonfires were lit on the hilltops to greet the rising sun, with sacrifice and magical rites designed to propitiate the mysterious forces of nature and protect the community from calamity. Centuries after Christianity superseded Druidism, the Beltane fires continued to burn all over the Highlands. In the eighteenth century Beltane was the great herds' festival, and many curious rites, of which the meaning was entirely forgotten, were preserved. In the nineteenth century the fires descended to the village knolls, where the bairns danced round the Beltane bonfires, roasted their eggs in the ashes, and rolled their Beltane bannocks down the hillside.

To the Druids, the most sacred form of water was dew, and to the dew of Beltane morning they attributed special virtue. Washing one's face in May dew is a rite, or a frolic, still practised all over Scotland. In Edinburgh, in the early hours of the 1st of May, bands of young girls may be seen making their way through the King's Park to " meet the dew " on the slopes of Arthur Seat (where the Beltane fires once blazed), or to St. Anthony's Well near by, where they kneel and drink the magic water, " wishing a wish " the while.

Wishing-wells are common in Scotland, but the most remarkable survival of pre-Druidic well-worship is the annual " pilgrimage " to the " Cloutie Well " on Culloden Moor, near Inverness, on the first Sunday of May. The " pilgrim " silvers the water with a coin, drinks and " wishes," and before leaving affixes a " clout " or a small piece of one of his garments to an adjacent bush, thereby casting off all his cares. People come in hundreds from far and wide —many by motor-bus—to witness, if not to take part in, the age-old rite.

In the course of time the festivals of Beltane and Midsummer were merged. To-day, the Feast of Summer Come Again is celebrated mainly in the Riding of the Marches, which is carried out in the Border burghs and in Lanark (Lanimer Day), Dumfries (Guid Nychburris Day), Linlithgow, Elgin, Musselburgh, and elsewhere. Some of the burghs trace their Riding for five hundred years, but they may well be centuries older. Their ostensible purpose was to see that the marches—boundary marks of the common lands attached to the burgh—had not been tampered with by rapacious neighbouring lairds, but they probably originated in the solemn circumambulating of sacred spots in order to aid the fertility of the fields. Traces of Druidism linger at Hawick in the gathering at the Mote to greet the dawn and the distribution of oak leaves.

The Selkirk Festival may be taken as a typical Border Riding. The proceedings begin on " the Nicht afore the Morn " with the Crying of the Burley through the wynds and ways of the old grey town, followed by the Bussing (decorating) of the Colours in the principal hall. As the night advances, communal spirits run high, and all night long the streets echo with footsteps and laughter and song.

At dawn, the town is wakened from a short sleep by the music of flute and drum, and soon the streets are thronged with people singing " Hail, Smiling Morn ! " Along the main street go the " Soutars o' Selkirk "—the town being formerly famous for its soutars or shoemakers—young and old, with arms linked, dancing from side to side with a gaiety that has to be seen to be believed. A terrific cheer greets the Standard-Bearer—the hero of the day— when the Provost hands the Burgh Standard into his keeping with the godspeed, " Safe Oot, Safe In ! "

At 7 a.m. a procession headed by the Provost, Councillors and Baillies sets forth. After them, on a magnificent mount, comes the Standard-Bearer, his bravely bussed banner fluttering in the breeze, and behind him are as many as a hundred and fifty riders. The crowd surges down to the river to watch the cavalcade cross the ford, speed up Lingley Glen, and disappear from view among the hills. Then the townsfolk go home to breakfast. Two hours later the crowd has reassembled at the Toll to await the return of the riders. Down the glen they come and through the ford, their spurs flashing above the sunlit water. The Standard-Bearer is well ahead, and as his steed pounds up the rise at the Toll he is greeted with tumultuous cheers. Riders and townsfolk now form into procession and make their way to the market-place for the last, and most moving ceremony, which commemorates the tragedy of Flodden. On a crimson-covered dais stands the solitary figure of the Standard-Bearer. The Burgh Band plays " The Soutars o' Selkirk," and there is an awed hush as the Standard-Bearer raises the flag and waves it rhythmically to and fro round his head, telling in movements more expressive than words the tale of the tragic September day in 1513, when, as the story goes, of the eighty men who had set out from Selkirk, one solitary horseman returned. Former Standard-Bearers in turn cast their flags, and last of all an ex-soldier. There is a two-minutes' silence, and then the low drone of the pipes takes shape in the lovely and deeply moving lament, " The Liltin'." With the memories of Flodden are mingled memories of the two World Wars, and of private bereavements as well. Thus, in sharing for a few brief hours their joys and sorrows and their common love of one particular spot of earth, the whole community is more closely knit together in that virtue so highly prized by the Scottish folk—" guid nychbourhood," or neighbourliness.

Midsummer Eve passes unnoticed in most parts of the country, but a great Midsummer fire still burns regularly on the summit of Cairnshee in the Deeside parish of Durris. The survival is due to a bequest made nearly two hundred years ago by a nostalgic Scot who as a lad had tended cattle on the braes of Durris and helped to " bigg " the bonfire, and who died a merchant prince in Twickenham.

The " Johnsmas " fires—Midsummer Day was dedicated by the Church to St. John the Baptist—died out in Orkney within living memory, but Midsummer Eve is celebrated in Kirkwall with midnight sports and dancing on the green.

Lammas. In the Lothians and the Borders, until the building of dykes and fences reduced the number of herds to a minimum, Lammas was celebrated as a herds' festival, which took the form of mock raids between the herds of adjacent parishes—each parish having its improvised "peel" or tower—followed by games, races, and an alfresco feast. To-day little remains of Lammas but the fairs at St. Andrews, Kirkwall, and other towns. A curious survival is found at South Queensferry—the Procession of the Burry Man, which takes place on the eve of the Ferry Fair. The Burry Man is clad loosely in flannels stuck all over with burs—the adhesive bur of the bur thistle, which grows profusely in the neighbourhood—and carries two staves garlanded with flowers. His resemblance to the Leaf Man of Central Europe and the Jack-in-the-Green of medieval England is too strong to be lightly dismissed. The Burry Man, who represents the Spirit of Vegetation, is properly associated with the Summer Festival, and it is probable that on its decline he was transferred to the main day of pageantry in the burgh—the day, or, more correctly, the eve of the Ferry Fair.

Hallowe'en. Samhuinn, or Hallowe'en, remains the most distinctive of all the Scottish festivals. In early times the Celtic year began with winter, and Hallowe'en was thus the Celtic New Year's Eve. As at Beltane, great fires burned on the hill-tops; but whereas those of Beltane were lit at dawn, the Hallowe'en fires were lit at dusk. These fires have burned down the centuries to our own time in an unbroken chain. In the sixties of last century, an Edinburgh sheriff, travelling from Dunkeld to Aberfeldy, counted no less than thirty bonfires on the hills, each having a ring of people dancing round it. Shortly before the first World War, "On a crisp autumn night, in a remote part of the Highlands," writes a correspondent to a Scottish newspaper, "we were looking over to where the dark mountains were silhouetted against the rising moon. For miles and miles the landscape was dotted at wide intervals with bonfires that blazed against the dark hill-side. The date was 31st October, and these bonfires were the direct descendants of the fires lit each year by the ancient Druids."

In the Lowlands the Hallowe'en fires have become a mere bairns' " bleeze."

At Hallowe'en, the season of earth's decay, our forefathers remembered their dead, and on this evening the souls of the departed were believed to visit their old haunts. Some years ago, a friend of the present writer, whilst " guizing " on Hallowe'en in the Hebrides, was solemnly welcomed by an old man as a *revenant.* And it was not only the ghosts of the departed that were abroad on

Plate 95   The Cuillin Hills, Skye, the most notable centre of rock-
climbing in Scotland

(*Photo : The Duke of Hamilton*)

Plate 96 (*Above*) The Procession of the Burry Man, South Queensferry
(*Photo: ' The Scotsman '*)

(*Below*) The dragon-galley of Up-helly-a', Shetland

this eerie night. All the queer, uncanny creatures of the other world were released that night. It was the great flitting-time of the fairies, who removed from one fairy hill to another, and the witches held a great "sabbath" on bleak moorland or wild shore, whither they flew on broomsticks or in sieves. It was reckoned unsafe to be abroad unless protected by fire lit at the sacred flame. Hence the turnip lanterns and the "can'le in a custock" (candle stuck in a hollowed-out cabbage stalk), and the blackened faces (done with the ashes of the bonfire) of the village bairns. The grotesque "fausse faces" worn by the guizards, and the pranks played by the youths on Hallowe'en represent the uncanny creatures of the other world and their mischievous pranks.

But perhaps Hallowe'en is best remembered to-day as a season of omens and auguries. The threshold of the New Year was naturally the time when our forefathers were most likely to pry into the future. Most of the vatic rites that survive (in the form of parlour games) are concerned with love and marriage, but originally they covered a wider field. Apples and hazel nuts play an important part in these rites, for the apple was the food of the Immortals and the talisman by which a mortal could enter the other world, whilst the hazel—"the magic tree that wizards loved"—was revered as the source and symbol of wisdom. The indoor Hallowe'en ceremonies invariably begin with the "douking" for apples in a large tub of water. The act of going through water to obtain apples is in all probability an ancient Druidic rite symbolizing the passing through water to Avalon or Apple-land, the land of the Immortals. Some of the immemorial out-door rites survive in the remoter rural areas. They are fully described in Burns's poem, "Hallowe'en." Hallowe'en to-day is pre-eminently the children's festival. What matter that the solemn rites of far-off times have become the frolics of our own if they serve to keep our racial memories green?

Yule. The term Yule covers the period from Yule E'en or Christmas Eve to Up-halli-day or Twelfth Night (6th January) and therefore includes both Christmas Day and Hogmanay or New Year's Eve. In pre-Reformation Scotland Christmas Day was mainly a religious celebration, the fun and feasting concentrating on the subsidiary festival, Uphalieday. After the Reformation the celebration of both Christmas and Up-halli-day was banned. New Year's Day is, of course, an arbitrary date that differs in various periods and various places. In ancient Scotland it was 1st November;

in Christian times, up to 1600, it was 25th March. The change of date to 1st January brought New Year's Day within the Yule period shortly after the banning of Christmas and Twelfth Night, with the result that much of the carnival spirit hitherto associated with Twelfth Night was transferred to New Year's Eve or Hogmanay. Thus the Yuletide merrymaking continued to centre round " the hinner end o' Yule." Many customs formerly associated with Yule E'en, such as the " redding " (tidying) of the house and the baking of the Yule bread, became transferred to Hogmanay, and as the festival increased in popularity, it attracted to itself many of the rites hitherto associated with the old Celtic Quarter Days, notably saining, guizing, divination, and first-footing.

First-footing, in the loose sense of the term, means visiting in the early hours of New Year morning. The " first-foot " is, strictly speaking, the first person (other than a member of the household) who crosses the threshold after midnight. The appearance of the first-foot is held to indicate the character of the luck that will attend the household throughout the year, and it is a matter of concern that he (or she) should be well-favoured. A well-set-up dark man is the prime favourite, and next to him a comely fair woman. It is important, too, that they should be people of good repute. An empty-handed first-foot signifies poverty and privation. The first-footers therefore invariably carry handsel, which may be anything from an orange to a bottle of whisky. After greeting the family, the first-foot pours out a glass of whisky from the bottle he carries, and this must be drunk by the head of the house, who, in turn, pours out a glass for each of his guests. The table is spread with the traditional Hogmanay fare, which includes two traditional cakes—a big round cake of shortbread, and Black Bun, a rich mixture of fruits, almonds, and spices moistened in brandy, enclosed in a pastry crust. The shortbread is a lineal descendant of the Yule bannock, which was baked between sunset and sunrise on Christmas Eve in honour of the Nativity, but which has a still earlier pagan origin, for the Shetland Yule-cakes are still nipped round the edge to symbolize the sun. Black Bun, on the other hand, is just the ancient Twelfth Cake. The first-footers must eat as well as drink, and frequently stay on for music and dancing. In some of the remoter parts of the country they still appear as " guizards." The first-footer visits only those families to whom he desires goodwill, and the attention is always welcome. The greater the number of first-footers, the more highly honoured the household.

The most notable survivals of the ancient Yule-fires are the Burning of the Clavie at Burghead, in Moray, and the festival of Up-helly-a' in Shetland. Whilst in many parts of the country local festivals have been allowed to decay, in Lerwick, as in the Border burghs, the process has been reversed, and the modern spectacle is far more imposing than that of earlier times when " fiery crates " were dragged to the pier-head by boisterous bands. To-day the crates are replaced by a full-sized, gaily painted replica of a Norse galley, complete with dragon head and tail, with ten oars on each side. Torches on slender poles are provided for the escort of guizards. At 7.30 on the evening of the festival the galley, mounted on iron wheels, is drawn to the mustering-place. By 8 o'clock an enormous crowd has gathered to witness the arrival of the Guizard Jarl, a splendid figure in winged helmet and glittering coat of mail, and his Viking squad. The brass and pipe bands are in readiness. A bugle call gives the signal for lighting up ; a second for the procession to move off. At its head is the great dragon-galley with the Guizard Jarl in the prow. Behind are her ranks of Vikings, the ruddy flare of the torchlight glancing on their coats of mail. Squads of guizards follow, and the procession passes through the main streets and along the front until it reaches the head of the pier. As the galley comes to rest, a gun is fired from the fort, and rockets go up from the ships in the harbour. The guizards form a flaming circle round the doomed vessel and join in the Up-helly-a' song. Amidst cheers the Guizard Jarl descends from the ship. A bugle call is sounded and accompanied with a tumultuous shout four or five hundred burning torches are flung into the galley. In a moment she is a ship of living fire. As she burns, the guizards sing their traditional song, " The Norseman's Home." An hour later, nothing is left but the iron wheels. The night is spent in dancing, feasting, and riotous merriment, the guizard squads going the round of the halls and of private houses, which are thrown open to all comers. The revellers usually reach home with the milk, and next day the shops are shut so that the town may " sleep off " the excitement. So ends the great winter carnival of the Shetlands.

Two other festivals fall to be mentioned—St. Andrew's Day (30th November), which is celebrated chiefly by Scots abroad, St. Andrew being the patron saint of Scotland ; and Burns Day (25th January), the anniversary of the poet's birth, which is celebrated in every nook and corner of Scotland, and indeed wherever a handful of Scots is to be found. At the Burns' Supper the humble haggis

SCOTLAND

is king of the feast ; homage is paid to Scotland's most loved poet ; the Immortal Memory is toasted, and the evening ends with the singing of his immortal songs.

To many people, however, the outstanding events in the Scottish calendar are the entirely modern ones associated with agriculture and sport. The leading agricultural event of the year is " The Highland " (the Highland and Agricultural Show), which, despite its name, now embraces the whole of Scotland. There are no finer stock-breeders than the Scots ; and their Aberdeen-Angus, Ayrshire and Highland herds, their Clydesdale breed of horses, their Shetland ponies, and their Highland and Cheviot sheep have achieved a world-wide fame. They may be seen at such auction sales as at Perth which attract many buyers from overseas. Nor are there finer gardeners, and many visitors will welcome the opportunity of visiting some of the most beautiful gardens in the country under the scheme initiated by the Scottish branch of the Queen's Institute of District Nursing. Details are published in *Visit Scotland's Gardens*, issued in spring and summer, by the General Organizer, Scotland's Garden Scheme, Cammalt, Fintry, Glasgow.

In the world of sport, the events most likely to interest visitors are the " Open " at St. Andrews, in which British and American golfers compete ; the " Clyde Fortnight," which draws lovers of yachting from far and wide ; and the Highland Gatherings at Braemar, Inverness, Oban, and elsewhere, when leading athletes take part in " throwing the hammer," " tossing the caber," and other Highland sports, and pipers and Highland dancers engage in contests that arouse no less interest and enthusiasm. These gatherings, however, are not genuine folk festivals like the Common Ridings ; they were instituted or reconstituted in comparatively recent times for the entertainment of the lairds' guests and the shooting tenants ; but they are exceedingly colourful and have definitely achieved a place in the Scottish calendar.

Curling and camanach, or shinty, are games as Scottish as golf, but only the winter visitor stands a chance of seeing such a memorable sight as the great Bonspiel, or curling match, at Carsebreck (held only after a severe spell of frost), when the Men of the North meet the Men of the South (of Scotland) in the " roaring game."

Lastly, the visitor is recommended to attend what is partly an agricultural and partly a sporting event—sheep-dog trials, when that most sagacious and hard-working of dogs, the Scotch collie, demonstrates his amazing skill in interpreting and responding to his master's will as expressed in his face, voice, and manner of whistling.

It is impossible to give in a work of this kind a complete guide to sporting and other events, or an exact date for all those already mentioned, but a monthly illustrated guide to leading events in Scotland is published, under the title *Take Note*, by the Scottish Tourist Board, 20 York Place, Edinburgh, from whom a copy may be had free on application.

PRINTED IN GREAT BRITAIN AT
THE PRESS OF THE PUBLISHERS

SCOTLAND
Mountain River & Plain

ATLANTIC OCEAN

OUTER HEBRIDES

Cape Wrath

Pentland Firth

Orkney Is.

To Shetland Is →

John o' Groats

Moray Firth

Loch Maree

Loch Ness

R. Spey

R. Don

R. Dee

GRAMPIAN MTS

△ Ben Nevis

NORTH SEA

R. Tay

SIDLAW HILLS

Firth of Tay

Loch Awe

△ Ben More

OCHIL HILLS

Loch Long

Ben Lomond △

Firth of Forth

Loch Lomond

R. Clyde

Firth of Clyde

R. Tweed

CHEVIOT HILLS

R. Nith

IRELAND

ENGLAND

Solway Firth